VICTOIRE

Also by Roland Philipps

A Spy Named Orphan: The Enigma of Donald Maclean

ROLAND PHILIPPS

VICTOIRE

A Wartime Story
of Resistance,
Collaboration
and Betrayal

THE BODLEY HEAD
LONDON

1 3 5 7 9 10 8 6 4 2

The Bodley Head, an imprint of Vintage, is part of
the Penguin Random House group of companies whose addresses
can be found at global.penguinrandomhouse.com.

Penguin
Random House
UK

First published by The Bodley Head in 2021

www.penguin.co.uk/vintage

A CIP catalogue record for this book is available from
the British Library

Hardback ISBN 9781847925817
Trade Paperback ISBN 9781847925824

Typeset in 11.85/14.5 pt Minion Pro
by Integra Software Services Pvt. Ltd, Pondicherry

Printed and bound in Great Britain by Clays Ltd, Elcograf S.p.A.

The authorised representative in the EEA is Penguin Random House
Ireland, Morrison Chambers, 32 Nassau Street, Dublin DO2 YH68.

Penguin Random House is committed to a sustainable future for
our business, our readers and our planet. This book is made from
Forest Stewardship Council® certified paper.

MIX
Paper from
responsible sources
FSC® C018179

For Nat

Contents

Prologue

Moulin-de-la-Rive, Brittany
12th/13th February 1942

The sliver of moon gave almost no light as a Lancashire-born engineer, an aristocratic French Resistance leader, a German military intelligence officer and a short figure in a black fur coat converged on a remote, chilly cove on the north-western edge of Hitler's Fortress Europe. They were awaiting the arrival of a Royal Navy boat to hurry all but one of them across the Channel to England.

The three men were brought together by the only woman of the bizarre party. Her coat that had seen better days and the battered red hat on top of its owner's cropped dark hair did not suit her code name of 'Victoire' as she stumbled myopically along in the darkness. Mathilde Carré's own war had already been eventful, and her impact on the men accompanying her critical. Her current code name was not her first in the twenty months since her country had been humiliated in its armistice with Germany: for one glorious year she had been known as 'La Chatte'.

Were the stakes not so mortally high, the choice of rendezvous might have smacked of that particularly British trait, an ironic sense of humour. Only hours earlier, the mighty battle cruisers *Scharnhorst* and *Gneisenau*, the pride of the Kriegsmarine, had slipped out of the harbour at Brest and steamed up the English Channel past this cove. Such naval effrontery was only possible because signals from 'The Cattery' transmitted to London on Carré's wavelength had indicated that the ships were 'quite unable to put to sea'. So much faith was put in her intelligence-gathering that this was believed even if other accomplished spies on the ground told a different story. An opportunity had been lost for the

RAF and the Royal Navy to strike a memorable blow in a low period.

Yet the Cat herself was now being smuggled out of France with the blessing and connivance of the Nazi occupiers of her country, to begin the next stage of a career that remains controversial as questions swirl around her patriotism, honesty and courage.

1

A Profound Need

The 'dirty, small black factory town' of Le Creusot in Burgundy where Mathilde-Lucie Belard was born in 1908 could never have nourished a girl with her ardent imagination. She was an advanced, solitary child, able to both walk and talk at the age of one, and spent her early years in the wholesome mountain air of the Haut-Jura in her grandparents' rambling eighteenth-century house with its steeply pitched roof, a paddock and a large garden.

Mathilde's father was an engineer in the steel industry that dominated Le Creusot, and so in love with her assertive mother Jeanne that Lily, as Mathilde was known in her family, believed that their 'amorous intimacy' would have 'disturbed' her even as a baby if they had not sent her to live with her maternal grandfather. She would come to look back on herself as 'a very miniature little lady', and whilst an early lack of parental guidance meant she struggled to parse emotional nuance in herself or read those around her, it instilled a spirited self-determination to try out all that life had to offer.

Her grandfather was an emotionally remote yet 'tender and indulgent' man who slipped Mathilde sugared almonds when she was reprimanded; he was eighty years her senior and shared his house with his spinster daughters, both in their thirties. Aunt Isoline and Aunt Lucie were contrasting and marked influences on their charge's developing character. Aunty 'Tine loved music, a party, stories and clothes, and opened Mathilde's mind to the possibility of a life of romance; Aunty 'Cie, nicknamed 'the Sad One' by her niece, was dutiful, virtuous, and 'a high-minded substitute for a real mother'. Mathilde loved Lucie's balanced calm but would share her periodic fits of depression, during which Lucie wrote poems she never dared to offer for publication. One of these involved a stream which Mathilde was told represented 'devotion, patriotism and sacrifice':

> In that desert which is my life
> There flows a charming brook,
> Fragrant with honey and nectar
> In which I have drowned many a regret …

The poem implanted a desire in Mathilde, 'at all costs, to die as a martyr for France', as she was to recall at a time when she was puzzling out the arc of her life. It was the first encapsulation of her romantic sense of her destiny, whose echo was to return to her twenty-six years later at a moment of devastating crisis to rally her innate heroism.

Her earliest memory was of 'weariness, cold sweat and a feeling of nausea'. She was undergoing scarlet fever, and on her recovery was fed a baked apple, the taste of which would instil 'childish joy' for the rest of her life; she could never drink champagne, given as medicine, without bringing her sickness to mind. She could not understand why 'the bells tolling wildly' at the start of the war in 1914 caused her aunts to be so tearful, and was unsure how to behave: all she could think to do was continue with her household duties of making her grandfather's bed and helping with meals. The skill that would be useful to her in the next war – of how to live with secrets whilst putting on a front of normality – was being imprinted early.

Mathilde learned to love nature in this period, and the thought of climbing roses and the scent of flowers was a great solace to her, particularly when she needed the distraction of daydreams, for the rest of her life. Her feeling for the area stayed with her and she knew that she would carry the house's smell and the feel of its rough walls to her grave.

Her independence and sense that she alone could forge her identity were reinforced by the fact that she only moved to live with her family, now in a flat in Paris, in 1915, aged seven. She had no clear impressions of her parents or her younger brother, Pierre, before then. Her father was a small man with a black beard who 'looked mild and good' to his watchful daughter. He was in army uniform in her first solid memory of him, on leave from the war in which he was to be awarded the Légion d'Honneur and the Croix de Guerre. Her mother was 'a large lady' in spectacles, perpetually about to 'fly into a passion'. After being the centre of attention in the Haut-Jura, Mathilde felt her parents were 'so in love' with one another that they excluded her from family life and 'explained nothing' to her whilst simultaneously 'reproaching her for being a mediocre pupil'. She was always circumspect with her mother Jeanne Belard and complained about her 'lack of affection', but hardly ever mentioned her father, a shadowy figure who was possibly withdrawn through his experiences in the war.

Despite the help Jeanne later tried to give her daughter at the most tumultuous moments of her life, Mathilde never integrated into her family or found it easy to forge empathetic relationships. Her self-directing streak would be her essential and influential compass in her later adventures, but one that came at the cost of the ability to recognise true attachment to others. At the same time, she was always torn between being engaged with hubbub and community and longing to escape to the peace of a rural existence; and was often at the mercy of events in her immobility between these extremes.

During her frequent stays in the mountains, Mathilde followed the progress of the war on the Sad One's map, and developed a hatred of 'the Prussians' or 'the Boche'. In the quiet environment where feelings were not shown or spoken of, she craved love and fantasised about being a war widow: she had observed that they were 'treated with solicitude, consideration and affection', and did not appear to contemplate the necessary stage prior to widow-hood.

She became closer to her brother when they caught whooping cough in 1919 and were quarantined together: it was an experience which inspired her 'fervent wish' to become a nurse, while Pierre was determined to be a general. This desire to serve complemented her 'profound need to love and please', her parents remembered. When she did not feel her love was reciprocated she asked to be sent away to school, but the thrill of departure for the Lycée Jeanne d'Arc in Orleans aged twelve soon tipped into despair at her first experience of incarceration: she believed herself unworldly, unpopular and lazy as she lurched from excitement to despair. In her craving for security, she made surprising choices, such as opting to 'remain an old-fashioned woman who knitted and looked after the house' rather than to 'become a modern, active woman' when offered the choice as an essay topic. She drank a bottle of ink in this crisis of identity, which, rather than causing any ill effects, merely turned her tongue blue. The passion that had led her to suicidal thoughts brought her back to the reality of her situation, as it was to do so to vital effect on two occasions in the first years of the Second World War.

*

At the age of sixteen Mathilde moved to a Paris *lycée*, and seized the freedoms of adulthood: she took herself to the art deco elegance of La Coupole for lemonade and to absorb the café's cosmopolitan atmosphere; she applied to sit for artists but at her interview realised that she had not understood 'what kinds of girls painters took for their models'; she met a man in his thirties, Philippe, when she was sightseeing at Saint-Julien-le-Pauvre who loved '*jeunes filles en fleurs*' but 'never kissed' her during the two years of their friendship. He encouraged her to read the radically modern works of Gide, Proust and Cocteau, and disappeared without any explanation from her life just as suddenly as he had entered it.

Following Mathilde's self-reliant upbringing which bypassed many of the usual experiences of childhood, it was perhaps unsurprising that when she gained two further admirers towards the end of her schooldays, they were both older men attracted by her charm and appealing vulnerability. It was as if she wished to accelerate her own steps towards becoming a grown-up and avoid the painful business of adolescent dating. Adolphe 'went into raptures over [her] hands, body and eyes', while Louis, the 'saner' of the two, was 'far more attracted to [her] brains and taste'. Both were smitten by her voice, which a later lover described as 'attractive ... rather low, but animated; [her] words [were] carefully phrased, cultured'. Her hands were indeed beautifully formed, and her myopic, slightly slanted, gem-like green eyes were compelling, the more so as vanity prevented her wearing her spectacles so that she moved near-hypnotically close in order to see her interlocutor. She was five feet tall, with a thin face, a small mouth and brown hair, and at this point suffered from what she termed a 'violent inferiority complex' from her mother's perceived undermining of her looks, taste and even that she did not 'know how to speak properly'. Her esteem was so low that when she was looking back over the drama of her life she could not recognise her own attributes and assumed that these two men could have been attracted to her only because she was 'irresistibly drawn towards evil'; she assumed herself worthless in the eyes of others. She was horrified when Adolphe pressed his 'bony knee' against her leg under the table at dinner with her parents, and cut him out of her life.

Mathilde failed her baccalaureate at the first attempt in her distraction and had to repeat her last year at school before progressing to the Sorbonne. She studied philosophy but her heart remained with the modern novelists. She always resisted Flaubert, as if Emma Bovary's path through life was some sort of painful premonition of her own search for connection and love. She listened to Bach while the momentous events of the times, the Depression and the rise of fascism, passed her by even as she longed for something to stir her out of her dream state. Another older boyfriend, Robert, owned a car and took her on trips to the Bois de Boulogne and Fontainebleau, as well as to the Louvre most Thursdays. Part of Robert's appeal was that he shared her romantic yearnings as he talked 'of love and of death', and was 'the epitome of dreams and love'; but she found it hard to return his affection amidst her own unfamiliarity with emotion. She was aware of his 'heart beating very fast' as they 'nestled together' companionably, but in response felt 'a bitterness' that she could not explain as he tried to draw out her intricately enigmatic personality. She decided that she wanted to follow Robert into studying medicine but her mother forbade it as 'not a suitable study for a well brought up girl' and pushed her towards the law.

At the end of her second year her inability to make the most of her gifts after her lost childhood overwhelmed her: the faltering romance with Robert ended, an arts review she had started with a fellow student went under, and she failed in her legal studies. She went to the Haut-Jura for her summer holiday but became aware that cynicism had 'killed the child I once was'; she now saw her aunts as 'ageing spinsters' and was oblivious that their 'tenderness was as sweet and as young as ever'. She realised she had become 'a complete egoist' and underwent the agony of being unable to escape her shame, admitting that the more she 'suffered' from what she had become, 'the more [she] denied everything in the nature of sweetness, sensibility and love'.

The quest for those ideals was to be a constant spur to Mathilde through her undoubted triumphs and the disappointments which her spirit and energy enabled her to overcome, and ultimately brought her peace. But as a younger woman, the struggle to give and receive love, or even to be accepted and sufficiently praised, was hard for her. She harnessed her powerful imagination to win a national short story competition, but even that achievement and attending the prize-giving banquet in her first evening dress, a 'periwinkle blue crêpe-georgette' creation, disappointed. The accomplishment 'neither delighted nor intoxicated' her as every-thing that happened 'seemed to ring false' and had only the 'slight excitement of the moment'. She was fantasising about her funeral in her early twenties as an occasion when the mourners could only express devotion to her, and told a friend that she would like to have Mozart's Requiem performed at it, an early and seemingly passing decision that was to have far-reaching consequences.

Further relentless self-questioning about her dislike of the law, her hostility towards her parents, and above all her 'periods of great depression', never clinically diagnosed in keeping with the times, would not let her settle. She considered studying at a psychiatric hospital; she tried to engage with emotions creatively and began, but never completed, novels and plays; she took up singing lessons with an acclaimed teacher – Duparc, Ravel, Chausson and Fauré were her favourites – and through these pursuits believed she might 'restore [her] balance'. But then she 'abandoned everything', dropped out of her studies, took a mundane job with an insurance company and rented a tiny room until her parents persuaded her to return home to save expense. She took her teaching certificate and became a supply teacher, but still could not escape 'the accursed blues' which left her 'worn out and drifting'.

When Mathilde was at her lowest, she removed herself from the humdrum by inventing 'fantastic, marvellous adventures' in which she would take the leading role. Often after these deep-seated heroic imaginings, her mood could just as suddenly shift, and she would emerge 'throbbing with life', singing to herself as she walked the Paris boulevards. Reaching for this more vigorous state was often to guide her decisions in the more dangerous world that was to come.

*

Mathilde Belard made her first escape in May 1932 at the age of twenty-four. She was in charge of a class of fifty ten-year-old 'urchins' and struggling to keep control when the neighbouring teacher heard the racket and stepped in to help. Maurice Carré was 'a handsome, well-dressed young man of about thirty' who stood out from his colleagues 'by his physique, ability and courtesy'. He was charming, an athlete who had only been kept out of the elite Saint-Cyr military academy by illness, a lover of Bach, Mozart, Gide, Proust and 'all modern theatre'; he taught her about painting. He told her that his father had been killed in the war and that as a result his 'dominating and vindictive' Corsican mother forbade him his desired career in the army. His air of authority calmed Mathilde's turbulent pupils at either end of the day and he was often waiting at the school gate to walk her home, or to attend plays and concerts.

The following October, Maurice invited her to a friend's flat and, 'looking very grave', proposed to her. He asked her to wait so that he could save some money as well as to persuade his mother of the suitability of the match. Mathilde was 'completely unmoved', as a teacher for a husband was not what her romantic imagination had conjured. Maurice acknowledged that she came from a 'superior class', despite the fact that her father's work was intermittent and her mother had recently told her there was no possibility of a dowry. She still considered her former boyfriend Robert her 'dream man', but suspected that even if his suit were still on the table, he was not stable enough to remain steadfast through her depressions; she was also aware enough of her emotions to wonder if the life of a doctor's wife would encourage the possibility of 'jealousy' as he became privy to his patients' secrets. In the end a formal change of her status in one of the few ways possible at the time was more important than anything. Mathilde recognised that the choice of husband was not to her driven by 'deep-seated loyalty', and the toss of a coin settled her decision: she sent a telegram to Maurice asking him to meet her that same evening at La Coupole, where she accepted his hand.

They married in secret. Mathilde endured a wedding night that was both painful and 'false, comic and a complete illusion', before returning home to lie that she had spent the night at a girlfriend's house. She continued to deny the most seismic event in her life to date as the couple maintained their bachelor living arrangements for the remaining two months of the school year, following which Maurice accepted a job as a schools inspector in Algeria. They planned to find happiness 2,500 kilometres from their 'hostile families'. When they came clean, Mathilde's father was, in fact, 'gently accepting' of his daughter's decision, yet still decided to leave it up to his Jura sisters-in-law to inform his wife of the tidings. Jeanne Belard found her son-in-law 'distant, a lamentable man', while Madame Carré, only informed of the marriage after her son's ship had sailed, disowned him in a one-line letter: 'You are no longer my son while you are the husband of that woman.'

The Belards saw the couple off to North Africa from the Gare de Lyon. At the age of twenty-five, Mathilde Carré was still searching for emotional fulfilment and escape and had forged the most available secure allegiance, one seemingly without much passion to guide it. But it had the advantage of taking her to a distant country in which she could forge new bonds and, she hoped, leave her depressions behind her. From now, she would be swept into a life that was always 'dictated by no kind of rational planning on her part' with all the consequences, both good and bad, of such an approach.

*

The dusty outpost of the French Empire that was the Algerian town of Aïn Séfra was only a partial success to one constantly seeking stimulus. The beauty of the Saharan landscape contrasted with their 'empty room whose only contents were an old official iron bed, a large cabin trunk and a few suitcases' left by their pensioned-off predecessors who were 'raddled' and as 'yellow as two old ivory carvings'. Mathilde revelled in the mountains, scrubby oases and desertscapes of North Africa, at finding her young charges' names 'straight out of *The Arabian Nights*', at knowing so much more about them and their families than she had of her Parisian pupils, and at having status as a cog in the French colonial machinery. She imbued her class with 'familiarity and love', 'spontaneity and gaiety', stories and singing. But alongside the new sensations of being valued and shaping young lives, she was simultaneously disheartened that she was a 'poor little schoolteacher' who might end up like her predecessors. She knew she was not living up to her dreams, and recreated her earlier image of herself as an 'extraordinary child' and as a 'well-beloved young girl of so much promise'. At other times she believed she was settling 'down to a future which seemed to have no bounds'. She was rarely consistent in her analysis of her powerful emotions, but always able to compellingly describe their extremes as she sought a balanced centre.

The greatest contradiction in Mathilde's seesawing responses, the one that tilted all the rest, was that she thought the marriage was 'as perfect as possible', yet was aware of 'the seeds of dissatisfaction, sadness and irritability' after a couple of years. She was 'desperate' to have a baby, and began to experience the lurches of negativity and self-loathing in which she felt that things 'will turn out badly'; she was aware that she 'spoiled everything [she] touched' as she failed to fall pregnant. The Carrés travelled to France and northern Italy in the summer holidays, and in Venice in 1935 Mathilde decided that her 'immense need to love' could only be fulfilled with a child, followed by the dawning, dramatically phrased realisation that she could 'no longer bear this life' without one. When Maurice went to Oran to carry out his annual military service later in the year, she spent time with an Arab friend, Mus, who had four children he spoke of tenderly; she even went as far as to briefly contemplate the 'temptation' of having a child with him, in order 'to form and direct, to nourish its mind', to put things right after her own childhood. The moment represents the potent combination of yearning and control within her that was to emerge repeatedly for both good and bad.

But before she could consider her next steps, the events that had made her 'world restless and unbalanced' – the Spanish Civil War, Hitler's repeated breaches of the Versailles Agreement as he rearmed, the Munich Conference and the betrayal of Czechoslovakia that paved the way for the looming war – came to a head in their last peacetime holiday in 1939. Mathilde had been growing increasingly miserable, and much as she hated herself for it, part of her was 'pleased' by the worsening situation and that 'everything was going to change' in her life once war came. As it was, everything shifted without political intervention: Maurice's brother had been killed in an aeroplane accident in May and Mathilde had written a condolence letter to the mother-in-law she had never met and who had 'shown no sign of life for six years'. She received a reply that 'accepted' her. When the two women met in Paris the following month, Madame Carré delivered a callous, devastating double blow: Maurice was probably unable to father children owing to an adolescent attack of mumps and, worse, his father had not been killed in the Great War, but had been an unfaithful man who had 'died in a madhouse', with strong implications of syphilis in the description. Mathilde knew she had enough trouble with her 'own sanity, instability' and 'morbid anxieties', and became terrified that Maurice might go 'mad' in turn.

*

The outbreak of hostilities solved her dilemma. On 18th September, two weeks after France declared war on Germany, the couple were in Oran, which was even busier and noisier than normal as Maurice's division prepared to embark for Syria. The harbour was filled with ships into which 'men, ammunition, mules, vehicles and supplies were hectically loaded', watched by a 'crowd of idlers, onlookers saying farewell to their loved ones, spies and dreamy Arabs'. In his affection for and understanding of the Arab world, Maurice had made the choice to go to defend the French League of Nations Mandate territory against an as yet unforeseen attack rather than fight on the threatened borders of his own country. Mathilde elided the rush of patriotism that overcame millions of her fellow citizens at this second conflict in just over two decades with her restless, hopeless grief about her childlessness and what she had just discovered about the Carré family to decide that her husband was taking the coward's path. When she looked back on this time from the fractured perspective of the maelstrom of the first two and a half years of war, reflecting on the mingling of 'joy, courage, idealism, excitement and anxiety, her stupid yet magnificent pride', she considered that this was the day her 'marriage ended'. In her absolute fashion, she considered her husband 'dead to her' from then on.

The war and Maurice's departure for Syria once again offered Mathilde the opportunity to start her life afresh. She believed a change 'would settle everything' for her as she still puzzled over her

'clear-cut impression that [she] was never what [she] was intended
to be'. She would at last be able to validate her sense of her latent
usefulness and, in another expression of the grandiose romanticis-
ing that kept her demons at bay, fulfil 'the great and beautiful task'
that had been hidden from her in the emotional emptiness of her
first thirty-two years.

*

It took Mathilde some time to get back. She had to pack up the Aïn
Séfra home of six years which now meant nothing to her and again
make her way north to Oran, where most of the shipping had been
requisitioned. After a few days she crammed on to a boat for
Marseilles, where she caught a train to Paris, by which time she was
'full of fire and wanted to get at the enemy'. She found her father
back in his Great War uniform and about to join the Paris Engineers
in the Charente; her brother was in a signals regiment. She took
one of the few options available for a woman and signed up for an
eleven-week nursing course with the Union des Femmes de France,
part of the Red Cross.

An early and comprehensive strike by the French and British
would have toppled Hitler's regime, but the only military action on
the ground was the French invasion of the Saar region which came
to a faltering halt as the German lines were reinforced in mid-
October. It was a tense time of political as well as military stasis.
Public opinion moved uneasily between fighting an all-out war
and what might be salvaged of the Third Republic by negotiation.
The Phoney War, in Paris as in London, was a period of suspended
reality characterised by confused bureaucracy, party-going and the
relaxation of moral codes; it was known as the *drôle de guerre* as if
the lack of fighting had a comic element even as Denmark and
Norway fell. Mathilde found it a 'ridiculous' period of 'incredible
light-heartedness', disliked the 'state of euphoria' in Paris, and cen-
soriously observed 'the great political speeches, mulled wines ... a
few war stories and victory songs referring to the Maginot and
Siegfried lines, propaganda, leg-pulling' and 'complete lack of

morality' as she went about her training. She longed to prove herself in the 'military zone' rather than looking after 'women and babies', and in her eagerness for action dismissed her less committed fellow trainees as 'jealous, petty [and] gossipy'.

*

The *drôle de guerre* came to an abrupt end in the early hours of 10th May 1940 as the Germans attacked on a 175-mile front in brutal violation of their repeated statements that they would respect the neutrality of Holland, Belgium and Luxembourg. Dive-bombers softened up any resistance, tank divisions smashed through the lines at their weakest points, and airborne troops landed behind enemy lines or directly on top of the supposedly impregnable fortifications designed for the static warfare of twenty-five years earlier. The Allied commanders had had neither time nor strategic impetus to implement the lessons of blitzkrieg in Poland or Norway and the result was failure on a deadly scale. Winston Churchill's first day as British prime minister dawned with the news of 'events ... of an order more terrible than anyone had foreseen'. Mathilde met an officer on a train who spread a rumour about a division on the front line which had been abandoned by their officers, leaving each of them with 'a little bit of money and a bottle of rum'. She was one of only three of her nursing intake of eighty with the skill and determination to qualify and had been at her post as matron at an emergency dressing station at Beauvais for ten days when the Maginot Line was smashed.

On the 14th, the unprecedented German tank advance – complete with combat engineers throwing up pontoon bridges to cross rivers and canals, and with each division accompanied by self-propelling artillery and a brigade of motorised infantry – established a thirty-mile wide bridgehead in the middle of the French lines at Sedan from where they began to push the Allied armies northwards to the Channel. Were it not for the evacuation of 198,000 troops of the British Expeditionary Force and 140,000 French and Belgians from Dunkirk, Britain would have been forced to sue for peace. As it was, nearly all their equipment, transport and weaponry was lost.

Mathilde was baffled and appalled as to how the sizeable and well-equipped armies were being routed, but had no time to ponder an answer as her patients arrived in increasing numbers. At first she saw a trickle of civilian refugees, whose domestic burns, piles, blisters and appendicitis frustrated her in her desire to experience battle. A few days later, the courtyard of the dressing station filled with 'dying men writhing in wheelbarrows', the bandaged walking wounded, and those so traumatised that they attacked imagined Germans 'with the proverbial strength of mad people'. The doctors, led by a commandant with a 'Rabelaisian bonhomie', and the two nurses, in their nun-like uniforms, worked around the clock, fortified by sandwiches and whisky. Mathilde's 'morale was high' as she excelled in her first encounter with war.

When the Luftwaffe started to bomb the retreating French, the work gratified much more elemental feelings in her. She and a student doctor went to a wood near Beauvais which was rumoured to contain many wounded. They drove along a road packed with infantry and civilians who hurled themselves into ditches when the strafing started up. They struggled against the flow of this stream and even though when they arrived they found the wood untouched, peaceful and carpeted with late-spring flowers, Mathilde acknowledged the 'strange thrill' in knowing each moment could be her last. At such times, 'the body lives, lives intensively … life is still everything, but it is already immaterial'. She acknowledged that her short sight meant that she saw much less of the terrifying detail of what was going on, yet was still able to take 'an almost sensual pleasure in real danger', *'une volupté extraordinaire'*. The craving for this arousal, alongside her immense courage, a yearning to be useful and loved in great causes, her intelligence and human instinct to survive, were to govern her next two years.

In most periods of history, Mathilde Carré's possibilities would have been unfulfilled, as she was acutely aware, but the lightning defeat of France's Third Republic in the late summer of 1940 was the perfect catalyst for circumstance, her human qualities and her psychology to combine into a life of adventure, danger and paradox; a life in which the very characteristics that led to her noble aspirations were simultaneously the flaws that precipitated her three-act tragedy.

2

A Useful Suicide

By September 1940, Mathilde Carré's world had 'crumbled about [her] ears', and the most valid way out of the 'hopeless mess' of her life so far would be to end it. She was about to cast herself into the River Garonne before a sudden change of heart: she would fling herself into the war instead.

Her disjointed upbringing and restless dissatisfaction had been brought to this crisis by the physical and spiritual agony of 'La Débâcle', the Fall of France, during which she had displayed a determination to serve when many others had given up. Now she, and France herself, was on the run; the country was divided in two and the 'Dark Years' had begun. Courage, compromise and complex allegiances would be needed. A chance meeting in a restaurant in the middle of the month, two days after her decision to live, would bring the curtain up on her next scene.

*

With the British Expeditionary Force and a large part of the French army out of the picture, 143 German divisions had launched an assault along a 400-mile front stretching from Abbeville to the Rhine on 6th June. The French mustered only sixty-five divisions and Beauvais was evacuated just ahead of the German bombers. Mathilde left the ruined city at dawn with a doctor who only managed to salvage a candlestick taken from his soldier son's bedside table. Their patients were abandoned to be tended by the enemy, and she took scant comfort that 'the dying on the stretchers did not understand' what was going on as the stunned 'living understood just as little'. They used the last of their petrol to get to Rouen, where they subsisted for three days on the milk and bread an elderly nun in a small almshouse could spare until they were able to board a train to Paris.

Mathilde was swept along by the waves of chaos overwhelming her country. She was in Paris only for a day, just enough time to learn that she had been awarded a medal by the Ministry of National Defence for her nursing work, before deployment to another emergency dressing station at Mantes. Within a few days 'the military rout' had caught up with them there too. The French army reminded Mathilde of a 'decapitated frog' twitching on the spit, 'convulsive movements which lasted until the signing of the Armistice'. She was fired by tales of courage, such as of the young Saint-Cyrien who defended a valley path to his last bullet, which he turned on himself rather than surrender. She despised a healthy soldier who came to their dressing station who either had to be a 'fifth columnist' or a deserter, and was later arrested with many of his cohort as he tried to swim a river to safety.

By now 'the Exodus' was fully under way as 2 million of the 5 million inhabitants of Paris and the Seine region fled without any government direction. Overall, 6–8 million citizens were heading for the south at an agonising rate of between three and twelve miles per day through a country with dwindling food stocks and resentful local inhabitants. Of the 23,000 residents of Chartres in May, only 800 remained a month later; ninety per cent of Lille's population of 200,000 were on the move. Mathilde experienced 'physical fear' for the first time when Mantes was bombed, which caused her 'an extraordinary feeling of elation'; she was 'calmed' by the heightened sensation of living on the outer edge of danger with no control over her fate. When another evacuation was ordered, she hitched a lift on an artillery lorry and once again arrived in a panic-stricken Paris, only to be despatched immediately to Orléans in the Loire Valley. She was 'furious and in despair' at the collapse of her country.

Mathilde and a colleague, Jane Smiro, joined the vast creeping throng heading towards the perceived safety of the Loire. Those who still had petrol crawled along in endless columns of cars, lorries, even hearses; bicycles and horse-drawn vehicles were brought out of barns and sheds, and wheelbarrows and prams were loaded with the elderly, the very young, and teetering mounds of mattresses and household possessions. A young resident of Angers noted in her diary on 17th June that the refugees were like exhausted 'automatons' walking 'towards a single vague goal: the south'. When the cars ran out of fuel they were abandoned, doors hanging open in the haste to get away from the screaming, strafing Stuka dive-bombers. Human and equine corpses were pushed to the sides of the road to allow the straggle to keep moving; the air soon began to stink in the summer heat. Antoine de Saint-Exupéry described the scene from the air looking as if 'some giant had kicked a massive anthill'; his wife Consuelo was fleeing with 'no transport, no possessions and almost no money' and did not 'know whether to cry or scream, beg or be silent, stay or go – but go where?' Mathilde was outraged at the sight of the 'people running away like cowards, following the example set by the army', and that there was no food to be had on arrival in overcrowded Orleans.

There was talk of a 'great battle' being planned on the Loire, and Mathilde's indignation, exacerbated by the discovery that her nursing unit had already left the city, was mollified when she found that officers from a tank battalion were billeted in the same chateau. Her spirits lifted still further when amongst them she found René Aubertin, a childhood friend from the Jura who was now a tank captain. Aubertin introduced her to 'a curious man with a Slav accent' of Russian extraction named Marc Marchal. Marchal was an 'intelligent and charming' scientist amongst whose distinctions was the presidency of the Association of French Chemists. By this stage any talk of fighting back was mere bravado, but the encounter with Aubertin did at least guarantee Mathilde a place in an army truck the following day. They managed only sixty kilometres and once again they were 'machine-gunned all along the road', at one point the bullets passing just in front of Mathilde's face. By now she no longer thrilled to danger, and felt neither the exhilaration

nor the 'physical shrivelling' of fear but rather disgust at the pusil-
lanimity of the hapless soldiers she had been 'bending over backwards' to help.

*

Verdun, a small city on the Belgian border, had held out against the
Germans for ten months in 1916. The bloody and heroic defence
cost 162,000 French and 100,000 German lives, and was led by
Philippe Pétain, earning him promotion to marshal of France.
Pétain had written what he presumed to be a posthumous citation,
referring to the 'sentiment of military honour', for Captain Charles
de Gaulle whose whole company had been wiped out. A quarter of
a century later, de Gaulle was to make much of the notion of honour, to his former commanding officer's detriment. The town that
had stood as the symbol of French valour and pride fell on one day
in 1940 with the loss of only 200 German lives, and the Anglophobe
Pétain became, in his mid-eighties, head of state. He and the
equally elderly supreme commander of a mere three weeks, General Weygand, were 'sodden with defeatism' and evacuated the
government to Tours for three days on 10th June before retreating
further to Bordeaux. The swastika was to be hoisted on the Eiffel
Tower and the Arc de Triomphe on the 14th without a single shot
fired by the French in defence of their capital. A solitary colonel
who tried to set up a machine-gun post at the Porte d'Orléans was
prevented by a police inspector.

*

Three days after Paris fell, Mathilde and Jane Smiro had arrived
unscathed but exhausted in a village between Tours and Bordeaux,
where they knocked on the door of a hôtel-Dieu, a hospital run by
nuns. Two tank corps officers had just been turned away at the
Judas grille despite the fact that one of the men was bleeding pro-
fusely from a head wound. The furious nurses went to find
bandages for the wounded man, Jean Merciaux, who proposed

after his treatment that they go to have a drink in a neighbouring café. On their return to the farm where he was billeted, he gave up his room to Mathilde and Jane, sleeping himself in the hay loft with his men. The next day, Jane 'attached herself to some airmen and disappeared' while Mathilde moved with the battalion to their new quarters in a seminary at Cazères-sur-Garonne. Merciaux had been educated at Saint-Cyr and served in the Foreign Legion; the war-seasoned Mathilde felt he 'knew the same world' as her and that 'they were already two old friends'. Three days later, she shared his billet in the bishop's cell, and decided she was in love for the first time. The couple spent their days socialising with Merciaux's brigade, playing bridge and draughts, and the battalion became a 'real family' to her in the unreality of the cessation of hostilities. Even the news that her father and three of her cousins were now prisoners and another cousin dead barely dimmed her new happiness.

For someone who had raged against the conduct of the war, any lingering shame or misery at the French capitulation left Mathilde when she realised in July that she had become pregnant under the enormous crucifix and assorted paintings of the Virgin in the bishop's cell. She 'brimmed over with life and joy'. For the first time she anticipated both giving and receiving unconditional love, and the 'prospect of a child gave ... an exceptional purity' to her ardour for Merciaux such as she had not felt for her husband. She felt 'there had never been a war or anything else unpleasant in [her] life'.

*

The lovers had met on the same day that the government requested an armistice. The treaty was signed on 22nd June, at Hitler's order in the same railway carriage in the forest of Compiègne as the signing of the treaty that had ended the Great War on such 'degrading' terms for the German people. That day, the British Cabinet in London approved Churchill's idea of an organisation, the Special Operations Executive (SOE), to 'set Europe ablaze'

through 'sabotage, secret subversive propaganda, the encourage-
ment of civil resistance in occupied areas [and] the stirring up of
insurrection' to overcome their current inability to fight conven-
tional warfare on the continent.

On 9th July, the French Parliament voted to abandon the Third
Republic. The new state would have as its motto *Travail, Famille,
Patrie* as a sterner and less idealistic replacement for the Revolutionary *Liberté, Egalité, Fraternité.* The Armistice divided France
into a northern zone and the coastline under direct German rule,
and a southern zone extending from the Spanish border to Nice,
and as far north as Bourges and Tours. The latter would be run by
Pétain's government, eventually from the spa town of Vichy, suitable because of its spacious hotels to house the various departments.
The occupied zone encompassed three-quarters of the country's
industrial wealth, its prime farmland and seventy per cent of its
population.

The 'Lion of Verdun' himself wished to avoid *Polonisation*,
the murders and privations which Poland was suffering under
direct military rule, yet was implicitly aligning the government
with the Nazi regime. In theory, he governed the occupied zone
as well as the unoccupied, but only took the short journey to
Paris once. He was trapped between the 'two scorpions' tails' of
the Armistice: 1.5 million captured Frenchmen remained in
German territory, enslaved hostages to extort obedience to the
Reich, and the country was to be bled dry to pay the cost of its
occupation. All but 100,000 troops of the French army, the same
number that Germany had been allowed to keep inside its borders in 1919, were disbanded and the fleet disarmed, but the huge
French Empire was left intact. Pétain stated to his countrymen
that 'if I could no longer be your sword, I wanted to be your
shield'. A new national anthem, 'Maréchal, nous voilà!', replaced
the 'Marseillaise'.

Hitler explained to Mussolini that he wanted 'a French government functioning on French territory' to run its own neutralised
country rather than having it 'flee abroad to London to continue
the war from there'. He saw it as an 'unpleasant responsibility' to

have to act in 'the administrative sphere', but realised that if France's armies had moved to North Africa to continue fighting, the Axis military effort would be 'dangerously dispersed ... offsetting the advantage of total military occupation of the continent'.

Was Pétain at that point the saviour of the French state, maintaining government with 'honour' as he promised, protecting the huge number of soldiers who now became prisoners rather than combatants – as many as had been killed in the previous war – or little better than a sympathiser awaiting Germany's ultimate victory? The Armistice seemed to keep some sort of hope alive for resistance to the Nazis and at least for the foreseeable future protected French Jews, despite appearing to recreate some sort of mythical pre-Revolutionary France based on traditional Catholic values.

For many French, the Armistice simply meant they had survived and could go about their business. They would be free of the threat of the revolutionary disorder of Communism, a state-subversive movement since the Communist Party had been banned at the point of the Nazi–Soviet Pact a year earlier. To some, the settlement was practical, even sensible: André Gide, arguably the leading author of the time, wrote in his journal (intended for publication) that coming to terms 'with yesterday's enemy is not cowardice but wisdom: as well as accepting what is inevitable'. To others, including the writer Jean Guéhenno, the agreement was so sickening that he could only feel 'pain, anger and shame'; he loathed the way the French radio said the marshal's name 'in the same way we would say "my love"'. Although the treaty was not due to take effect until the 25th, soldiers laid down their arms at once: Rommel, driving his men forwards to Brittany, found those from whom he feared attack standing by the side of the road; the French Colonel Charly was shot by his own men after he ordered them to fight out of an encirclement near the Maginot Line.

Hitler was careful not to overplay his hand. He had got a swift and cheap peace, leaving a semblance of government which spared German manpower to serve elsewhere, and gained an income of about 20 million francs per day as payment for the Occupation.* The Reich claimed the fruits of French industry in the north and grain quotas which started at a manageable 550,000 tons but were at 1.2 million tons by 1942 to feed the German troops on the Russian front.

Some, led by General de Gaulle, already in exile with his Free French, favoured fighting on, despite the hopeless situation and the potentially dire repercussions. His first broadcast from London on 19th June announced that 'The flame of French resistance can never go out', but many of his compatriots felt that his was not the right path: of the 1,600 men in London's White City camp following the evacuation from Dunkirk, only 152 chose to sign up with the Free French over repatriation.

For a few, resistance was pointless unless it was within their country's borders. Many believed the invaders would go home following the inevitable collapse of Britain and most just wanted to live in peace with their families: between 50,000 and 90,000 of their countrymen had been killed and twice as many wounded in the last six weeks and the tally of 1.3 million dead and 4 million wounded from the previous war remained etched on to memories.

Life was changed for those that found their homes in the occupied zone. The *tricoleur* flag had been replaced by the swastika; there were few French vehicles on the road; German soldiers were served first in shops, and with the rate of exchange at twenty francs to the Reichsmark, eight francs more than before the victory, they soon cleared the shelves. Jobs were not yet as rare as they were to become, food was reasonably plentiful and bicycles

---

* Exchange rates during the war are hard to calculate as currency flow ceased, but at the rate SOE offered in 1942 to an agent in London, 20 million francs equates approximately to £115,000 in the currency of the day, or somewhere over £6 million in 2018 values. The Germans reckoned that it had cost the French 30 million francs per day to maintain their army, so this was an affordable tax. This rate of exchange will be used throughout.

commanded only a small premium. André Gide commented in his diary on 9th July that 'If German dominance meant abundance, nine-tenths of Frenchmen would accept it, three-quarters of them with a smile.' Survival and relative stability were paramount. Sartre pointed out that it was 'necessary to work' so as not to 'perish', and 'necessary for the peasant to grow beets', even if half of them went to Germany; and that the railway engineers' courage 'saved hundreds of lives' as they brought rations into Paris and smuggled resisters around the country, yet they simultaneously aided the occupiers as the locomotives and rolling stock could be seized at any time to serve war aims. For the next four years, 'every one of our actions was ambiguous' and 'a subtle venom poisoned even the noblest undertakings'.

Most nations, including the United States, Canada and Australia, recognised Pétain's government as legitimate, but Vichy cut off diplomatic relations with Britain after Churchill ordered the French ships fired upon at Mers-el-Kébir in Algeria on 3rd July to prevent them from falling into German hands; 1,297 French lives were lost, and bitterness sundered the recent alliance. The midshipman nephew of Mathilde's doctor-companion in the flight from Mantes had been killed in the attack at Mers-el-Kébir, and the uncle blamed 'those traitors at Vichy' for their refusal to surrender the fleet rather than the British for the attack when they encountered each other later in the year. Pétain – who dated back to before the Entente Cordiale of 1904 brought nearly 1,000 years of intermittent conflict between Britain and France to an end – regarded his northern neighbour as a foe, and one who preferred to fight his wars on French soil.

For the politicians, an armistice was preferable to the looming unconditional surrender without hope of negotiation; for the population, it was a relief to be out of the war and at peace again. Hitler shelved his invasion plans for Britain, Operation Sealion, in the autumn of 1940, but had printed plans which threatened a considerably more restrictive life than anything imposed on the occupied zone in France, let alone Vichy with its 'semi-independent regime': all able-bodied British men between the ages of seventeen and forty-five were 'to be interned and, as far as possible, removed to the mainland'. Eleven million would effectively be enslaved to work on the continent. The 'welfare of the [remaining] inhabitants' was to be considered 'only in so far as they contribute directly or indirectly towards the maintenance of law and order and the securing of the country's labour force for the requirements of the troops and the German war economy'.

The prosecutor at Pétain's post-war trial entitled his memoirs *Four Years to Erase from Our History*, and attempts to remove the marshal from French consciousness started in 1944. There are now hundreds of streets and squares named after de Gaulle, including the former place de l'Etoile where the Arc de Triomphe stands; the last of those named after Pétain, in a village of forty inhabitants near Verdun, changed its name in 2013. A Resistance hero described the atmosphere in 1940 as 'full of fear and the face-saving feeling that after all France was still a country'. Whatever compromises were to come, however 'xenophobic and repressive' the 'moral and political asphyxiation' later, at the time the Armistice could be seen as the least bad result of catastrophic diplomatic, political and military failures going back seven years or more. Questions about the ends of patriotism, motive and survival become much easier with hindsight, particularly from 1942 on as the symbols of French nationality disappeared and deprivations increased. In the end, the Vichy government, as de Gaulle well understood, was 'potentially more traumatic than the defeat of 1940 and the German occupation, because Vichy was the creation of France itself'. Many of the wounds opened by the Armistice, with all its philosophical, political and patriotic paradoxes, have not fully healed to this day.

*

All Mathilde's energy was focused on her love for Jean and their unborn child as they arrived in Toulouse in August. In contrast to the anguish she had felt over the previous weeks, now for her 'defeat had vanished'. Her war would be in many ways emblematic of the choices facing her country. French politicians and civilians alike were frequently forced into complex doubleness and temporary betrayal to survive during the Dark Years, but questions around her country's motives and morality did not affect her at that moment. Toulouse's warm Romanesque bricks contrasted with the ornate spa architecture and ironwork in the new seat of government, and its strong left-wing tradition and proximity to the escape route over the Pyrenees into neutral Spain made it a natural meeting point for those determined to continue the struggle. It even had a statue of Joan of Arc in the main square for inspiration. Merciaux was awaiting his transfer to the Foreign Legion and North Africa, and she considered she 'had never been so happy in [her] life'.

A miscarriage in early September changed everything. Mathilde was heartbroken as hope 'fled'. The departed Merciaux was no longer a noble war hero but 'a man like any other', as her great love was shattered by this calamity. The passionate player in her own melodrama decided that life had nothing more to offer as she conflated her personal torment with that of her country: first France, now she had been defeated; she was in despair at her repeated failures and her blank future. She looked at the 'balance sheet' of her life and vowed to drown herself in the turbid waters of the Garonne. But her indefatigable pride reasserted itself. She would serve her country after all and if necessary 'commit a useful suicide'.

Calmed by the reassertion of her spirit and always swift to act on her impulses, Mathilde sought out the British consul to discuss her options. He suggested that rather than resuming her nursing career with the Free French in England, 'in France another field of action lay open to patriots'. The British had lost the land war, the air war was in the balance and the Nazis now had 'access to three seas'; they could only fight on against the most powerful military machine the world had ever seen with 'the invisible weapon, intelligence'. With little idea of how she would get into this undefined sphere of action and no further guidance from the consul, Mathilde decided to stay in the city and see what happened.

Her path became clear the very next day, 17th September. She had put on her only suit, a grey one, to go out to dinner with her 'featherbrained friend' Mimi Muet, who was beautifully turned out in black with a fashionable hat that Mathilde knew showed up her own tousled hair. They went to La Frégate in the middle of the city. The smoke-filled restaurant was packed. When the waiter asked whether the women might allow a small man with close-set, blue-grey eyes and 'an appalling French accent' to join their table, they had no hesitation in agreeing. The newcomer, who seemed to vibrate with energy, introduced himself as Armand Borni. Mathilde's next dramatic role, in one of the most influential partnerships of the Second World War, was about to begin.

3

La Chatte

Armand Borni chose to walk Mathilde Carré rather than Mimi
Muet back to her lodgings that night. Although he had an eye for
female beauty and appreciated Mimi's stylish turnout, what drew
him to Mathilde was that she was 'intelligent, cheerful and like a
Spitfire' for her dynamism. She saw 'a man about the same height
and age as myself', a 'thin, muscular' figure 'with a long narrow
face, rather large nose', poor teeth and 'eyes which must originally
have been clear and attractive' before a flying accident had ren-
dered them permanently bloodshot. He told her that he was the
son of a French oil engineer, brought up in Romania, conscripted
in the French mobilisation and now, like her, washed up in
Toulouse – which at least explained the combination of his French
name and thick foreign accent. They agreed to meet the next day at
11 a.m. at the Café Tortoni in the place du Capitole, the city's 'bee-
hive'. There Borni told her that it was 'absolutely vital and of great
urgency' that he found someone to improve his French. In Mathilde
he had spotted a drive that matched his own; she had yet to find
her own next steps after her miscarriage and her passionate affir-
mation on the banks of the Garonne, and responded to his
'confidence and enthusiasm ... intelligence and willpower' to find
her own zest returning.

They started work in his hotel room immediately and, although
it became expedient for each of them to deny it later, became lovers
in their shared secrecy, uncertainty and 'the great affection'
between them. As their 'friendship became intimate', Borni started
to tell Carré his story, and to consider that she might take a star
part in his remarkable plan.

*

Armand Borni was a *nom de guerre* for Roman Czerniawski, and Mathilde soon realised that she was teaching a remarkably self-assured patriot, whose every other thought was of his native Poland and of how to 'restore the Polish nation' that had been in existence for only twenty-one years before its dismemberment in 1939; he was 'perfectly prepared (at times, almost anxious) to die for it'. The combination of his 'great daring and initiative' and his belief that 'every problem' he saw was 'bound up with the Polish people' made Roman a courageous and committed spy. What Mathilde appreciated as his speed of thought and charm – he spoke 'very quickly' and was 'always smiling' – won her trust and loyalty. And his 'intensely dramatic and egoistical nature', attributed by his taller, patrician English spy counterparts to his stature at only five feet and five inches, made him the perfect colleague in their shared adventures.

Roman had been born in 1910, the son of a well-off financier in a part of Poland that became Ukrainian following the collapse of the Austro-Hungarian Empire in 1918. He was a fighter pilot until a serious crash left him partially sighted and deskbound at Aviation Command in Warsaw – his 'Spitfire' compliment to Mathilde was high praise in its reference to the new British fighter he admired above all others. He developed an interest in intelligence to become 'a man who lives and thinks spying', and after the Germans destroyed his beloved country, he went first to Romania and, under threat of internment there, escaped on forged documents to Paris. The remnants of the Polish forces were regrouping as best they could, and he was put in charge of the Deuxième Bureau, the military intelligence unit, of the 1st Polish Armoured Division. Always keen to disseminate his wisdom, he wrote a treatise called *The Duties of a Deuxième Bureau of a Large Unit*. Although he was not called upon to fight in 1940, by the time of his dinner at La Frégate he had added the French Croix de Guerre to his Polish one with its two bars.

At the Fall of France, Czerniawski's commanding officer, General Duch, ordered his troops to make their way from Alsace-Lorraine through enemy lines to regroup in Toulouse. Czerniawski's first port of call was to a blonde, twenty-one-year-old widow whose lover he had become while billeted with her in Lunéville, Lorraine, just before his division went to the front. He left three days later with Renée Borni's late husband Armand's papers, identity, clothes and bicycle, which he rode 300 miles through the German columns to arrive in Paris in July. He was depressed by the deserted boulevards, the swastikas and the shuttered drabness of the 'gay, bustling city' he remembered from pre-war days, and was puzzling how best to get to Toulouse when he was hailed from a café table on the Champs-Elysées by 'the smiling faces of Lieut. Krótki, ADC to General Duch, and Lieut. Czyż', his coding officer. The two lieutenants recounted how they had gone to the mayor of Hurbache's empty office as their division dispersed and taken the rubber stamp they found there to make 'official' identity cards, and now moved about freely.

This meeting, and an encounter with the wife of Captain Kossowski, a Polish officer who was a prisoner-of-war in Alsace, led to Roman's epiphany. He decided to ride Borni's trusty bicycle to this captain with a false identity card to enable an escape bid. German soldiers were everywhere as he pedalled along in the unconvincing disguise of a Polish art student off to visit a distant cousin in hospital, and it struck him that an ability to interpret 'every signpost, every sign on a truck, every distinguishing mark of any sort ... like lines in an open book' would be invaluable. He was breathless with excitement more than exertion as he envisaged 'small cells of resistance, multiplying themselves with great speed' across occupied Europe. Integrated with these was the possibility of 'small invisible cells of fighting units, blowing up vital centres of lines of communication, impeding and limiting all free movement of conquerors, spreading terror and touching deeply the soul and morale of the enemy troops'. As the previous war had been changed by aerial combat, so this one would be enhanced by the 'Fourth Force: *Underground ...* '

Roman's vision was of a network 'which would become indispensable in the endless intricacies of contemporary warfare'. British intelligence had been 'virtually obliterated in the 1940 debacle' and 'in order to win, the British must get out of the fog in which they were waging their desperate fight', as one of their own undercover MI6 officers in France put it. At the same time as Roman was formulating his idea of an entire resistance and intelligence movement combined, SOE was still self-confessedly 'puling in its cradle'. He made his way south with only his brainwave and the new map published by the ever-efficient Michelin tyre company that showed the frontiers between 'Zone O' and 'Zone Nono' to guide him.

*

General Duch asked Roman to find a route for stranded Polish soldiers to escape to England. A 'most unusual travel agency' with a network of trustworthy 'contraband and smuggling people' on both side of the Pyrenees who could either get men out through the 'wild mountain passes' or through the frontiers with forged papers was set up. Roman perfected a hectographic printing method which involved imprinting an inked image on to a taut gelatine pad and then back on to cards and documents to look like official-looking, if often rather smudged, stamps. By the end of the year, nearly 20,000 of Roman's countrymen, about a quarter of the troops under General Sikorski's command in France, had arrived in England by one means or another.

He took particular satisfaction in exfiltrating Duch himself, but not before the 'cool, calculating and experienced general' had introduced him to Colonel Wincenty Zarembski of Polish intelligence, code-named Tudor, the chief of a network in Marseilles with a radio link to London. Zarembski was startled by the diminutive captain's ambition but won over by his passionate prediction that the Polish and French had moved from shock and fear to annoyance and impatience, and would shortly be 'screaming for action'. He gave Roman's network his backing and blessing. As the two Poles parted, the new network organiser half-murmured what was to become his creed – 'Every day and in every way against the Boche.'

The aims, resources and results of F1 (for France 1) were limited. As the Poles were wary of making one Frenchman feel he was spying on another, which would endanger lives in a country of opportunism and divided loyalties, they were constrained to use mainly Polish agents. Their operations in the unoccupied zone were to establish how far the Vichy government was collaborating with the Third Reich, if military installations and airfields were being used by the enemy, and what industries were involved in the German war machine. Roman realised that he would have to push his work into the danger of the occupied north to make a difference on the scale he craved.

He had enough self-knowledge to realise that he was better at providing ideas and energy than practicalities in a field where detail was invaluable and could save lives. He needed an efficient headquarters staff, ideally with 'some sort of constant companion-secretary', a native French-speaker, to deal with the French agents and material, not least as few French would take orders from a Pole. He took the code name 'Walenty' (Valentin) and began the work of launching his outfit, which began with 'two unusual men and one even more unusual woman'. The first man was the Balkans representative for the Telegraph Agency Express (a pre-war cover job for an intelligence operative) called Józef Radziminski, known as 'Buster Keaton' for his similarity to the deadpan silent movie star. Through Radziminski came Philippe Autier, whom Mathilde found 'thin and frail ... with enormous glasses ... rather from a bygone era, mannered and gentle'. Autier had such exquisite social graces that Czerniawski felt he could pass as 'an Englishman speaking perfect French', yet he also had the French attributes of an enjoyment of 'all aspects of good living and good wine'.

Autier might have filled the role of French agent-runner and handler of their material, but Roman thought two men constantly seen together could look suspicious. Not entirely without self-interest, he envisaged someone 'of pleasant appearance, with a great deal of personality necessary for the successful making of contacts; and a quiet, elegant manner; an intelligent woman with

an orderly mind, brave but careful' to be his partner in the enterprise. It was with these requirements in mind that after a busy day
helping escapers that he decided to dine at La Frégate on 17th
September. It was an expensive choice, but one that held 'more possibilities perhaps to find interesting people'. And there he spotted
his 'unusual woman'.

*

Mathilde took some French essays to Roman's room and asked
him to read them aloud, stopping him frequently to correct his
accent. She asked him to call her 'Lily', as her close friends did, or
'Micheline'. He became passionate and poignant as he spoke of 'his
destroyed Poland, of his fellow officers imprisoned by the Germans,
of his father and mother … of his little fiancée Eva'. He told her that
despite the crushing evidence to the contrary, 'he would not accept
that Poland had been defeated', and she was captivated by his conviction, responding to the boldness and moral certainty he
radiated. Her desire to live for France 'even if it involves great
danger … even if it amounts to suicide' was rekindled. She found
common ground in their intelligence and pride, admired his 'literary, poetic and artistic feelings' and knew from the start that he,
like her, 'refused to be conquered'.

They worked, talked and made love every day. Mathilde impressed Roman with tales of her father's service in the previous war
and her pride in her brother's graduation from Saint-Cyr. Roman
saw that she, like him, 'already knew the meaning of war – and
defeat' as she unwittingly auditioned for a new role. He trusted her,
seeing a mix of impetuosity and courage that matched his own,
and recognised that she was 'intelligent, eager for adventure and
might render [him] great services'. He began to drop comments
about an organisation that could inform and disrupt lines of
communication and installations. Towards the end of September
he mentioned his current work and his need for a 'companion-
secretary', without hiding from her the dangers of prison, torture
and death.

For her part, Mathilde was 'ready for all sacrifices' and she gave voice to her inner wish for glory as she said, 'Perhaps … perhaps I will become a second Jeanne d'Arc.' As Roman already saw himself as the 'Joan of Arc of Poland', according to a fellow spy, the two idealists seemed perfectly suited to realise what was now a joint, revolutionary intelligence vision.

*

In mid-October, Jean Merciaux left Mathilde's life for the last time. They had not seen much of each other since her miscarriage and the encounters were 'torture for both of us', but Merciaux asked that she join him in Morocco as soon as she had the right papers. It would have been simple to get an identity card, but she was now committed to another path. To prevent any wavering in her determination, Roman took her on a trip to begin her indoctrination and training. They went to Marseilles, Lyons, Vichy and Limoges, where he introduced her to Józef 'Buster' Radziminski and Philippe Autier.

Roman was following the proper tradecraft in revealing information on a need-to-know basis – 'less to say if pressed hard', as he put it. Radziminski was soon to leave F1, but Autier and Mathilde hit it off right away: they started scheming about which of their contacts in Vichy would be worth cultivating to get 'interesting information' for London. Roman gave her a code name as he began to teach her the rudiments of spycraft. He commented that she was able to walk 'so quietly' in her 'soft shoes' that she reminded him of a cat. 'La Chatte' pointed out that she could 'scratch as well'. It was a marker of the delicacy of her equilibrium as well as a veiled threat.

She was frustrated by Vichy. In the autumn sunshine, there was no sense of 'worry or defeat, everything spoke of a gentle and easy way of life' that was at odds with reality. It had also become a place of suspicion. On 24th October, Pétain's kingmaker and successor as prime minister, Pierre Laval, shook Hitler's hand in the tiny railway station of the village of Montoire-sur-le-Loir in the occupied zone. Two days later, Pétain also met the Führer, although with 'very little idea of what he was doing'. Their meeting had no agenda and once Hitler realised that the marshal was not going to get involved in a military agreement, 'he fell back on generalities'. Pétain announced at the moment of his handshake that 'I enter today into the way of collaboration', and brought a new, wartime nuance to a word that at the time represented 'the hopes of a pro-foundly humiliated nation', but later became a synonym for treason. His supporters characterised *une collaboration à raison* as a commonsensical compromise, helpfulness snatched from the jaws of the defeat. It was one of the defining symbolic moments of Franco-German co-operation that opened the way to full-blooded resistance, and a permanent ambivalence. On his only visit to Paris in April 1944, Pétain was greeted with great affection; General de Gaulle was to receive a near-identical welcome four months later, after the Liberation, with the same 'elegant motorised policemen escorting' each of the men, 'the same pretty Parisiennes throwing flowers, and the same delirious crowds singing the "Marseillaise"'.

The two agents and their new colleague were made aware of how careful they would need to be soon after their arrival. The German Armistice Commission was based in Wiesbaden, but had a controlling influence in the Vichy police department to ensure adherence to the terms of the Armistice. Roman checked in to a different hotel to Mathilde and Autier, and left his registration form on the concierge's desk, only to find a policeman scrutinis-ing it when he returned from the bathroom. He had put the Alsatian town of Hurbache as his birthplace on his false papers: his division had been based there so he could summon some knowledge of the place, and it explained the mayor's stamp pur-loined by his colleagues on the forgery. His strange accent passed muster, but the amiable gendarme knew Hurbache well enough to start asking him what news of 'old Jean-Pierre' and 'Huguenot'. The Pole was able to escape with the excuse that he was keeping his girlfriend waiting, and swiftly booked himself into a larger, busier establishment.

Mathilde came under suspicion of a different kind when she ran into Captain André Achard, an old acquaintance from Algerian

days who was now working in the air ministry. She introduced him
to her companion, who was exuding his usual energetic high spirits, and Achard, suspicious both of the foreigner in the paranoid
town and of Mathilde's personal loyalties when her husband was
off in the army, asked her to call on him at his office later. He wanted
to know if this Captain Borni 'was her husband … or her future
lover?' She took the novice's foolish risk of telling him the truth
about Roman, and her honesty paid off as Achard had 'influence in
Deuxième Bureau circles'. He 'had no love for Great Britain', which
he maintained had abandoned them after Dunkirk, but told
Mathilde that the British were 'essential to save France from the
Germans' as he pledged his support. Such calculations had to be
taken on the balance between emotion and practicality for the next
four years.

The trip was not a recruitment success. Their contacts were tied
up in the peculiar and delicate business of the government, and at
least one person who could have engineered 'some useful opportunities in occupied France' pointed out that any organised resistance
could destroy the fragile power balance between Pétain's government and the Reich.

*

While they were in the south, Roman was wary of Mathilde's 'emotional and enthusiastic approach' to life as she hurled herself into
his world, but back in Toulouse, away from the mistrust and mach-
inations of Vichy, he reflected that he 'felt quite safe' enough with
her 'after watching her under difficult conditions of travel' to show
his full hand, including his plans to move to the occupied zone to
give his dream reality. He acknowledged that she had an energy
and courage that complemented his own, she could give him legiti-
macy to allay the suspicions of any enemy or collaborator, and lend
him credibility in the eyes of the French agents.

He made the most of the gravity of his 'very important undertaking' as he discussed detailed plans 'to create this new network'
reporting from occupied Paris to the Polish government-in-exile

and MI6 in London. Mathilde understood that this was 'a very serious business' with a start-up date of 15th November, just over a month away. Apart from his bad French and lack of contacts, she was moved to hear that she was 'the only person [he] could trust and who possesses all the qualities necessary for this work', including that she was 'intelligent, brave and gay'. He would be 'the general' and she his 'colonel, chief of staff, pilot-major and Spitfire'. She responded that she was at the service of her 'General Toto', to use her flirtatious name for him, possibly a reference to Dorothy's loyal, energetic dog from the recently released *Wizard of Oz*. A few busy weeks after her suicidal thoughts by the Garonne, Mathilde now believed '*la victoire du monde*' was within their grasp.

One last bit of personal business needed settling before her next heroic chapter could begin. Maurice Carré, back from Syria, sent a telegram from Marseilles to say he was on his way to Toulouse. Mathilde found her husband 'cross-grained, ill and very disagreeable' and they had a ferocious row. Now that she had imbibed from Roman's deep well of patriotism she thought Maurice if anything 'pro-Nazi and hating the British', whom he assumed, not without justification, were sure to lose the war. She regarded him as more than ever a coward, refused to return to Africa with him, and suggested that he join de Gaulle where at least he would 'immediately be made a major' in the organisation which had abandoned their country. Neither Maurice nor many of his comrades took that route: of the 35,000 troops returning from Syria after the armistice signed at Acre of July 1941, only 5,500 joined up with de Gaulle; the rest returned to France. The Carrés were to meet for the last time a few days later. When Maurice went on to show courage in battle, Mathilde admitted that her behaviour towards him had been 'unforgivable', one of only two such 'actions' in her life that deserved such condemnation.

For now, she could get on with her own war. She returned to Vichy to exploit her new acquaintanceships and learn some spycraft. Achard lined up two officials from his 'Deuxième Bureau circles', Captain Simoneau and Dr Bernard, who taught her how to write with invisible ink by using alum dissolved in water; running a hot iron over the message would bring it back. Roman, always damning about French intelligence matters, dismissed their trade-craft as 'based on films'. The monocled Simoneau, whose 'beautiful hands and fine features' did not escape her notice, gave her a crash course in the markings of the Wehrmacht, how the red of the artil-lery must not be confused with the red of the staff officers, and how yellow was worn both by signallers and by cavalry.

While Mathilde was in the occupied zone pursuing her espio-nage education, de Gaulle put out his Brazzaville Manifesto, which argued that the Vichy government was illegitimate, yet did not call for armed resistance. At the same time the British Foreign Office panjandrum Sir William Strang opined in his usual unemphatic style that the British had to be careful not to 'ride two horses at once' as they were 'still gingering up' to the Vichy regime. Mathilde never interested herself in diplomacy or politics and was oblivious to these manoeuvrings; but she intuitively knew where the best fun and gossip was to be had and spent her evenings sipping gin in Vichy's Les Ambassadeurs hotel amidst the American journalists.

*

14th November 1940 saw former prime minister Neville Chamberlain's funeral as well of one of the most devastating raids of the Blitz: 544 civilians were killed in Coventry alone, but only one of the 515 German aircraft that dealt the terror was shot down. It was an auspi-cious day for Mathilde and Roman to head north to set up. She could travel as she had resurrected her Red Cross credentials and applied to 'go to Paris to continue her work as a nurse', but Roman took a secret midnight bus that deposited him in a farmyard on the demar-cation line between the zones. An old man came round, cap in hand, and the passengers threw in 'the equivalent of a few days' wages' before he led them cross-country on foot for some miles, stopping to avoid the sentries' rounds which were regulated with German effi-ciency. Eventually the illegal travellers were far enough inside the occupied zone for those with forged papers to be able to board trains and buses.

Mathilde's first visit since the Armistice found the capital in the throes of an air raid. She was shocked to see only German military vehicles on the roads, jackbooted soldiers on the streets and red banners with swastikas hanging from the public buildings. The French *tricoleur* had been banned after the Armistice and a sixteen-year-old boy who had tied the flag to the lightning conductor of Nantes Cathedral two days earlier had been executed; news of his death had spread across France 'like a powder trail'. The elegant place de l'Opéra 'had been made hideous by the forest of Wehrmacht military signposts' whose blocky Gothic lettering was another heavy-handed reminder of the city's rulers. Radio-France and the daily papers had just started to run a competition asking listeners and readers to identify the sources of Anglophobic quotations such as: 'Impious England, fatal executioner of all that France held divine, murdered grace with Mary, Queen of Scots, inspiration with Joan of Arc, genius with Napoleon.'* The curfew, which ran from ten o'clock at night until five the following morning deadened the place. Clocks had been moved to Berlin time, an hour ahead of the southern part of the country and two hours ahead of Britain, which meant it remained symbolically dark until late on the mornings of that numbingly cold winter.

The mortality rate was already on the rise and by 1942 was to be forty per cent higher than it had been from 1932–8; deaths from tuberculosis more than doubled. There were constant power cuts as much of the coal that ran the power stations was cut off by the British shipping blockade; the rest was mostly diverted to the Ruhr Valley to keep the weapons factories open. October's *Statut des Juifs* had freed the Nazis to begin the French paperwork of the Final Solution.

Rationing had hit Parisian style and palates hard from September, with 'everything good' in short supply, 'from butter to clothes, from tobacco and wine to salt, from petrol to coffee'; meat was hard to come by. Since September, the ration had been about half the calories necessary for good health: 250 grams of bread and 15 grams

---

* The answer was Alexandre Dumas.

of fat per day, 185 grams of meat and, cruelly, only 40 grams of cheese a week; 500 grams of sugar a month. Dogs had been killed to save food. Mathilde succinctly registered that 'the city had no soul left'.

She broke the news of her final parting from Maurice and Roman's imminent arrival to her mother, who was 'overwhelmed and shocked' in her 'bourgeois dismay' at a divorce in the family and Mathilde's proposed living arrangements. On no basis other than knowledge of her daughter's impetuous nature, she also warned her about 'the difficulties of such work' when the network idea was explained to her. However, she came around to the new dispensation after some pleading, and agreed to receive this Polish airman.

Roman reached Paris in the late afternoon and travelled from the Gare d'Austerlitz to meet Mathilde at the flat on the avenue des Gobelins. He was now to be known as Armand Carré, a cousin of the family, with his questionable French once again a result of his Romanian upbringing. Madame Belard was taken with his bravado as he recounted his journey, but at the same time marked him down as 'vain, and rash'. What 'astonished' her was that her daughter had 'feelings' for a man who was so unremarkable in looks, with 'un physique quelconque'. She could not comprehend that the flat Mathilde had found was intended as their espionage headquarters rather than a love nest.

The official start date of the network that soon became appreciated by the London espionage chiefs as their 'sole regular source of information from France' was two days later. In that desperate year alone, Great Britain lost 2.73 million tons of shipping with only 221,935 tons of new warships built, and was trapped behind her cliffs. The following eighteen months were to make Mathilde Carré at once an acclaimed heroine across the Channel and a reviled villain in her own country.

4

The Big Network

The network was audacious, original and not to be equalled for the rest of the war. Owing to the combination of Mathilde Carré's efficiency, Roman Czerniawski's visionary idealism and their combined dramatic flair and optimism, it was conjured into being within mere days of their arrival in Paris.

Roman had already settled on a name: he used to read an aviation bulletin called *Interavia* which was packed with succinct information and he wanted the reports from Paris to imitate its straightforward style; the network would be international: he was a Pole, most of the agents would be French and their work was intended to be of use to all the Allies. He agreed 'Interallié' with Colonel Zarembski moments before Mathilde arrived in the Toulouse hotel room for one of their daily language lessons. Zarembski courteously bowed as he took his leave. It was the only time the head of Polish military intelligence was to meet one of his star operatives.

*

Mathilde took Roman to inspect their premises before the curfew. They walked quickly through the streets of the Observatory district to the Faubourg Saint-Jacques and a stuccoed, seven-storeyed building opposite the Cochin hospital that had itself been built as a clinic. He was delighted by the large room on the top floor she had rented from a penurious artist called Arthault: it had a flat roof accessed either by an exterior staircase or through the attic which gave the possibility of a radio aerial in future. It was taller than the neighbouring buildings and offered views on all sides to the river, the Observatory and the Luxembourg Gardens; north were the great towers of Nôtre-Dame, and to the west the dome of Les Invalides, the final resting-place of Napoleon. Roman recognised that the rooftop would be useful for 'night observation' of neighbourhood movements. The one aspect of their work that needed settling right away now that the network was about to become reality was their relationship, and they agreed on that first day that they should 'cease to exist for each other as man and woman and become merely pals in intelligence work'. Mathilde returned to her relieved mother for the night.

Roman was too wound up to sleep and by the time Mathilde arrived in the morning, he had crystallised his thoughts. They could pick up 'scraps of information' and go around 'making contacts', but urgency did not allow a gradual evolution. He had refined his concept to one unprecedented in its scope, scale and simplicity: the occupied zone would be broken down into segments; even within these, the difficulty faced by agents trying to travel around by train and bicycle, checking on 'all points of interest', returning to write their report, deliver it, collect fresh instructions and then set off again for fresh observations would be time-consuming as well as conspicuous to any suspicious gendarme, informant or busybody. Such a repetitively furtive organisation would require hundreds of recruits with little time to vet them, and would be both 'uneconomical and dangerous'.

There would be an organic spider's web of sectors, each with a head based in a major town; below that person would be a hierarchy of locally appointed agents and subagents spreading out across the sector and feeding back to regional centres, unknown to those on the edges. Fewer reports would find their way to Paris and out to the Allies, a smaller headquarters staff would be necessary and only a few cells at any given moment would represent a security risk. Roman had spent the night with his map and the railway timetables and was ready for Mathilde to take the lead in implementing and populating the network.

Mathilde and Roman were like 'two urchins' that first day as they fizzed with their 'ideals and pride'. They made a list of tasks: to find agents, to 'organise France', their own work and liaison with Marseilles and London, to get a radio and 'have a budget' for her to manage. And within a matter of hours, they were ready to put their plans into action.

*

The previous week had carried intimations of a perilous future under German rule after an autumn during which Sartre noted that the occupiers had conducted themselves 'with restraint and diligence', displaying 'at times a naïve goodwill'. A group of students from the Sorbonne and various *lycées* had gathered as usual to lay a wreath at the Tomb of the Unknown Soldier at the Arc de Triomphe to commemorate the 1918 armistice. There had been small, peaceful protests for a few weeks in the Latin Quarter and propaganda messages transmitted by the BBC that urged demonstrations at war memorials. The French police dispersed the small crowd at the arch with baton charges, but German soldiers followed up with machine-gun fire. Several demonstrators were wounded and over one hundred arrested.

The fuse for the first non-belligerent death was lit on 10th November. A twenty-eight-year-old engineer, Jacques Bonsergent, had been part of a group which had accidentally jostled some soldiers. In the shouting match that followed, one of his companions raised his fist to a sergeant and Bonsergent was arrested, seemingly for no greater crime than being a witness to a minor quarrel. He appeared before a military tribunal on 5th December at which he inexplicably took full responsibility for the incident and was condemned to death. Two days before the first Christmas of the Occupation, Bonsergent was shot at Vincennes prison. The Germans stuck posters on kiosks and in Métro stations that claimed his execution was for 'an act of violence toward a member of the German army'. Life in occupied Paris suddenly seemed more arbitrary, even as the majority of the city's population went about its daily business as best it could.

*

Mathilde rented another two rooms on the next floor down, one for each of them, while the painter's studio became the operations room. By the time she had finished her negotiations, Roman had worked the sectors out on his Michelin map. There were to be six-teen of them, starting with Sector A, running from Bordeaux to the Spanish border, then radiating north. C, D, E and F would take in the coast from Brest to Calais and the Belgian border, before spiralling back to K west of Paris. Paris itself and annexed Alsace were separate sectors. The agents in each sector would have code names that would correspond to their letter – for example, in the critical coastal C Sector, César was a fisherman from Roscoff, a father of nine who was prepared to risk his life by carrying mes-sages to and from British ships and submarines in the Channel in his small boat; the sector head, known as Coco, was Jacques Collardey, a twenty-year-old pilot towards whom Mathilde felt great affection, characterising him as a 'Paris ragamuffin ... pos-sessing all the light-heartedness of youth'. Collardey was 'a success with all the women', particularly after he 'grew himself a mous-tache to prove himself a man', in Mathilde's view. In espionage terms, his greatest success was befriending a Brest photographer who supplied copies of all the prints ordered by the Wehrmacht. The affection between the carefree ragamuffin and Mathilde was to have devastating repercussions.

Now that the Gestapo's reputation for extraction of information by torture had been established in Eastern Europe, it was vital to give the civilian recruits some guidelines to keep the network safe and ensure codes of practice and discipline to enable them to pass on intelligence of the highest quality and consistency. Mathilde and Roman sat down on that first day to write their instruction manual. Mathilde, who had already confessed that she had never read a spy story in her life 'or even seen a film of this type', was an

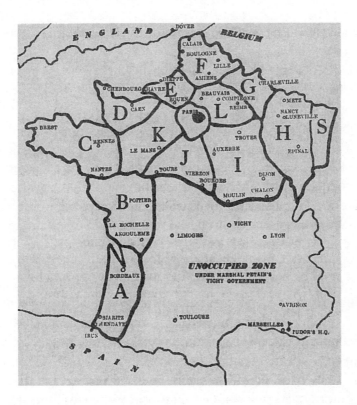

eager student as well as an enthusiastic editor and typist as she was anointed Interallié's chief of staff.

They created a spy's handbook for the ages. They would report 'information on the land forces, Luftwaffe and navy, munition dumps, stocks of fuel and electric power stations, troop movements, chemical warfare, industry, press, politics and propaganda', the whole structure and panoply of war. The document they wrote that day headed 'Information Service' was remarkable both in its ambition and its comprehensiveness. Its nineteen pages began with an exhortation: what will 'succeed' in the 'invaded territories' are the 'strong, dynamic and confident elements' that do not merely 'passively wait for a miracle'. Information – military, propaganda and counter-propaganda – would win the day. The Germans will oppose any 'liberators' looking for information; the Gestapo and the French police 'under German pressure' will quash or control anyone they have 'bought' or 'whose souls they have enslaved'. Even in defeat, it is up to a nation to decide whether it has been 'conquered'. Paris under the Wehrmacht had fired Roman to fresh imaginative heights and Mathilde had found a new-found intensity alongside him.

The practical part of the document was trickier. Agents had to be able to learn and pass on the German order of battle in detail, and Roman had not dared carry his reference material over the demarcation line; even his capacious memory could not hold the many markings and subdivisions of the occupying forces. In a characteristic moment of courage mixed with imprudence, he went to visit the military bookshop in the boulevard Saint-Germain. Amongst the histories and dictionaries was a volume that should have been banned – the thin, yellow *Guide de l'interprête*, a pre-war Deuxième Bureau primer with concise charts of all German units and their identification marks. If a shop assistant had informed on him, Interallié would have been still-born and his war, if not his life, over.

As well as calling on potential agents' finer feelings, the pair were aware of the lure of money as an incentive to resist or collaborate. They offered between 500* and 2,000 francs as a reward for the 'enormous effort and expenses incurred' to identify each division, including the commander's name and transport capability; the same amounts for anyone who came up with any 'good initiatives' for future espionage; 5,000 francs for persuading a fisherman to courier messages to British ships or leave them in specially adapted lobster pots.

There was a detailed section on tradecraft. Agents were urged not to be too obvious as they checked for a tail. 'Do not look mysterious or conspiratorial'; 'talk in a low voice in public places'; when talking to another member of the network of the opposite sex, 'always look cheerful, as if having *une conversation amoureuse*'; 'avoid banter'; 'write legibly in tiny letters' and 'be precise'. The list

---

* 500 francs had a purchasing power approximately equivalent to £3 at the time.

of instructions was so comprehensive that it enabled the necessarily novice spies they would be recruiting to produce top-class material immediately, and drop it off at the network's first 'postbox' on the fifth floor at 27 rue de la Michodière: 'box 20, not 20B or 20C … learn the address by heart' and do not 'dawdle or chat' while in or around the building. There were even sample reports as templates.

Roman's dynamic confidence stoked his chief of staff's patriotism to the point that she wrote 'each of your efforts is sacred to your country' to her as yet unknown spies.

*

Over the next few days they turned what was a set-up based on vigorous thought, a few maps and a banned book into an essential network with strength in numbers and depth of penetration. It was a unique feat.

As Roman 'knew very few people in Paris and … spoke French inadequately' with the added danger that to the unattuned ear he might even sound German, the bulk of the recruitment fell to Mathilde. She signed up her childhood friend and summer companion in 'La Débâcle', René Aubertin, on her first day in Paris. Aubertin 'had never seen the girl he had known from childhood so enthusiastic or so sure of herself' and once again talked about his 'curious' chemist friend, Marc Marchal, who in a respectful nod to his fifty-one distinguished years was code-named Oncle Marco.

Philippe Autier, the early recruit for F1 in Vichy France, now furnished them with an introductory letter (written in pencil, in case of the emergency need for erasure) to his cousin Maître Michel Brault of the Paris bar. Brault refused to become an agent as he had his sights set on getting to London and working for the Free French, but was to play a crucial role in Mathilde's life. He was the type of settled figure to whom she often turned, while Roman, more circumspect about anyone who did not launch themselves wholeheartedly into his organisation, showed an unusual cynicism when he decided that Brault's real aim was to 'make money' by selling

their reports to the Deuxième Bureau, and was displaying patriotism merely 'for sentimental reasons and to be able to boast of it
later on'. The lawyer was at least 'an honest and conscientious man'
with 'a lot of good practical hints and suggestions'. Mathilde and
Brault met 'two or three times a week' in the early days and the
'handsome, tall, middle-aged' figure with his 'charming manners'
performed several introductions that paid off, and one, a year later,
that was to twice prove a godsend to her.

One Brault contact was Henri Boussel, 'Traffic Officer of the
Northern Railway', who provided 'information relating to troop
movements and requests by the German staff for train allocations'.
Mathilde failed to realise the importance of such 'friends in top
circles of the French Railways' until her more experienced 'General'
gave an example of their intelligence value: it took seventy-two
trains running at twenty-minute intervals to move a division, prior
knowledge of which could reveal a strategic shift by the enemy as
well as a potential bombing or sabotage target.

In 'the confusion of thought and conflicting loyalties' that typi-
fied Paris throughout the war and long after, it was hard to calculate
whom to trust. Mathilde was the instinctive assessor of potential
agents, learning to draw them out to the point where they would
declare for France or de Gaulle. Her old friend Mireille was married to Charles Lejeune, a police inspector in Paris who was
invaluable as an interpreter of the dizzying number of German
regulations, as a provider of blank cartes d'identité, and for his
access to inside knowledge. He became chief of R Sector, Paris. The
Lejeunes lived at 6 avenue Lamarck, where Mireille was the concierge, such a good cover for a variety of visitors that she managed
one of the network's 'postboxes', a delivery point for the agent
reports. Mireille put Mathilde on to an Alsatian couple down the
street, the Hugentoblers, who loathed the occupiers. Richard
Hugentobler chatted to Germans in bars and cafés around the city
while his wife, another concierge, managed a third postbox and
became 'devoted' to Mathilde.

The agent who was to unleash the most dramatic and dangerous
moments of the entire war for Mathilde and Roman, alongside

dozens of other spies both known and unknown to them, seemed a routine recruitment in those mid-November days: Jean Lucien Kieffer, or 'Kiki' as he was also known, was a 'cheerful, cheeky' pilot with a round face and a 'broad and solid' physique, notable for permanently wearing a beret. He was an engineer in his late twenties whose work was 'very efficient and intelligent' even by Roman's exacting standards. Mathilde and Roman both considered Kieffer 'able and trustworthy', their instincts at the point of recruitment as sound as ever. They could not have foreseen the results of their well-founded faith.

Some agents were sent by the Deuxième Bureau or arrived by word of mouth via Aubertin and Brault in the later weeks of 1940. A young air-force lieutenant with access to information about aerodromes in the Paris region provided a stolen copy of the German 'red book' which contained photographs of all Luftwaffe aeroplanes which Roman copied by hand to enable the agents to tell 'a Junkers from a Messerschmitt etc.'

Gaston Lurton had a radio shop near the demarcation line in Tours and became head of J Sector towards the end of the month. He was 'a stout, honest fellow' who was 'ready for anything', including locating crossing points to and from the unoccupied zone on his horse, smuggling letters and documents, collecting information and weapons for the Resistance and fomenting propaganda through his extensive local connections. He knew someone who made dies for embossing the yellow identity cards provided by Lejeune, and had 'a printer friend' who provided them with 'excellently printed demobilisation forms'. Lurton and his sector were so important that against her better judgement Mathilde had to sign up his mistress, 'an elderly café servant' known as Jeannine-Ernestine, who was of limited use because in spite of her 'courage and patriotism' she 'was so stupid' that she once reported that a German 'division has left without giving a forwarding address'.

Pierre de Froment had served with Jean Merciaux and Mathilde seized on a chance encounter with him to provide military information from Brittany and later to train agents in Lille and Amiens. Simoneau of the Deuxième referred 'a young sergeant-pilot with

fair hair and a baby face … a typical, good-natured Parisian, courageous and loyal but always grousing' called Jacques Laboureau, the
son of a Montmartre music dealer who provided Luftwaffe intelligence as 'Jackie'. Laboureau found Mathilde 'ambitious and
intriguing', and in turn recommended a friend of his called Jean
Carbonnier. Carbonnier was a fat, fifty-year-old commercial traveller, which gave him the excuse to move around D Sector, which
he headed. Mathilde spotted Carbonnier as a man of vigorous
appetites who was dangerously fond of 'la dive bouteille', and who
had stockpiled his flat with black-market provisions including
'exquisite chocolates' which gave Roman 'great happiness'.

Another Simoneau contact was Pierre d'Harcourt who was
Interallié's vital, if unorthodox, link with the Deuxième Bureau,
fulfilling Simoneau's instructions to 'give any information you feel
may be of help … even if you are giving it to us as well'. The
Deuxième was not ashamed to infiltrate an intelligence-gathering
organisation that followed a different chain of command, a sign of
how hard it was already to operate independently in Vichy.
D'Harcourt was overweight, unhealthy and short-sighted, and
appeared an 'elderly, rather indolent, dreamy scholar' to Mathilde,
but she came to appreciate his 'cold, logical power of reasoning,
calm and courage … to obtain results'.

*

Roman was always 'rather reserved around the French' because
of his 'conversational handicap' so left these recruits to Mathilde
with 'absolute confidence', but he brought in some of his exiled
countrymen. Colonel Zarembski suggested an old friend from a
Franco-Polish family called Lucien de Rocquigny. De Rocquigny
was a 'small, delicately built' aristocrat, an exquisite pianist with
'greying hair and thin, sensitive hands'. Mathilde was smitten by
his 'gentleness, goodness' and 'youthful freshness'. He had been the
pre-war editor of the Echo de Varsowie, a newspaper that had been
essential reading for every foreigner in Warsaw, and had escaped
Poland via Hungary to look for a way to avenge himself on its

destroyers. His role was to study all the French and German press material for anything that would give away troop positions or movements, right down to news snippets that might say 'Local man, captain of 7th Cavalry Regiment, married today ... ' or 'Brave man from the barracks of 15th Infantry Regiment helped to save people from huge fire ... ' In a 'Vichy and Paris press' which was made up of 'the malpractice, distortions, omissions, and lies that constitute news reporting' in what Jean Guéhenno called 'this European prison', such nuggets were all de Rocquigny had to go on. Anything to help guide the RAF to its targets was welcomed.

Prince Wladimir de Korczak Lipski, descendant of a twelfth-century Hungarian king, had fought for the British in the First World War and was a commercial artist, which gave him access to 'small French industry' as well as forgery skills. His wife had been killed by the Germans in Warsaw and he was dedicated to revenge. The sharp and watchful man had already worked for F1 and 'knew the outskirts of Paris like the back of his hand'. 'L'Observateur' was confident that 'a walk in the country, a chat in the local bistro and the information would flow in'. His sixteen-year-old daughter, Lydia, also joined the network under the code name 'Cipinka', meaning 'little chicken', her father's pet name for her. Lydia was studying at the Industrial Design College and therefore able to draw plans of factories and military installations to a minute scale.

Stanislaw Lach, whom Roman had met in Marseilles, arrived in the third week of November. He was suitably unmemorable for any suspicious watchers, a 'tall, thin Pole of indeterminate age with a muddy complexion and a small black moustache'. Roman put him down as 'a typical Polish porter, a gossip and a drinker', but he was also 'calm and brave' and superbly efficient. Lach used his previous employment on the Polish railways and in the Citroën factory in Paris to good use to earn the code name 'Rapide' as the first network courier. He spent many nights pedalling his bicycle fifty kilometres to hide in the bushes near the aerodrome of Melun-Villaroche, counting the German bombers out and back again from their blitzing of English cities to pass on an idea of the effectiveness of British flak. Armand's unwaveringly loyal former ADC, Lieutenant Bernard Krótki, signed up as 'Christian'.

*

Interallié was an unparalleled creation in speed and scope. Roman was full of praise for 'Lily's tireless efforts' in moving around the city 'from one appointment to another, bringing each time new contacts' and 'new possibilities' as he refined the handbook in the studio. She was encouraged to be as observant as possible, and always to wear her spectacles regardless of whom she might meet. She could then see enough to ask what 'GFP' on a soldier's epaulettes might mean and to learn that it was Geheime Feldpolizei, the Military Police.

Most of the Paris agents and chiefs of the sectors were in place, trained and gathering intelligence by late November, only three weeks after the network's birth. The initial information was about the occupying forces in each sector, particularly on the coasts of Brittany, Normandy and around the Pas de Calais, C to F sectors, but the guidelines were universally applicable. An agent might ask a wine merchant what sales he was making to the local barracks; just hanging out in cafés, restaurants 'and other localities in the town' might produce gossip and occupiers' details. The names and addresses of the commanding officers in each town and the registration numbers of military vehicles were always useful. For example, 'two officers of the 58th Infantry Regiment and four men of the 2nd Artillery Regiment. The barracks: Barracks X occupied by the signal corps, the sentry bears the number 63. The names of the officers discovered: Colonel von X lives in the last villa as you leave the town on the right leading to B ...'

An agent looking at Luftwaffe installations should provide a sketch of the airfield, show the sheds and hangars (including those already destroyed), the numbers of genuine aircraft, any dummies, and the location of power stations, munitions dumps and fuel tanks as guidance for bombing raids intended to paralyse local industrial and military capabilities with few civilian casualties.

Details of camouflage, anti-aircraft guns and other defences, whether or not the field was being further expanded, the numbers and types of vehicles entering the place, were all potentially valuable. Railway watchers were asked to note how many trains travelled in which direction over what period, what regiments were on them, and what was painted on the sides of the goods wagons.

The Paris zone was the most important for industrial information. Sketches of factories and defences were needed, what and how much of it they were producing, who was on the board of management. The ratio of German to French workers could be an indication of the degree of secrecy around a product, or whether there might be enough employees to incite sabotage; an intimation of morale could influence fifth-column incursions and propaganda. Chemical factories needed special attention in case of the development of new weapons, and Marchal's expertise would be critical when powders could be got out for analysis.

Before the sector heads had their subnetworks in place, Roman had the idea of sending them to lurk near the different *routes nationales* out of Paris as a fact-gathering exercise. He assumed that even the outlying units would have to send vehicles and officers to the capital regularly, so a rough map could be drawn of which divisions were where. After this, the agents scattered: 'Albert' went to the Bordeaux region already aware that there were two or three divisions on his patch, as well as to check on how many German and Italian submarines were in port; 'Charles' went to Brittany to spy on two divisions there; 'Fernand', a French Reserve officer and industrialist contact of Marchal, headed for F Sector, the Amiens–Dunkirk area; René Bourdon was to check the units in I Sector, on the eastern frontier with Germany; Lurton went home to Tours.

*

Intelligence was useless unless it could arrive in London. When Pierre d'Harcourt had carried his own intelligence to Vichy, his methods of transmission looked distinctly amateur: apart from the occasional flash of inspiration such as when he persuaded the prefect of Nevers' driver to smuggle documents for him, he occasionally sent papers tied to an arrow fired over a river on the demarcation line. Or, in summer, bathing parties would be held on both banks and his man would swim between them unnoticed by the guards. Interallié worked in altogether more secure and bolder ways.

The agents left their scraps of paper in one of the two postboxes in avenue Lamarck. As visitors needed to call on the concierge, they were unlikely to be remarked upon by snoopers. Mathilde would 'move swiftly from one appointment to another' in her 'black fur coat, red hat and often small, flat, red shoes' to collect the reports from Mireille Lejeune and Madame Hugentobler and bring them back to the office. There they would be collated, coded and typed up on the flimsy paper normally used for keeping carbon copies of letters.

Only Mathilde and Roman knew the code, which was simple, ingenious and tough to crack. The French word to be sent was looked up in Kielski's standard French–Polish dictionary and a reference given based on the page number and the line on that page on which the word appeared. If 'production' was to be sent and it appeared on the twentieth line of page 365, that was set up as 36520. Proper names were spelt out according to the letters 'of the alphabet which appeared at the top of each section of the dictionary'. Once all the words were written down as groups of numbers, the variables were added: the date was coded; for example, 10th May would have two sets of numbers, one for the date and one for the month. These variables were then added on to every pair of groups. On arrival in London, the variables were stripped out and then reference to the dictionary enabled the rest to be decrypted.

Mathilde typed the coded reports up on Tuesday nights. There were never more than sixteen pages, the maximum number that could be folded flat and put in an envelope without being too thick for purpose. She handed the package to Lach over a cup of ersatz coffee in the Café Européen opposite the Gare de Lyon on Wednesday, following which the courier boarded the eleven o'clock

Marseilles express and made his way to the first-class carriage immediately behind the engine. As soon as the train started to move, Lach would go to the lavatory, which held a toilet on the tiles rather than a hole in the floor on discoloured linoleum as elsewhere; above the toilet was a sign reading '*Replacez le couvercle après l'usage*' to encourage male passengers to lower the seat. He would unscrew this and put the papers behind it. The thin envelope did not produce a noticeable gap between the sign and the wall, and Lach added the tradecraft refinement of putting his handkerchief on the end of the screwdriver to prevent any telltale scratch marks on the screw-head.

However nondescript Lach was and however well forged his papers, someone travelling weekly in both directions on the same route stood a good chance of attracting attention, so he rarely crossed the demarcation line. He alighted in Dijon while the train continued on. A woman from the Tudor network boarded at Avignon in the unoccupied zone, unscrewed the sign to take Lach's papers to Marseilles, and replaced them with anything that he needed to pick up as he reboarded the Paris-bound train in Dijon. The flimsy pages contained no mention of Interallié or its locations should they fall into the wrong hands. Only one report was ever lost, but was rediscovered 'several weeks later' safely in place. It turned out that the first-class carriage had been uncoupled in Marseilles for repairs.

*

Interallié's fast start was expensive. Rent, bribes, false documents, payments for information and expenses all mounted up, and Roman was always 'over-generous ... with no idea of the true value of money', unlike his beady chief of staff. Madame Belard, who also took messages for Aubertin and Marchal, had given the pair a small loan, but it reached the point in December when they were down to their last centimes. They visited the pawnbroker with Roman's camera and were offered 1,200 francs. When Roman produced his papers in the name of Captain Armand Borni, the owner took pity on him as a French officer down on his luck and upped the loan to 1,500 francs.*

Word finally arrived that the Polish government-in-exile and British secret service were sending 1.5 million francs† via Lisbon to Zarembski in Marseilles, and Lach was sent over the line to bring some of it back. He could not run the risk of being searched on the train with huge sums in cash, so had to cross on foot. He chose a place near Montceau-les-Mines, south-west of Dijon where he had been tipped off that the sentries changed over at midday. However, just as he emerged from the wood on to the road that ran along the border, he was spotted and 'sprayed with bullets'. He leapt into a hedge and escaped behind the line again to hide up in a tailor's house. By this time the station was surrounded by soldiers. The tailor bought a ticket and as the Paris train came in, Lach crossed the tracks to clamber aboard from the side away from the platform. It was their first truly narrow squeak.

*

The partners revelled in their venture: they were 'always laughing' and as they dined together in the blackout, their 'hearts were full of light'. Mathilde was buoyant, her 'life had grown wings'; she did not always know 'what [she] was doing' but felt 'entirely confident', and now believed that if 'one wished for something with enough fervour, it would be granted'. She was working with 'the best people' and felt fulfilled for the first time that she could remember, important, living in constant jeopardy and making a difference to the war.

Interallié was the only network worthy of the name in the occupied zone, serving Vichy as well as Britain. But Mathilde and Roman knew their intelligence had to flow more quickly for it to be of real use. An urgent report sent out of sequence ran the risk of not arriving in time for it to be acted upon; a suspicious border guard could unmask the train toilet ploy and lead to a trap, exposure and

---

* Approximately £8.50; £470 in 2018 values.
† Approximately £8,500; £470,000 in 2018 values.

a tortured confession from Lach. On Christmas Eve 1940, Roman spent hours with a wet pencil drawing a passable impression of a smudged German stamp on his *carte d'identité* before heading over the border on a bus with Lurton to Colonel Zerambski's Villa Mimosa in Marseilles to discuss the acquisition of a radio, complete with operator.

Mathilde went to her parents' flat. Arsène Belard had just been released from prison owing to his age and he told her that Maurice Carré was now in the army in North Africa and wanted her back in his life. He had written 'despairing letters' to them, to Captain Achard in Vichy and even to Marshal Pétain about her. But the fearlessly committed spy was anticipating the year ahead too keenly to look backwards.

5

In Every Way

By the end of 1940 Interallié had populated occupied France with agents, clearly laid out its working methods and instituted a delivery system that it was already hoping to upgrade. It had the energy and aspiration to become 'the fourth force' in warfare, 'indispensable' to Britain, France and Poland in the face of further, seemingly inevitable defeats. The 'Walenty reports', as they were known in London after Roman's code name, were already deemed by their British recipients as 'of the utmost value and the best source of military information in France at that time'. 1941 was to be the year in which it produced essential, unique intelligence to live up to its own exhortation to scheme 'every day and in every way against the Boche'. It was a bleak and terrifying time for many French citizens, and one in which Mathilde's character, her courage and her recklessness, her patriotism and her moral codes were all to be tested to their limits.

*

Roman returned from the unoccupied zone on 2nd January after a hair-raising journey which included dropping his wallet and false papers on the bus carrying him over the border. He had had a reviving Alpine holiday in Megève 'with a petite blonde' called Madeleine Lecquelec, and arrived back with a radio set the size of a portable typewriter and its operator, Fernand Gane, as well as his committed new mistress-recruit. 'One supposes he had got bored of La Chatte', a bemused British spy digesting the romantic liaisons at

Interallié headquarters commented. Madeleine was about thirty, married to a dentist with two daughters, 'no beauty but ... with a lot of charm and a love of sport'. Mathilde, who took the view that her partner 'found celibacy unbearable', went to Rouen early in 1941 to ask the dentist, whom she considered 'a caricature of Dostoevsky's "eternal husband"', if his wife could travel frequently to Paris. The dentist 'played his role so well' that even though he often 'came to fetch her back', his wife still 'came often'. Madeleine's initiation into intelligence and resistance was to be brutally punished during the last two years of the war in a series of concentration camps.

Eventually, it had to be admitted that the wireless transmitter 'looked very nice but did not work'. Gane was a prickly figure in his late thirties whom Mathilde 'never found sympathetic' and she noticed that even the ebullient Roman 'was trying to hide that he felt the same'. Gane had been wounded during the German invasion and had returned to his peacetime occupation as a 'publicity agent'. The only obvious solution to the weak radio signal, which could transmit its Morse code but not receive, seemed to be to rig up an antenna on the flat roof of the studio, leaving it open to detection from an upward-looking neighbour. Gane and his colleague Max Desplaces, a civil servant in the police department, checked and rechecked the set-up but eventually it was decided that Mathilde and Gane should go south for expert advice.

Before this mission, they had to move their headquarters for fear their strenuous radio efforts had been intercepted, as they needed more space for the even larger scale of the intelligence work that they were envisaging, and because Mathilde was getting fractious in the unheated studio during the coal shortage in that first winter of the Occupation. She was brought down by her 'weariness' and the 'uncertainty of [her] future' and had 'a vision of the African sun', even of still being able to 'lean' on Maurice's calm strength, and had to remind herself as she queued for food that she had opted for a life of engagement and danger over her schoolgirl choice of bucolic peace and knitting; she 'had no right to weaken or to harbour regrets'.

She found a new apartment on the rue du Colonel-Moll, which exemplified the well-attested espionage technique of hiding in plain sight in that the other two flats on their floor were occupied by some Gestapo officers and 'some old Russian collaborators'. Mathilde created cover for herself by chatting up 'Monsieur Gestapo' whenever she saw him, to the point that the Germans called her their 'lift flirt' as they 'vied with each other for courtesies'. They were persuaded that the flat 'was occupied by gay young things who played dance music all day' and her passing friendliness was a welcome change from the sullen resentment of most Parisians. The concierge on the ground floor was a 'Germanophobe' who had been 'bayoneted in the buttocks' by the Nazis. Mathilde told this ally that her 'cousin Armand' was experimenting with gazogènes, substitute fuels, most often wood or charcoal carried in huge stoves on the roofs of cars, so the concierge was not to be surprised if he acted a bit oddly or if there were surprising noises: 'You know – these scientists!'

A further security hazard was their ancient 'maid of all work', Marie, a Basque who had been a servant in the building since she was young and displayed a 'devoted affection' towards Mathilde. Marie was strongly 'anti-Boche' and used to write encouraging letters to Winston Churchill denouncing 'offensive foreigners and undesirable French people', letting him know that Radio Paris told lies, and suggesting 'about a hundred people like her' whom he could call upon for help. These were sent via a friend to be posted in Vichy France, leaving Marie to channel her patriotic feelings through her venerable, one-eyed dog, John, whose English name became 'a symbol, even a cult' of her Anglophilia. The friend must have binned these letters in Paris as by that time the only authorised personal correspondence between the two zones were printed cards with a checklist of the sender's state of health, which might be 'tired', 'slightly seriously ill', or 'wounded', and a limited list of other bulletins, including that there was a shortage of 'provisions and money' or that someone had 'passed the examination'; there was only one sign-off, 'Affectionately. Love'.

The flat was ideal both as headquarters and home. Mathilde took it upon herself to ensure there were always fresh flowers, mimosas if possible and sweet-smelling pine cones 'in every corner', but its big dining-room-office 'horrified' Maître Brault with its 'open display' of intelligence documents and 'the great staff maps on which the exact positions of Wehrmacht units had all been marked' spread across the table. Roman slept on the sofa in the salon in the centre of the apartment, while Mathilde had the only bedroom off its corner now that they were living together 'like brother and sister'. Once she did rush into the salon in 'an elegant and sheer blue nightdress' to share an idea that had taken root during the night only for him to 'noisily flounce out'; she made it clear to him after this that she 'thought of him only as a companion in the war and a fellow idealist'. The bathroom at least became her 'private domain' since she liked to bathe frequently, while he 'did not like water'. The dissatisfied Kieffer, who could never resist an opportunity to be snide about his superiors, was definite that they could not have been lovers as she was 'always reproaching Armand for being too dirty'.

They soon settled into a routine of a late start and a gossipy breakfast before getting down to work. Initially they also lunched together in the apartment, but as they were constrained in what they could say in front of Marie, Mathilde started going to her mother's most days where she caught up with Madame Belard's thoughts gleaned from BBC broadcasts. Sometimes the favourites de Rocquigny and Aubertin stopped by for supper, and then they would work on into the night, distilling and encrypting the day's intelligence. More often than not, Roman would play a record that had just been released by Billie Holiday, 'Gloomy Sunday', often known as 'the Hungarian suicide song', about a lover driven by war to take his own life. It was an uncharacteristic favourite for a man of his optimistic ebullience.

In the frustrating absence of a working transmitter, or 'piano' in their code, Mathilde stuck to her old routine of setting off each Monday morning to go to Mireille Lejeune's *conciergerie* to pick up the previous day's reports from the sector heads. These 'often asked

for a meeting to explain something further', or money needed to be
handed over before they returned home. Monday evenings involved
'pulling the reports apart … to extract the salient points' as some
agents, despite the clarity of the briefing manual, put in anything of
conceivable value. Mathilde would give them 'hell for mistakes/
omissions of dates or names' and frequently 'reprimanded them
for inefficiency' the following week. Aubertin would come in to
redraw the sketch-maps and military insignia sent from the field
on to flimsy paper while Roman moved bits of tracing paper around
his Michelin maps to track divisional manoeuvres before adding
his comments on the 'general situation'.

*

These laborious methods of working could not continue as
Interallié grew and refined its techniques, and Mathilde and Gane
left for the unoccupied zone in mid-February to sort out the radio.
The atmosphere had become more threatening in the past three
months: soldiers who had kept a lackadaisical eye on the demarcation line had now been replaced by 'professional customs men'
with motorbikes and dogs, and there were police checks on trains
which included questioning anyone with mud on their boots in
case they had travelled cross-country. That month one man had
already been shot for an illegal crossing and many more imprisoned in Tours.

They had planned to cross at Vierzon but Gane's contact was
nowhere to be seen, so they moved on to Poitiers, where a railway
worker told them to walk a further twelve miles through the rain to
Fleury. They stopped at a hotel, but kept going when the proprie-
tress informed them about a railway employee who could show
them a good spot to cross the line when the guard thinned out.
After waiting near the railway, they struggled up to their waists
through a bog that straddled the line and had a bad scare when
they emerged on being challenged by what turned out to be a
sheepdog. Eighteen hours after they had left the Gare d'Austerlitz,
the pair entered the Zone Nono to be met by a local schoolmaster

who cleaned them up and helped Mathilde to the Vichy bus while Gane went on to Marseilles.

Vichy had changed in the past three months since the pro-Nazi Admiral Darlan had become vice president of the Council. Darlan believed that the war could result only in German victory or stalemate, and either way would end up in two power blocs, 'a European one dominated by Germany and an Anglo-Saxon one dominated by America'. Darlan even hoped for an outright German victory rather than a negotiated peace with Britain as that way France and Germany could carve up the British Empire and condemn the old enemy to the status of a 'third-class dominion'.

Mathilde found the atmosphere in Vichy 'slowly becoming collaborationist and apathetic' and was disappointed that her 'friends' enthusiasm had waned and they had grown stale'. She realised that Simoneau had lost power and influence in the toothless Deuxième Bureau. He had become, in the newly minted word that carried a dejected loss of any sense of ideology, 'envichysés', institutionalised by the strange town and times just at the very point when she was energised by her Resistance work.

It was a relief to meet Gane in Lyons. He had been in touch with the Tudor technicians as well as collecting 50,000 francs* from Zarembski, and was confident that what he needed was a larger transmitter. They set off back for Paris on foot at midnight led by a *passeur*, a new breed of guide who claimed he had poison darts against dogs, and who was almost certainly giving a cut from his exorbitant fee both to the French guards who waved them through and to the German sentries who appeared not to hear the twenty-strong party pass. *Passeurs* were not above murdering clients who failed to keep up, particularly on the arduous crossings of the Pyrenees.

During their tortuous travels, Gane told Mathilde about his mistress, 'as well as his wife and his daughter'. The former was Monique Deschamps, 'an intelligent and practical woman' who was 'very emancipated and had started her studies in medicine'.

---

* Nearly £300; about £16,500 at 2018 values.

Mathilde agreed that Deschamps be considered as an agent, and a couple of days later met 'Moustique'. The new recruit had 'bright mahogany-red hair cut short' and a 'cigarette constantly stuck between her lips' which gave her a look of 'a certain arrogance and that she "couldn't give a shit"'. Mathilde never mentioned Deschamps with much enthusiasm although she professed to find her 'truly amusing' company. In the end she could not forgive the 'one time she slept with' Roman that year. Mathilde let her know that such behaviour was against the rules, although it never seemed much of an issue otherwise in the network, but the payback for her strictness was to hear 'all the details of their lovemaking' from Deschamps, whom she now deemed 'more cunning and astute than actually clever'.

*

Jean Carbonnier, the fat commercial traveller who ran D Sector on the Cherbourg peninsula, was arrested by the Gestapo in March as the German grip on the occupied zone tightened that cold spring. All Mathilde knew was that 'having drunk more than usual one evening, somewhere between Cherbourg and Caen he opened his mouth too wide'. His house was thoroughly searched and his extensive inventory of luxuries taken away for German use but 'not much pressure' was put on him. The Gestapo 'did not deal at all efficiently with his arrest', failing to question Carbonnier closely about any Resistance activities since he was to be 'charged and shot for black-market activities' anyway. The arrest of the sector head of such an important area 'disturbed them a great deal', and Mathilde decided to visit the letter drops on different days of the week rather than on a more noticeable regular day; she would now empty them on the 4th, 14th and 24th of each month. Gane was moved to an apartment in the vast Palais Berlitz on the corner of the rue de la Michodière to start work on the new transmitter.

Marchal was gathering information about German troop and supply movements through his contacts on the railways as well as in the chemical and gas industries. The scientist with his 'high-domed forehead' worked with 'great precision', not reporting on an assignment until he was 'sure he had all the data'. He once broke into a factory carrying out 'special research on germ warfare' near Vincennes on 18th January, to be surprised by a night-watchman. He escaped with 'a bleeding jaw and torn clothes' alongside an increased appetite for front-line resistance. When he had served in the Rhineland in 1919 Marchal had met a German named Oscar Steininger, since when the two 'highly intelligent, artistic men of the world' had remained close. Mathilde used to dine with them and extract intelligence from Steininger on his monthly visits from Berlin 'to deal with the administration of property belonging to British subjects'. She believed her friendship with Steininger both pleased Marchal and made him 'a bit jealous, unnecessarily'.

Now she had earned her spurs, Mathilde started to play more of a front-line, intelligence-gathering role herself. She went with Marchal to Orly aerodrome, a Luftwaffe base just outside Paris, and spotted that the café opposite was sporting a 'For Sale' sign. She pretended to be a potential purchaser and asked if her 'architectural adviser' could go around the building. While she employed her charm to keep the owner on the ground floor, the putative architect upstairs jotted down 'full details not only of the Luftwaffe planes using the runways but also of the hangars and the anti-aircraft installations'.

Her sense of her own invincibility, in combination with the engaging frisson of danger, could occasionally lead to foolhardiness. Once as she scurried between appointments, she stopped for a cup of tea at the Café Dumesnil at Montparnasse station. The room was more or less empty but an officer with perfect French insisted on sitting at her table to ask her for some 'information'. She got in first by saying she would like to know what the flash on his shoulder signified as she 'didn't recognise it'. The officer boasted that he was responsible for all Luftwaffe supplies for the Bordeaux region, and they went on to discuss German propaganda, how surprised the Nazi government had been that France had accepted the Armistice terms, and his view that Britain would win the war eventually as Hitler would take too many risks 'like gamblers always do'. When he finally got around to his request, she was able to tell him where he could buy a box of tennis balls before she rushed back to write up the encounter.

When she took her greatest risk, it was her 'very impudence and daring' which saved her. She went to the tiny port of Saint-Pol-de-Léon in Brittany to recruit fishermen to drop messages offshore. The trip turned out to be futile as the men took the prudent path of remaining silent rather than jeopardise their jobs and families so she went on to Brest to inspect the RAF damage on its dockyards. She found the inhabitants 'staunchly pro-British' and proud to keep their shops open amidst the destruction like the Blitzed Londoners. To show solidarity, Mathilde decided that 'nothing would be wittier than to speak with a broad English accent'. She even had the 'nerve' to go for supper to a restaurant designated for German officers and to employ her 'feigned nasal' tones there.

German intelligence was efficient that day. When she arrived back in Paris on the night-train Mathilde noticed 'a tall man on the platform' looking at her 'with marked interest'. She went to have breakfast in the station café and was followed in. He was a Gestapo officer alerted from Brest that 'a young woman in a black fur coat and a red hat with a pronounced English accent was on the Paris train'. Mathilde employed 'all her charm' and nerve to pass off her prank: there had been so much talk of the raids that she had gone 'as an inquisitive woman with time on her hands' to see the damage, and that she had put on the accent 'to amuse myself' and 'to see the reactions of the townspeople'. The Gestapo man, Max, laughed uproariously at this fine example of Parisian humour, and told her about his Irish mother in Dublin, his badly wounded ankle and how much he hated his job. He begged her to lunch with him. She was glad to get home to change and empty her incriminating jottings out of her handbag before they met again at the Gare du Nord where they enjoyed a 'very amiable meal' before Max caught his train to Berlin.

*

Zarembski flagged up that the transmitter needed a more 'highly professional and skilled man' than Gane to carry out 'the steady and efficient work', so in early April Roman decided to follow the route through Fleury to Marseilles to consult with the intelligence chief. He returned with the 'tall, blond, slim' Janucsz Włodarczyk, a naval radio-telegrapher who had been running the station in the Polish Embassy in Paris until 1940. Roman had complete trust in Włodarczyk's 'nice, quiet behaviour and obvious inner strength', every bit of which he would need over the next two years, but the chauvinistic Gane felt usurped by his arrival, and the seeds of dissent were sown.

Despite the potential fault lines inherent in the network between the nationalities and the competing egos, Mathilde and Roman remained the closest of colleagues. He suffered a blow when his mother died, the first shock of which he got through by getting plastered at dinner with two friends and Mathilde. The men drank numerous toasts 'to his Poland and his family' and hurled their glasses into the fireplace and Roman spent the drunken small hours with his deputy sitting on his bed as he reminisced about the country of his youth that he was desperate to restore.

On 1st May they were on the move again after Roman feared he might have been followed home. They went to an apartment rented by Mathilde under the name of Madame Donadieu at 3 place du Trocadéro, but she suspected the landlady of taking too close an interest in the comings and goings, so Roman went back to rue du Colonel-Moll a couple of months later and she moved on again, to rue Grenelle. From then on, they only stayed anywhere for a few weeks. Security for the expanding network became a high priority in the increased German surveillance as Berlin planned its invasion of Russia and needed its western flank to be quiescent in order to divert troops and attention eastwards.

*

They were finally ready to test their powerful transmitter on 10th May. No bursts of radio waves could be too long for fear of discovery, so they arranged four attempts and persuaded the anxious Roman not to bother them at least on the first two occasions as they 'establish[ed] the link in technical code'. Mathilde would be known as 'La Chatte' on the airwaves, Roman as 'Valentin' or 'Walenty', and the network as 'La Famille'. The very first encrypted message, 'From Interallié Stop Very happy to establish the direct link Stop Valentin', got through to London.

Valentin himself had been sent to a nearby café to prevent his anxiety infecting the group. At four o'clock, Gane moved through the tables and asked if the seat opposite was free. He ordered himself a cup of coffee, putting his copy of that day's *Paris-Soir* between them. A moment later, Roman got up, switched his own paper for Gane's and said a polite farewell. 'Bursting with impatience', he was back in the flat before he extracted a piece of paper with a pencilled string of five-figure groups from inside the newspaper. He stripped out the numbers representing the date and day of the week, got down Kielski's *Dictionary* and turned its pages to key in each word until he had deciphered 'To Interallié Stop Congratulations … ' Mathilde and Roman 'clapped hands and danced with joy around the big desk' in the office. Eleven months after the Armistice and seven since they had arrived in Paris, the founders of the great network were at last able to get their intelligence out immediately.

*

Speed of delivery ramped up the danger of discovery. Włodarczyk, Desplaces and Gane transmitted four times a day on four different wavelengths, but did not dare have their radios live for more than five to ten minutes at a time as scanners operated from the headquarters of the Abwehr, the German military intelligence service. They also changed wavelength every three minutes in sync with the expert 'London Side', long enough to send up to a hundred groups of five figures, each group representing a word taken from the dictionary that served as a cipher.

The peeved Gane proved himself by getting together enough spare parts to build more radios and over the next couple of months they set up stations in the original Interallié base near the Observatory and a room the other side of the Arc de Triomphe in the place Pereire, where Włodarczyk lived. He trained up two more operators to work from the Trocadéro flat, the preferred main location as it had a corner room at the end of a long corridor where the transmitter key tapping out its Morse code ran less risk of being overheard (although Roman once arrived to find the hall light flickering in time with the dots and dashes as the current running through the heavy cable to the rooftop antenna was interfering with the building's supply).

More information of ever-greater usefulness flowed to blacked-out, bomb-damaged London. Mathilde moved swiftly between the radios and postboxes, meeting agents and sector heads and typing up the reports; Roman coded and decoded for most of the day. They started photographing papers after he located a camera in a second-hand shop that held sufficient 16 mm film for a hundred photographs rather than the standard eight, sixteen or thirty-two. They found a lens for short-distance work and used a large wardrobe as a makeshift studio and darkroom. Aubertin worked out a way of shading colour directly on to the film with fine nibs and Indian ink, as was needed for detail such as the insignia of German units. The reports now varied between twenty and fifty negative photographs, occasionally up to over a hundred, and were packed into tubes and packets that had contained medicines before being given to Lach. If any should be opened, the exposure to the light would render them unreadable. Now that the flimsy paper in the first-class toilet had been abandoned, the courier went straight through to Marseilles where one of Tudor's men took the films on to Madrid and Lisbon, whence they travelled by air to London.

Reliance on Lach was risky in itself, as his frequent crossing of the demarcation line was liable to attract attention; also, he often carried cash on his return trip which would be very hard to explain away. A partial solution came about in the form of Gane's lover Monique Deschamps. The diminutive and vivacious 'Moustique' had cut a swathe through Interallié: Mathilde admitted Deschamps 'worked well' even if she 'quarrelled the entire time with her lover and tried to sleep with all the boys'. Lejeune once came to Mathilde to complain that he had found Deschamps in her favourite Laboureau's bed, to which the chief of staff turned a blind eye. But as she heard more and more of this sort of thing she 'grew angry' and shouted at her underling to 'Make love with them all ... but for heaven's sake work.'

Mathilde cracked both the operational and the personnel problems by engineering that Deschamps go to head up the critical A Sector on the Atlantic coast to find another way into Spain for important material. Deschamps arrived in the 'contact office' on the top floor of the Berlitz building to say that she had fixed up for the cousin of one of her agents, 'an old family servant', to carry mail to the border post of Hendaye, from where it would be taken on to the Spanish town of Irun. After the fees for all involved were settled and Roman had grumbled at how 'these border people have lived on contraband profits for centuries', a service was set up by which a love-gift of what appeared to be cosmetics would leave Paris each Thursday on the 8 a.m. train and be carried over into Spain the following morning.

The reliable radio meant that they could be of even greater service to the London spies, although the arrival of a visitor from England further highlighted the increasing jeopardy of their environment. Michel Coulomb was parachuted in by SIS and a message came via Lach that Mathilde was to go to the Comtesse de Dampierre's house at Neuilly to meet the 'stolid' operative who needed Interallié's help to connect to London. Coulomb got off his first message in early June but when the reply came in and Mathilde went back to Neuilly to pass it on, he had gone. He had been betrayed to the Gestapo alongside Pierre d'Harcourt and shot in the leg at a Métro station in the Bois de Boulogne as he tried to escape. The 'young, very modern and cute' Colette de Dampierre was also arrested and sentenced to death; she was reprieved to work in the factory that made goods for the Lévitan department store, a favourite haunt of Nazi officers after it had been seized from its Jewish owners.

D'Harcourt, whose age and size gave him no chance to escape, had Mathilde's telephone number on him, but the Gestapo failed to follow up on the incriminating evidence. It was another lucky break.

*

Mathilde was now spending three days a week collecting, collating, abbreviating, correcting, and supplementing intelligence 'with additional remarks', as Roman looked over the paperwork and carried out his cypher work. 'Clean, precise and methodical', she then typed everything up for photographing under seven headings behind a cover page headed 'INTERALLIÉ' and the report number in a circle. 'General Situation' acted as a contents page; three sections for 'Army', 'Navy' and 'Air Force' then gave an analysis by sector. Chapters on 'Transport and Communications', 'War Industry' and 'Review of the Press' followed. Marchal, who was also a member of the Vichy-based Patrie organisation, provided any chemical or engineering news.

The flat resembled the editorial office of a weekly newspaper as everything was prepared: papers were shuffled and voices raised as transmission day came around; there was a wardrobe with a metal stand that held Roman's camera as he took the photographs to leave by train for Madrid; de Rocquigny, Aubertin, Krótki and Marchal moved in and out of the room. Roman justified the danger of this noticeable activity by pointing out that each time a pilot took off from a British airfield he was risking his life. But the headquarters workload was impossible to sustain. What changed the dynamics of Interallié came to Roman when he was talking to Paul Martin, head of H Sector. Martin mentioned the small Lorraine town of Lunéville on his patch and Roman remembered the young, blonde widow whose husband's identity and bicycle he had taken. Not only did Roman hope to rekindle their affair of the previous summer, but he knew he could trust Renée Borni. Even better, he knew she would be able to race through the addition and subtraction of the coding work.

Renée Borni arrived at the end of June and was code-named Violette. On some level Roman realised that it was a high-risk strategy to introduce another woman into the office as he listed the differences between her and Mathilde that were 'too big to allow them to be friends': Mathilde 'was not exactly pretty, but interesting to men, sophisticated ... *une femme de lettres* with a Sorbonne background ... ambitious, very often nervous and highly strung ... She bored of people who did not share her interests.' Against this, 'Renée was pretty, young ... quiet but vivacious, had no high-school education ... no interest in literature or the theatre ... liked going to cafés and restaurants'. Yet despite these differences he did not anticipate any reason for jealousy as he welcomed Renée into the network and into his bed, and went out to lunch with her and Mathilde to brief her on 'her new and unusual life'.

For her part, the 'sophisticated' Mathilde undertook to train the newcomer in matters both agency and Paris, giving her 'all the necessary tips so that she could smarten herself up' and stop looking like 'a typical little provincial woman'. She took pride in the 'swift and successful' transformation she wrought, but got in digs such as that Borni 'was a girl with no education'. Mathilde rarely praised her female colleagues, but admitted that Renée 'did the tiring and unrewarding work' of encoding 'admirably', which greatly increased the speed of decryption and freed Roman to do more intelligence work. Mathilde was at least mollified by the arrival in the evenings of Maître Brault's secretary, Ginette, who had 'the strong qualities of a true woman' to help her out with the typing and collation of the reports.

*

That summer of 1941 was one of intense activity and change for Interallié as both input and output multiplied in response to France's changing backdrop. There were now between 150 and 250 agents and subagents at any one time and the material flowing from them was ever more detailed and precise. Mathilde and

Roman dealt with daily requests from London asking for 'more information about the "Cathedral" division about to leave for the Russian front ... more about the installation on the Atlantic coast of the 47s taken from the Maginot Line', and the like.

The Nazis further constricted the occupied zone: on 14th May the first Jews were taken to concentration camps and laws forbidding them to travel from Vichy France were implemented in late September; they were compelled to carry identity cards and put Star of David posters in the windows of their business premises; all bicycles had to be registered with a number plate and owners had to have both hands on the handlebars at all times to lessen ride-by attacks. Pressure on French industry and agriculture to arm and feed a Wehrmacht committed on two fronts was stepped up, and demands made 'to establish much more material assistance than before from occupied Western Europe'. France became Germany's main source of labour, raw materials and manufactured goods. Patriots found themselves physically and psychologically restricted by degrees.

Interallié's personnel shifted and altered alongside the often-transient loyalties of wartime. Jacques Laboureau had already left in March for 'personal reasons', whether or not because of his relationship with Monique Deschamps is unclear; Deschamps herself wrote to say that she was 'bored' and wanted to be in Paris with Gane; jolly Gaston Lurton gave up as head of J Sector, to be succeeded by the dim Jeannine-Ernestine. The head of G Sector, who had managed to extract 10,000 francs* out of Mathilde 'by pretending that the Gestapo were after him', rejoined his old air squadron. A twenty-year-old pilot took over B Sector, and 'a Jew who changed the money for the organisation on the black market' ran F Sector. Intelligence-gathering for some was a form of employment rather than a patriotic duty as more small networks sprang up; Interallié occasionally lost agents for 'better pay and conditions of work', such as a Pole who claimed he was on his way to England

---

* Approximately £60; about £3,300 at 2018 values.

to continue the struggle from there, but was thought by Roman to have absconded to a rival outfit, with the ensuing security risk. There were, in fact, no networks to touch Interallié for its reach across the whole of occupied France and its ability to transmit to England.

Their reputation and their radios made them a natural point of contact for all those wishing to subvert the German occupation. Brault introduced them to a Russian who ran escape lines for enemy combatants in France, but before Mathilde 'could fix up any satisfactory arrangements, he disappeared'. 'A Franco-Scottish gunnery officer', Lieutenant Roger Mitchell, was an early SOE agent put in touch with Roman by Zarembski. Mitchell, who spoke French so well that he 'could easily pass for a Frenchman of good family' moved in and out of their lives as he arranged landing and pick-up zones through Włodarczyk, with whom he was 'well in', and used the Hugentoblers' avenue Lamarck postbox. Roman was very taken by the glamour of his 'excellent new companion' with his tales of undercover work, surreptitious parachute jumps and hurried pick-ups from fields lit by flares, and the two men became firm friends.

Mathilde and Roman were still moving frequently: in mid-July he went to the rue Picot leaving her in the place Pereire; at the end of the month they both returned to rue du Colonel-Moll; she went to 3 rue Cortot, Montmartre, in August and he joined her in October, but as 'the two witches' who oversaw the house accused him of being a 'fifth columnist' owing to his furtive callers he was soon off again, this time with Renée to a first-floor flat 500 metres away at 8 rue Villa Léandre. Włodarczyk had been transmitting from the top-floor attic of the house since September following two previous moves himself.

The terraced, three-storey, brick house with the tree in its tiny front garden was in a cobbled cul-de-sac adjoining the avenue Junot which stretched up towards the gleaming dome of Sacré-Coeur. It was to become the main Interallié headquarters and its most infamous address. Countless transmissions – that opened 'La Chatte Communiqué' and closed when time allowed with the resounding motto of the network, 'Tous les jours et par tous les moyens contre les Boches! Vive la Liberté!'* – were despatched from the attic room in its gable. Mathilde as usual made the place as homely as possible, although she tended to rush in and out when not going about her duties; she also sometime stayed at 6 avenue Lamarck, the same building as her friends Charles and Mireille Lejeune, where she escaped the witches' beady censure.

*

London was relieved to get the 'steady stream of good and reliable reports' from Interallié at a dire time: Rommel had landed in Libya in mid-February; in April, a month when British shipping losses ran at 688,000 tons, Yugoslavia had collapsed and the Germans had invaded Greece and Crete; after the invasion of Russia in June the Germans found themselves fighting Total War and ruthlessly started to seek out 'the enemy within' who might disrupt their occupation. Pétain felt his control falling away in this 'ill wind' and broadcast in August that 'anxiety is spreading, doubt is taking hold. The authority of my government is being challenged, its orders are often being carried out badly.' Alphonse Moser, a young German naval subaltern with a desk job in the Admiralty building, became the first of the occupying forces to die by assassination when a young résistant fired two shots at him as he boarded the Métro at the Barbès-Roucheouart station in Montmartre. By the end of the year there had been sixty-eight such attacks despite the declaration of the Hostage Ordinance in response to Moser's death: now any French person arrested 'for whatever reason shall be considered a hostage', and in future 'a number of hostages corresponding to the gravity of the crime shall be shot'. 'The nightmare is beginning', the collaborationist newspaper La Gerbe commented.

The sector heads and headquarters staff were reporting to Mathilde on the ammunition and fuel depots, the power stations,

---

* 'Every day and in every way against the Boche! Long live Liberty!'

industry, factory and chemical developments, troop movements, port loading and unloading, ships in dock for repair or being stocked for a mission, the emblems on the conning towers of submarine supply vessels, invasion exercises, the erection of pillboxes along the Atlantic and Channel coasts. The devoted de Rocquigny added press and propaganda reports. The sectors from Brest to Calais reported the installation of radar posts, and London asked for more detail on location and design.

It was important for the British to know that the two largest battle cruisers in the world, the *Scharnhorst* and the *Gneisenau*, built in 1935 in defiance of German undertakings at Versailles and the scourge of the Royal Navy in the disastrous Norwegian campaign, had been in dock in Brest since March. Regular updates from Interallié were required on the progress of repairs as well as to guide the ultimately futile RAF bombs, and London decided Mathilde's reports were the most reliable on that vital subject.

Roman felt a 'wonderful sense of fulfilment' when, after checking and rechecking the reports and his maps, he realised that Interallié had located the entire German order of battle in France. 'There was no room for any other division' in the entire country. He called for a celebration dinner with Mathilde, Aubertin and Renée Borni that became memorable as it was the first time he had eaten 'green frogs'. Shortly after, he had another one of his epiphanies: by calibrating the shoulder tabs and vehicle markings of each unit of the twenty-two German divisions in France, he could break them down to individual regiments and even companies. Mathilde had to listen to a dream one morning in which Field Marshal Rundstedt looked 'astonished and cross' at the network map on the wall of the latest paper-strewn office adjoining Roman and Renée's bedroom.

As the value of the reports improved, occasionally more information was demanded than was feasible. The day after the Afrika Korps arrived in Tripoli, Włodarczyk took a message that read 'Urgent and important Stop Can you find out which German armoured divisions landed in Africa Stop', which annoyed Mathilde and Roman for its presumption. But their luck held as Roman had time to kill between two appointments that evening and looked in at a cinema on the Champs-Elysées just in time to catch a newsreel of a march-past of the corps. As the dust settled around the tanks, he caught the emblem of a Panzer division he could identify. Interallié's reputation was intact.

*

One afternoon Mathilde heard the short-long-short ring on the bell which indicated the arrival of urgent news, and after a brief conversation rushed into Roman's office to say that one of Oncle Marco's railway contacts had divulged that Hermann Göring had just left Paris by train to inspect Luftwaffe bases in the north-east and would be returning to the capital the following evening. They had his full itinerary and the timetable was sent on their next contact at 4.15: 'Most Urgent and Most Important Marshal Göring special train left Paris 2pm today and proceeds on the route ... ' The network chiefs stood over Włodarczyk as he tapped out the message, and were excited when the confirmation signal came back from London.

The next incoming contact was at 7.30 p.m. but there was no mention of their coup. They listened out for news of Göring's death on the radio in vain. The following day, Mathilde spoke again to the SNCF employee who had endangered his life to bring them the intelligence. He was tearful as he described how he had watched the *Reichsmarschall*'s train shunt unmarked into its siding. She shared his 'disbelief and anger', but tried to keep up his morale by mentioning some of the triumphs in which he had played a part. The reply to their signal did not arrive for another two days: 'RE Göring train sorry news too late to use for RAF Stop'.

Major Zychoń of Polish intelligence in London later told Roman the sorry story. The message had arrived at the radio station on a day when the officer in charge was young, inexperienced and anyway absent. By the time he got back, the last motorbike dispatch rider had already left, so it languished in his tray until the following morning before being forwarded to Polish headquarters at the

Hotel Rubens, near Victoria Station. There it was receipted and numbered and sent for decrypting in the usual way but did not reach the Operational Studies Room until Göring had returned to Paris. Roman extracted a promise that such oversight would not reoccur with their riskily won material, but never got the chance to test the reassurances.

*

Threats increased again that second autumn of the Occupation. Spot checks of papers on the Métro started up, and although the headquarters team still had passable forgeries, it was distinctly unsettling. They had a scare which would be comical in other circumstances when an agent left a report in the Berlitz postbox inside the wrapping of a bar of chocolate, and, for cover, attached a letter of complaint to the manufacturer about the inferior quality of their product. Roman asked Renée Borni to deliver it to Mathilde only to find out that she had posted it instead. After a brief panic, they decided that when the manufacturer discovered the intelligence about German forces in Le Mans district they would be 'scared to death' and destroy it. A courier from Simoneau was caught on the demarcation line, but Abwehr complacency meant he was not 'properly investigated' before being shot; a thorough exploration would have led to their 'complete destruction'.

Overall, Interallié was deemed 'perfectly designed and carefully organised' and working to maximum effect by October 1941. Roman was justified in his boast that his 'Big Network ... was now the last stronghold of Allied resistance against Germany' and Mathilde was without question its 'cornerstone ... and the intelligence, industry and keenness she brought to the task inspired total confidence'.

Roman was even asked to go to London 'for a personal consultation'. He was to be accorded the honour of being the first aeroplane pick-up in the occupied zone. Mathilde, known affectionately by her colleagues as 'the Colonel', would run things in his absence. She recorded that she felt 'a new burst of energy' at the responsibility.

Her aim, as foreseen by Lucien de Rocquigny, to 'be mixed up in great international affairs' was no longer 'eating her up', and her British counterparts, whom she had yet to meet, regarded her as 'an amazing woman'. The restless uncertainty of her earlier life was calmed and her need to live in the heightened sensation of peril more than satisfied as she seemed to be fulfilling the fantasy of being a second Joan of Arc that had saved her on the banks of the River Garonne only a year earlier.

6

Family Betrayal

Roman was always alert to the possibility of glamorous tales of clandestine derring-do when he heard Roger Mitchell's secret doorbell ring at the rue Villa Léandre house, and was delighted when the SOE man told him that he had been asked to organise Roman's exfiltration to visit the high-ups of the Polish government-in-exile and the security services in London. Interallié was at its zenith, and Roman and Mathilde had every reason to be proud of their extraordinary creation, born of his ingenuity and infectious patriotism, and her more complex cocktail of characteristics, of which loyalty to her country, efficiency and a yearning for useful connection were dominant. Roman knew recognition was as important to his essential deputy as it was to him, and had sent a request ahead that 'some British war decoration be bestowed on her'. It might be seen as ironic, however, that the very period at which Roman was celebrating their triumphs would be the one when the network was tested to its limits, and Mathilde's own strengths and defects were to play a part in the wider moral hotch-potch of occupied France, with its rich and bitter variety of opportunities for betrayal: mercenary, ideological, emotional, practical and, as often as not, accidental.

*

Mitchell was initially surprised by Roman's choice of venue for Operation Pick-Up. Until now the flimsy-looking British Lysander aeroplane made the most of its short landing and take-off by coming down in a field for as little time as possible in the relative safety of the south. Now Roman proposed leaving from an aero-drome at Compiègne, in the middle of occupied territory. Yet his brazen plan had flair and made counter-intuitive sense: the last place the enemy would take note of a landing and take-off was at a small aerodrome. Mitchell told London that he approved the dou-ble bluff and the signal came back to Włodarczyk: 'We agree for Compiègne. Keep constant watch there for German activities. Will fix date.' The operation would be near the October full moon in three weeks.

Roman was energised by 'a new adventure', his first visit to 'the very centre of the resistance against the Germans'. He had never even spoken directly to most of his 'intelligence bosses and col-leagues'. In a newly created piece of spycraft, he made plans to carry his secrets in a gramophone case with the mechanism removed and a record on top in the belief it would be less noticeable than a suitcase. Renée was worried for him but Mathilde was 'glad' as she set about analysing their financial and equipment needs for the future for analysis in London. Roman gave her 'the right to send and sign radio messages', appraise all incoming material, and have sole responsibility for Interallié's affairs in his absence.

The local L Sector agents had verified that the infantry battalion stationed a mile away never emerged at night and on 1st October, Squadron Leader John 'Whippy'* Nesbitt-Dufort, guided by Mitchell's torch, brought his Lysander in to land. He greeted Roman with his entire knowledge of French – 'C'est la vie! C'est la guerre!' – before whirling him off to RAF Tangmere on the south coast of England. 'Walenty' was met by Flight Lieutenant Philipson, given dinner by the station commander and driven through the blackout to bomb-damaged London by 'a lovely girl'. The *Paris-Soir* that fell out of his pocket would be on King George VI's breakfast table as a memento of the historic operation.

*

---

* So nicknamed because he had once made a forced landing among the ani-mals of Whipsnade Zoo.

The warmth in Britain contrasted with the atmosphere in Paris as it became clear that without Roman's powerful belief in and almost innocent enthusiasm for intelligence-gathering, the clash of its unfettered personalities could destabilise the network. And it fell to the volatile temperament of Mathilde to deal with the fallout of the paranoia and insurrection.

The discord began with François Tabet, a former soldier and a friend of Mathilde's who had just been recruited by her to help Włodarczyk on the radio. Tabet lacked the single-minded urgency of his Polish superior and became the subject of 'unfavourable reports'. Roman agreed with Włodarczyk that Tabet was 'a man without principles, a consummate cad' and it had been decided to send him 'off into the country on indefinite leave of absence'. But they needed another operator to run 'a small wireless transmitter' from Brittany 'to direct the sea passage'. Mathilde's plan was that Tabet should return to the fold, but Włodarczyk's view that he was 'too unreliable' overruled her. There was concern that Tabet knew too much to cut him loose. In true SOE style, Mitchell considered for a while that they might resort to 'bumping him off' but in the end he was thought unlikely to be 'a menace to the organisation' and was banished into the swirl of part-time agents scattered across France.

The only new security precaution was a fresh postbox, which Mitchell suggested should be in a busy meeting place where comings and goings would not attract attention. Café La Palette on the boulevard Montparnasse was chosen, and the drop-person was the café's elderly female lavatory attendant who could plausibly enter the cubicles where documents had been left. It was the only postbox not chosen by Mathilde.

She herself became unmoored without Roman, who had been her handler and guide as well as her partner in many ways. He had saved her in Toulouse, and without his praise for her 'exceptional bravery', upon which he always commented, she was submerged by her esteem, which caused her to lash out when she encountered rivalry from others. The ambitious Fernand Gane, slighted over his radio-building expertise, had got back in with Roman by praising

Renée's work at every turn, which had not gone unnoticed by Mathilde. Gane had been sent to head up K Sector but his resentment at being 'relegated', as he saw it, from headquarters staff bubbled up in the chief's absence. He undermined Mathilde directly by saying he had heard there was a file on her in Vichy as an 'agent double', although he was unable to explain for 'what two parties she was working'.

The unease of Mathilde's relationship with Monique Deschamps had been reinforced in her imagination in the summer when she had joined her and Gane for dinner in the Hôtel du Louvre. Mathilde had arrived late, and 'had to leave the table several times with violent colic and fits of vomiting'. Not long after, she was having one of her periodic lunches at Chez Dominique to debrief its eavesdropping head waiter; he told her that a couple 'were plotting against' her and 'might easily try and poison' her. What was more, they looked like Gane and Deschamps. Her friend Tabet had further fuelled her paranoia when he let slip that Gane had tried to poison him too, apparently out of sheer spite. These needless seeds took root during Roman's absence.

Even more troubling to Mathilde's fragility was that Gane and Deschamps 'became very friendly' with Renée Borni after Roman left. Mathilde's perceived enemies' fraternisation with the naïve young widow, who had 'believed in their friendship as [Mathilde] had done', was hard to take without Roman's bolstering presence. A tangled story came via Mireille Lejeune's policeman husband that 'schemes were afoot' to poison Roman 'on his return', although the 'chief danger to him personally was through his girlfriends'; apparently he needed to make a choice between them. This strange, unsourced rumour of undefined assailants heightened the unease in the atmosphere prevalent at a dark point of the war.

The real and imagined stresses took a toll on Mathilde's 'physical powers of resistance' and her 'nerves' in the first days of November. She slept badly and drank huge quantities of coffee and brandy in the belief that they kept her 'up to scratch'. She disassociated as so often at times of stress and felt she was 'floating on air' as she slid back into her childhood need for escape. She craved 'a miracle' that 'a good fairy' could produce 'a little house' for her alone, a place into which she could withdraw from the world when her foundations were crumbling.

*

London struck Roman as calm after the febrility of Paris. He was lionised by his exiled countrymen and by the British spy chiefs, who considered that he 'had organised his agents in a masterly fashion'. On his first morning he was taken to the MI6 building near St James's Park, where the Polish intelligence liaison officer offered to speak to him in any one of seven languages, then walked over to the headquarters of the Polish General Staff in Buckingham Palace Road. Colonel Gano, the head of intelligence, who struck him as 'quiet, polite' and more like the 'head of some business firm' than an accomplished spy chief, introduced him to Roman's hero General Sikorski, prime minister and commander-in-chief. The two men spent hours together discussing his work and techniques, and how he might best pass on his experience to others.

He got his first taste of Allied politics when he suggested that he might meet de Gaulle and his staff, as some of his French agents were 'full of admiration' for the Free French. The senior Poles 'shifted uneasily' at this suggestion and fobbed him off by saying they did not want to change a system that was working so well. It might not help their idealistic colleague's devotion to his work to learn of the fault lines between the prickly French general, the British government and its allies, and SOE.

Roman's one free evening was spent being shown the sights of London from the top deck of a bus by Mitchell's fiancée. Otherwise he was kept hard at it until a few days into his stay when he was summoned to read a decrypted wireless message in the Hotel Rubens: 'Important Stop La Chatte to Valentin Stop Have serious trouble with Kent and Friends Stop They refuse to co-operate and threaten secession Stop'. He was dumbfounded, but played the situation down to his superiors as the result of Gane's potential to be 'unpleasant ... and make threats' and La Chatte's oversensitivity.

Nevertheless, he was alarmed enough to decide to return home immediately.

Roman made the third parachute jump of his life two days later, into a rain-sodden melon field outside Tours, after spending less than a quarter of the time he had planned in England. His frustration was considerably lightened by the award of the Cross of the Virtuti Militari, the Polish equivalent of the Victoria Cross or the highest level of the German Iron Cross, to which it bore a distinct resemblance. The medal was accompanied by an exhortation from his countrymen that he keep up his standards: if the Germans were to continue to make ground in Russia, it would be vital to know their movements and dispositions before the war ended with a negotiated peace that annihilated Poland.

Already anxious about what he might find, Roman was further unsettled to be tapped on the shoulder by his agent Janina at Tours railway station. She informed him that someone in her sector had been captured by the Gestapo either because of his Interallié links or for his work for a local outfit. The man kept arms in his flat, so any connection to the Big Network was potentially fatal. Roman hurried Janina away in case she was under surveillance and told her to report to Paris in two weeks, after which, all being well, he would give her 1,000 francs, and she should remain underground for the duration.

He rushed from the Gare d'Austerlitz to the rue Villa Léandre just in time to report his safe arrival in the four o'clock transmission, then tackled 'the considerable confusion inside the Organisation' that had been exposed in his brief absence. 'The Chief's girl', as Renée Borni was known in London, confirmed that Gane's chauvinism had played a part in the falling-out, as he found it galling to be given orders by a Pole or by a woman he did not respect. It emerged that Gane had even tried to bully Mathilde into teaching him the coding system, with all the attendant security implications.

Mathilde had recovered from her dissociative state and was relieved to see her partner again, especially when he told her that his medal was really for all of them. Not only that, but he reiterated that he had 'arranged for her to receive a British military medal' of her own. He had told SIS that she had 'contributed more effort and nerves and lived in worse conditions than any RAF bomber pilot' and that 'her work was not inferior to any British intelligence officer in France'. He squared away Gane by dangling the promise of autonomy over his own radio if he was more co-operative.

The unease within the network was a reflection of its scale and importance, as well as of the danger of a structure built around personalities: the edifice could be threatened by the flaws and foibles of individuals. The discovery of any one agent could lead to collapse unless they were united in their aims. There were repeated reminders of the growing ruthlessness of the occupiers: when the *Feldkommandant* in Nantes was killed by 'cowardly criminals paid by England and Moscow' on 20th October, fifty hostages, many of whom were thought to have Resistance connections, were executed by firing squad with fifty more to be killed on the 23rd if nobody came forward with information; alternatively, 15 million francs* was on offer for information. Just before the deadline, Pétain came on the radio and 'denounced foreign plots, hatched in England, and invited [the French] to become informers'. None did, which meant another ninety-five hostages were shot, forty-seven more were sentenced to death in the courts and others sent to the camps as slave labour. The Vichy government had compromised itself further as it crossed another morally complex line in an attempt to preserve French lives.

Changes had to be made to prevent Interallié's people overwhelming its purpose. On Mitchell's advice, Mathilde and Roman began to discuss the division of the organisation into three parts, army, air force and coastal. Some of their wares were being shared with the new Soviet allies, who had commented that the network was misnamed given that they had no Russian agents. Roman had been asked in London to come up with another name and had settled on 'Progress', which he was planning to unveil on their

---

* Approximately £85,000; £4.7 million at 2018 values. It is questionable whether the Germans ever intended to honour such an extravagant reward.

anniversary in November. They had worked hard and been dealt some lucky hands in the great distance he and Mathilde had travelled since they had crossed over from the unoccupied zone eleven months earlier. Although in wartime luck often seemed to be a finite resource.

*

The trouble started in D Sector, which had survived the network's first near-disaster in March after the hard-drinking Jean Carbonnier had gone to the firing squad as a black marketeer without giving away the greater prize. D was acknowledged by Mathilde as the 'most-exposed sector' as it covered the heavily scrutinised Cherbourg peninsula and the crucial northern ports, including Caen. High-value intelligence flowed from it, and a reliable figure was needed to take Carbonnier's place.

One of Mathilde's earliest and most celebrated recruits had been the clever, beret-wearing airman Jean Lucien 'Raoul' Kieffer. Kieffer had had a tumultuous few weeks: he was 'desperately anxious' to get into the war proper, and finally had persuaded Mathilde and Roman, who considered his 'services too valuable to be dispensed with', to put him in touch with an 'escape organisation'. He got across the demarcation line and on to the border, but the fascist-leaning Spanish authorities caught him, beat him up and repatriated him, only for him to be arrested in the unoccupied zone for his illegal crossing of the border the other way. He eventually made his way back to Paris where he took Carbonnier's place in D Sector under the code name of 'Désiré', as well as starting an affair with his subagent Charlotte Buffet, a painter. The sound strategy of moving Kieffer, and his subsequent flouting of the much-broken espionage rule about agents and subagents remaining out of each other's beds, were to have dire consequences for Interallié.

The ambitious new sector head had an immediate narrow escape when he was investigating an aerodrome near the coast and was spotted by a sentry, but managed to talk his way out of the predicament with the implausible excuse that he had got lost. He then began to 'reorganise' his area, notably establishing a vital link with some fishermen who took mail to an island about thirty kilometres west of their home town of Granville which they left in 'old fishermen's sheds now not in use' to be picked up by British submarines.

There had been an air raid in Cherbourg in the week of Roman's trip, the evening after which an elderly toper called Mabire was sitting in a bar with a German corporal. The two men worked in the local Luftwaffe fuel depot and Mabire did not mind the company he kept so long as he was stood a drink. He garrulously confided that he had been questioned by his neighbour, Madame Buffet, in the air-raid shelter about how many aeroplanes and of which type were using the depot. The dutiful corporal, uneasy in his French outpost, passed this conversation on to his superiors who in turn notified German counter-intelligence branch Abwehr IIIF in Paris.

Nothing would normally have come of such a tip-off. But with the Resistance gathering strength and RAF raids on military targets on the increase, Abwehr IIIF was increasingly the butt of official criticism and unofficial teasing about their lack of results. Even more damning was the practically simultaneous alarm rung by a municipal worker in Cherbourg docks, Emile Lemeur. Lemeur had been supplying occasional information to Madame Buffet, and it is not clear why he turned traitor. He too was a drinker and maybe needed the money, had become fearful for his life should he be caught, or suspected that when the Germans won the war collaboration would play in his favour. Lemeur went to the local Geheime Feldpolizei office to confess that he had been trafficking the names and tonnages of ships using the harbour.

Cherbourg was known by the Abwehr 'to stink of spies' but these reports reaped unanticipated dividends. The headquarters of the unit which dealt with Brittany and Normandy was based in a luxurious villa in Maisons-Laffitte in the north-western suburbs of Paris that had been commandeered from the French actor Harry Baur after his unjustified arrest as an accomplice in his wife's fictitious spying. Hauptmann Erich Borchers had been enjoying his life in the extreme comfort of the villa, away from the responsibilities and fidelity of home, and was irritated at being ordered to the coast. He was a tall, cadaverous man in his early forties who appeared much older owing to his bald pate and white moustache; he had been a journalist in the Rhineland before the war and was hampered in his job by his limited French. So his first call on arrival in the port was to the local branch of the GFP to request an interpreter. The unranked Hugo Bleicher stepped into the job and into his part as the leading man in the central act of Mathilde Carré's drama.

*

Bleicher was not in sympathy with his country's rulers. The son of the owner of a successful bicycle shop near Lake Constance, he had been educated at Ravensburg University and been a teenage prisoner of the British at Abbeville in the First World War, an experience which left him with decent English and excellent French alongside a strong dislike of the British, the poor treatment of captives and warfare in general. He did not rate Nazi methods or ideology, and was determined to work in his own way to prove both wrong. As a result, he became one of the most successful Abwehr operatives of the entire war.

His impression of the organisation's officers was that they were not much use at counter-intelligence, but 'to make themselves really indispensable' they had become 'adept at supplying the head office in Berlin with black-market goods unobtainable in Germany'. He distrusted, even 'felt repugnance' for the Gestapo and 'euphemistically referred to them as his "concurrents"'. He was an energetic, zealous man of divided allegiances and psychological astuteness, physically strong, now running to fat, short-sighted, with brown hair and eyes, a red face and, as seen by an adversary, a 'clumsy gait like an elephant'.

Bleicher had worked as a salesman for a chemical firm in Hamburg and enjoyed his well-regulated life with his wife and son in the suburbs, until he had answered a circular from the city's

Chamber of Commerce in August 1939 to be a censorship reader, utilising his French. This was, in fact, a cover to become 'part of the secret field police force for the occupied countries of Europe' and after the Armistice he was posted to Caen. There he fell for Suzanne Laurent, the striking, convent-educated brunette *patronne* of the Pelican Bar. Laurent was a widowed mother in her mid-twenties who Bleicher realised 'loved the invader more than she loved her country'. Her clientele had never been drawn much from the tight-fisted French of the area, and had shifted with the war from English tourists to German occupiers. She grew 'tired of business' and when her lover moved to Saint-Lô, she followed him. She got used to hiding in the linen cupboard, the cellar or the loft of his requisitioned house as it was illegal under GFP rules for a non-commissioned officer to keep a mistress.

Life in the Cherbourg branch of the GFP was dull. Bleicher identified missing prisoners of war and looked out for anti-German graffiti artists or propagandists who slipped pamphlets into schoolbooks; the number of futile denunciations between neighbours bearing old grudges alone generated a massive amount of paperwork, and with his high opinion of his own talents coupled with his resentment at still remaining at the lowest military level, he considered himself 'a flower blooming unseen'.

On 3rd October, Bleicher was 'holding the fort' in the office in the place Napoléon when 'a man in a shabby raincoat and green hat' and a temper about his wild goose chase stormed in. Captain Borchers of the Abwehr Saint-Germain needed an interpreter to sort out a 'totally muddled espionage case' and if Bleicher managed it, he would get him released from the police and into intelligence. Bleicher jumped to, and was astonished to be brought before 'a drunken fellow who seemed unable to utter an articulate sentence'. Lemeur told all he knew for a 'bounty of 3,000 francs'*. From this undemanding interview in a field office emerged the formidable spymaster who, although barely promoted within the service for which he felt 'distrust and repugnance', was acknowledged by his

---

* Approximately £17; £940 at 2018 values.

counterparts in England and America as 'a man of great ability and ingenuity, and a specialist in running double agents'.

*

The pitiful Lemeur was the bathetic catalyst for the swift unravelling of all Mathilde and Roman had achieved over the past year, the barely imaginable figure who determined the rest of their lives. He snitched about Kieffer's 'mistress, a certain Madame Buffet' whom he had met once and who had asked that he pass on any tidbits from the docks. It was the second time Buffet's name had cropped up, and she was picked up.

The wayward Kieffer's cooling desire for Charlotte Buffet became the mundane cause of the fraying of the next strand of the rope. Buffet knew that the sector head was 'no longer interested in' her and reported him 'out of jealousy', according to Mathilde. Presumably fear would have led her to a confession anyway once she was in German hands, but either way Borchers and Bleicher knew from the lovers' pillow talk that the man they wanted worked for 'a clandestine organisation based in Paris' and came regularly to Cherbourg to debrief his agents, after which he would return to the capital where the information was 'sent to London either by radio or by a special courier'.

*

When Kieffer returned to Paris in the last days of October and was trusted enough to be given a role in the logistical planning of Mitchell's exfiltration, he still had no knowledge of where Mathilde worked, who else was at the top of the organisation, or even what it was called. Productivity had not faltered during her period in charge of the rue Villa Léandre office, even if the emotional levels had been raised. But professionalism had now been restored as Roman mapped out the secure re-formation of the network as Progress, and composed the last two, triumphant, reports under the Interallié name. No. 99 was to 'contain the Order of Battle of the German Land Forces in France' and No. 100 'the Order of Battle of the German Air Force in France'. Mathilde, who had regained her equilibrium and rushed about the city as before, noticed that Kieffer remained 'strangely restless'. Mitchell too commented that he had 'expressed ... disgruntlement at only having communication with the chief of the organisation through a post-box cleared three days a month' when he heard about the new drop in the La Palette toilets.

The Germans knew that Kieffer was due for his monthly visit to his sector early in November. Borchers had soon lost interest in the case and wanted to get back to the fleshpots of Paris, so appointed Bleicher 'as the man most competent to carry out the arrest'. The former policeman assumed that he was about to net a small-time operator and was pleased to be left alone by his 'impatient and inefficient' new superior. He was in place at Cherbourg station as the Paris train pulled in. Kieffer was easy to spot as he wore his 'airman's leather jacket' as predicted by Madame Buffet, whose tradecraft had been found dangerously awry: a search of her house revealed 'a certain number of questionnaires' for agents as well as 'plans of the organisation and maps of the *département*' that condemned her to imprisonment. She would not have escaped with her life later in the war.

When Kieffer had walked 500 yards from the station, Bleicher ordered the Gestapo driver to pull up alongside his prey. They bundled the unresisting sector head into their car and started to interrogate him. Kieffer quickly folded, saying ruefully, 'It's a pity you've caught me. I should have caused you a lot of trouble in Normandy.' He admitted that he was part of an 'information organisation based in Paris, but he didn't know the address of its chief', only that he went by the name of 'Armand'.

Kieffer was at the start of his new career as a double-dealing informer that gave him the life of intrigue and importance he craved, as well as saved his life for all he knew. For his part, Bleicher was proud that 'a short verbal process' was all it took to get this information, and delighted to be seconded to Maisons-Laffitte for a fortnight on the back of it. He booked rooms in the Hôtel de

Genève, next to the Gare Saint-Lazare, and Suzanne Laurent joined
him to sample the delights of the capital. The next morning at midday, the irritable Borchers introduced him to the chief of
counter-intelligence, Major Eschig, who gave him the authority to
carry on interrogating his prisoner and find the mysterious
Armand.

*

Kieffer showed some flickering of conscience when he offered up
that he had a rendezvous with 'an agent from head office' in the
place de l'Opéra in three days and he was 'ready to go' to fulfil the
appointment. On the day, Bleicher went to the square for a futile
afternoon's walking around. Far from showing the rage of the
thwarted, the newly minted Abwehr agent travelled back to Fresnes
prison to start practising the technique of reasonable negotiation
that was to make him so formidable. His days in uniform were over
as he hurled himself into 'a world of treason, espionage, subversive
activities and double-crossing'.

He had 'a long conversation' with his prisoner, who 'finally
admitted' that he had hoped his ploy would deceive the Abwehr.
The German pointed out that they would find the top people in the
organisation soon enough and that if any of them came before a
military court there was a 'good chance that these *grosses têtes*
would be shot'. Kieffer crumbled completely in the face of such rea-
sonableness. He pleaded that he would be unable to 'stand
imprisonment' and asked that none of 'his comrades' be 'put to
death' and that any who agreed to work for the Abwehr be 'set free',
to which Bleicher agreed; the prospect of more turncoats suited
him.

Kieffer considered presenting 'his sector as an isolated and independent organisation' trying to 'establish a sea-route' for 'its own
needs' but that was not likely to be believed, he later justified. He
told the Feldwebel that he was ready to 'play', but that he genuinely
did not know the address of 'Centrale'; the best he could offer was
'Christian', whom he regarded as 'Armand's adjutant'. Bleicher

ordered Kieffer to tell this Christian that he wanted to report to Armand personally on the search for courier-fishermen, and to return with the address of headquarters.

'Christian' was Lieutenant Bernard Krótki, the cheerful optimist and former professor of languages who had greeted Roman on the Champs-Elysées just after the Armistice. Roman loved Krótki, who sang Italian songs and 'was full of ideas', and had recently made his unswerving ally his 'personal assistant'.

Mathilde had noticed that Kieffer was the only sector head not to put in a report when the postbox at La Palette was emptied on the previous day, 14th November. She asked her 'dear friend' and agent Claude Jouffret who often 'gave her general help' to make contact. Jouffret found Kieffer at his usual hotel and the sector head demanded a personal meeting with the chief. When Roman heard this, he was 'greatly astonished', but at the same time needed to hear about the 'new naval route'. Although he did not 'sense any danger', his training resisted the meeting and he asked Krótki to go speak to Kieffer again. Their second encounter was set for two o'clock next day at the Café Monte Carlo on avenue Wagram.

That Sunday was a happy one for all of the headquarters staff, and for Mathilde and Roman in particular. It was a year to the day since they had started Interallié and they were feeling upbeat, united and excited by their future. Mathilde had asked the BBC to send *un message personnel* in their broadcast at 9.15 when La Famille was gathered: '"Many happy returns to our Family in France on the occasion of the Anniversary", followed by some French melody if possible.'

*

Krótki left the harmonious gathering in the rue Villa Léandre for the Monte Carlo just after lunch. He and Kieffer spoke for half an hour or so on the terrace, adhering to the Interallié manual by making their encounter seem convivial without drawing attention to themselves, and Kieffer handed over some notes about the 'naval route' he had cobbled together that morning. Bleicher was behind a newspaper at a corner table.

Roman was disappointed as he 'glanced through the data', which 'were so indefinite as to be of no use at all'. He had to decide whether to go 'and see Désiré in person in order to discuss the matter with him or to send Krótki once again with a list of definite questions'. Pressure of time saved him for now: he was desperate to mark the anniversary with reports 99 and 100, the glorious climax of an extraordinary year of intelligence, so wrote 'a list of questions on a scrap of paper' which included whether there was actually a fisherman to carry out the role and, if so, the precise plan so that the Royal Navy could be told the co-ordinates. He despatched Krótki back to the Monte Carlo. It was nearly six o'clock, and he reminded his friend that they would be having 'black coffee and liqueur' in a couple of hours and 'was very anxious' that Krótki 'be present'. It was the last time the two comrades were to meet.

*

The party that evening consisted of Mathilde, Renée Borni, Claude Jouffret, Lieutenant Lecourt, René Aubertin, Włodarczyk and Roman. Mathilde bought a bottle of champagne, of which only half was drunk in the 'very calm, dignified and not noisy atmosphere'. They were moved and proud when they heard over the radio, *'Nous souhaitons bon anniversaire à notre Famille en France'* and asked Włodarczyk to reply with their war-cry: *'Le jour de notre anniversaire je transmets au nom de l'organisation notre maxime de combat: "Tous les jours et par tous les moyens contre les Boches! Vive la Liberté!"'* Everyone left before curfew.

Mathilde did not heed Krótki's non-appearance as she was used to his 'unpunctuality and lack of discipline': recently the absent-minded academic 'had explained that he had to take a bath' when he had failed to appear for a meeting. Before falling asleep, Roman reflected with satisfaction on his colleagues' commitment, although Mathilde felt 'overworked and a little tired'.

By four o'clock the following afternoon, Roman was starting to worry. He kept looking out of the window to see if the house was being watched. At dusk, 'strange coincidences' started to occur: there were several 'wrong telephone connections'; 'some unknown individual' brought the landlady men's suiting material 'to sell at a comparatively low price'; he thought he heard machine-gun shots. He and Borni left the house at eight to go out to supper and he 'noticed an elderly individual' on the street 'who made some distinct movement betraying his interest in us'. But he decided he 'was oversensitive and let the incident go', and besides, he was on the way to one of his favourite restaurants, La Franquette, to continue the celebrations of the night before. He said to his girlfriend that she should call on Krótki the following morning, 'observing all security measures', to check on him.

*

Mathilde, Roman, Borni, Aubertin and Włodarczyk had been betrayed before they had even begun their champagne and coffee and before the congratulatory exchange on the BBC.

As soon as Krótki had arrived back at the Monte Carlo, he had been seized, bundled into a car and driven at high speed to the late-Victorian fortress-prison in the town of Fresnes, ten kilometres south of Paris. The prison was in the bottom of a damp valley, its ground-floor cells were 'partly rotten' and the food was 'indescribably bad'; it took a strong spirit to stay there more than a night or two, as Kieffer had just discovered.

Bleicher started to interrogate Krótki. The loyal Pole at first 'refused to reply' and then denied any knowledge of Armand or his whereabouts, at which point Bleicher made a risky counter-espionage move based on his appraisal of Kieffer's psychology over the past few days: he sent him in as a stool pigeon. Kieffer was pushed into the cell to tell Krótki that he too had just been captured; they must have been spotted together earlier. It was easy to persuade the trusting Pole 'to give him the address of the Villa Léandre in Montmartre'. Bleicher left immediately to plot with Major Eschig how to effect Abwehr IIIF's first great triumph of the war and 'bring down the headquarters' of this organisation of which they still knew almost nothing.

*

Mathilde was ignorant of Krótki's continued absence, and went about her Monday business contentedly, ending the day with Mireille Lejeune. As usual, she found her old friend 'sweet, devoted and full of common sense', and accepted her invitation to stay over after the curfew. Nearby, Roman was finding it hard to maintain his habitual good cheer at La Franquette. Borni was surprised when he asked the restaurant violinist to play 'the Hungarian suicide song', 'Gloomy Sunday', rather than something more fitting for such a dinner. 'The sad, fascinating melody' stuck in his head for the rest of the evening and for months to come. He could never bear to hear it again.

The couple got back home just before ten o'clock. Włodarczyk had been transmitting reports 99 and 100, which consisted of 1,000 groups of numbers, on his six o'clock contact with London, but had had to sign off with 200 groups still to go. He had destroyed what had already been sent; the remainder had been coded, but the whole text was still *en clair* on Roman's untidy desk. Borni went to bed. The two men had another discussion about 'the technical possibilities' of using a small 'radio correspondence set received from London for maintaining liaison while the naval route Cherbourg–London was set in operation' before Włodarczyk too went to his room. Roman wrote some notes 'connected with the move and reorganisation' and joined Borni at around three in the morning.

At six o'clock he was jolted awake by thunderous feet and shouting German voices on the stairs. There was a 'beating at the door', which was smashed open. 'A shot was fired blindly' and five men in Gestapo uniform with one in a mackintosh and a beret 'rushed into the room'. Roman felt strangely calm. He asked to be allowed to get dressed. Bleicher was 'the individual in mufti', and even though he did not even know Roman Czerniawski's name, he could not resist exclaiming in his first dawn arrest that 'I am the fisherman from Cherbourg. I was not looking for small fry, I went straight for the head.' Fifteen minutes later, Roman was speeding through the blacked-out empty streets to be interrogated. 'An ordinary denunciation' by a drunken docker in Cherbourg a month earlier had sparked the fuse that was now destroying his and Mathilde's dreams.

7

Trapped

The curtain rose on a suitable backdrop on Tuesday 18th November: it was cold and foggy, and Paris was hard to make out in the mist from the heights of Montmartre. The misery of the second winter of the war was made worse by the shortage of coal and overcoats; people were plugging the holes in their shoes with newspaper; they would be soled in wood soon as French leather was used to belt and boot the Wehrmacht. If the first act of Mathilde Carré's wartime drama had been made vivid and important by her own passion, needs and courage, the second brought devastation, shock, and decisions made without reference to her most redemptive characteristics. The ensuing, hectic four months were the most tumultuous, condemned and ambiguous period of her life.

Roman Czerniawski had been taken to the Gestapo headquarters at the Hôtel Edouard VII in the avenue de l'Opéra where he was punched on arrival by the duty officer in the marble-floored foyer for shaking his hat on to the floor as he could not otherwise remove it while handcuffed. His landlady, Madame Blavette, was brought in with her two nieces, and was astonished to see her tenant; she had been kept in complete ignorance of what was going on under her roof, but was not believed and spent four months in prison. Roman gave a false name in the hope that the gleeful Germans would continue to assume he was a small-time resister, one of 'those bandits of the Hôtel Continental in Brest' as they had shouted on his arrival. But soon after Madame Blavette's appearance the papers gathered up in the flat were brought. He did not need to hear his real name called to realise the game was up. He was taken to Fresnes prison at ten that morning, just as his deputy was arriving at the Café Lamarck for her appointment with her 'general help' and agent Claude Jouffret.

*

Bleicher and his henchmen had made such a racket with their storm tactics, heavy boots and gunshot that Włodarczyk and another radio operator, Georges, who was staying, had the opportunity of escape from the maid's single room in the attic. They knotted their bedsheets and lowered themselves down the back of the building on to a neighbour's roof with a breakable skylight. As they abseiled past Roman's flat, Włodarczyk 'could hear a German telephoning' inside. Georges sustained some bloody injuries and once they had made their way to his cousin's house they finished dressing their wounds and 'supplementing [their] wardrobe'. They tried various local telephones, but found two call boxes and a telephone in a local café out of order, which Włodarczyk melodramatically ascribed to the Gestapo cutting the network.

He eventually managed to ring Krótki, who did not answer, as he was still in Fresnes, ignorant of the consequences of his conversation with Kieffer. Włodarczyk next got hold of Max Desplaces who passed on messages to Gane and Monique Deschamps, enabling them to flee for the demarcation line. At midday he met up with Georges once more, and told him to get word to La Chatte, but later heard she had been taken; he 'assumed that she had poisoned herself' by taking one of the 'pills she always carried on her' – something she never mentioned in her own account, and possibly a self-dramatising legend she had put around the network. He tried to contact London from the rue Manuel Hidalgo radio at the appointed time in the afternoon, but that failed as London expected to receive on the 'No. 1 crystals', which were now in the possession of Hugo Bleicher. Włodarczyk fled and three days later, 'dropping with exhaustion', he walked across the demarcation line. Georges' fate remains unknown.

*

Bleicher remained behind as the Gestapo took the manacled Roman away. Given that Bleicher already possessed 'the archived copies of his messages', he did not 'even have to ask' the terrified Renée Borni to 'reveal all she knew about the organisation'. Borni had been patronised by Mathilde, had fought with her only the previous month, almost certainly assumed that her lover was on his way to his death and that she was to share his fate after her confrontation with this red-faced, bulky, armed German. Despite her later protestations that she did not even know Mathilde's address, Borni gave up 'the existence of Madame Carré alias La Chatte alias Micheline' at once. Her almost mythic punishment for this quick betrayal was that she would have to continue to live, work and eventually be judged alongside her colleague and victim.

For now, she was taken to the hall to await the day's visitors. Jouffret, the go-between with Kieffer two days previously, had an appointment just before ten prior to his meeting with Mathilde, and was arrested 'as soon as he crossed the threshold'. The only word that he heard Borni say was '*Oui*' when she was asked to confirm that he 'was indeed "Michel"' before he too was on his way to the Edouard VII.

Mathilde was waiting 300 metres away in the café next to the Lamarck Métro station. She was in her fur coat and had been passing the time by telephoning her mother and fixing a restaurant at which to meet Marc Marchal for lunch. After quarter of an hour, she gave up and returned to Mireille Lejeune's. Mireille was agog with the talk from the dairy: the Gestapo were searching the avenue Junot, which abutted the rue Villa Léandre, and Mathilde must not go near. But Mathilde's reckless commitment determined her to collect some money stashed there and hide some documents brought by Aubertin to the anniversary party. If she did not return, her friend was to burn the papers kept in a blue suitcase and hide the 137,000 francs belonging to the network.

She did not move with her usual scurrying haste as she pieced together Kieffer's, Krótki's and now the loyal Jouffret's absence with what she had just heard. She focused on anything else. She noticed that winter had fully taken hold, and that there was not a single leaf left on the Montmartre vine, and that there were more Germans than usual at the avenue Lamarck crossroads. When a military policeman stopped her to ask for her papers, she was quite calm in showing them: her *carte d'identité* gave her parents' address and stated she worked there as her father's secretary. She was 'waved on her way'. She 'flirted with the idea of going into the Vieux Châlet Café' where the Anglophile owner could keep her safe for a while if things were as tricky as they were starting to appear, but that might cause trouble for him.

The policeman who had just stopped her woke up to his orders and reappeared to ask what she was doing so far from home. She noticed a print and philately shop on the other side of the place du Tertre, and was quick with the lie that she was planning to buy a stamp for her lunch date. But the shop was shut, so she had to keep walking. In her frozen trance, it did not occur to her to go in any other direction than towards her own building. Just as she turned the corner and saw the splintered door hanging off its hinges, the same policeman and a Gestapo NCO called Tritche came up behind her. Tritche, a model of Aryan manhood who was loathed by Bleicher for being 'stupid, conceited and completely Nazified', seized her arm and said, 'You've kept us waiting, Madame.'

She was walked to a car that had been parked by the great white edifice of Sacré-Coeur at the city's highest point; the spot now held a certain irony as the church was built as a symbol of penance for the previous defeat of France by the Prussians seventy years before. Mathilde might have remembered her twenty-first birthday, when she had been there with a group of friends speculating about their futures – someone had predicted that all of Paris would come to admire her. She floated free once again as always at times of crisis, and looked down on herself to see a 'poor, anonymous creature who would be shot next day'. She realised that she had fulfilled her desire to make her mark in the war, her 'useful suicide'. Before the car turned downhill towards the place de l'Opéra, it passed Renée Borni on the corner of the rue Villa Léandre next to a large, bespectacled man in a mackintosh. He pointed at the car and asked Borni a question, to which she gave a defeated nod.

*

Mathilde was taken to the Edouard VII, where she passed Jouffret in handcuffs. She gave the details of her family and husband, and attested to her pure Aryan descent, as had been required since the previous month. At one o'clock she, Madame Blavette and the concierge's nieces, who were cursing and shouting 'like viragos', were put in a van together and driven back up the hill to La Santé prison in eastern Montparnasse.

La Santé was a terrible, dark, misnamed, mid-Victorian place of despair, like Fresnes, divided into different sections for French and German use. Only one prisoner had ever escaped in its history, by the use of forged papers. Mathilde's cell was four metres by two and a half, 'icy cold, damp and stinking', the toilet a hole in the floor in one corner. She knew that La Santé had seen the execution of six *résistants* from the Patriotes Antifascistes group that August and September, yet betrayed no fear for her own fate, high-handedly demanding a mattress and sheets for the board that served as a bed.

She was fed what might be her last meal: a hunk of unidentifiable meat, vegetable, bread and ersatz coffee. She settled herself on the soggy mattress with her fur coat for warmth. She listened to the clocks of the prison, neighbouring hospital, churches and convents sound the hours through the night and thought 'calmly' of her death, perhaps as the inevitable completion of her desire fourteen months earlier to be 'a second Jeanne d'Arc'. We do not know if her Sorbonne philosophy studies included Nietzsche's aphorism that 'the thought of suicide is a great consolation: by means of it one gets successfully through many a bad night', but it perhaps proved true for her, as by morning she had concluded that however 'noble' an end she might have, she did not want La Santé to be her last home on earth.

*

'Four warders and two German women' crowded into Mathilde's cell as the neighbourhood clocks sounded an inharmonious, unsynchronised eight chimes. Such a wake-up committee may have sparked her fluctuating sense of her esteem, or her will to live may never truly have deserted her; or her instinct to survive, and maybe to serve again, won the day. Whatever the combination of motives and factors, Mathilde's collaboration began after one night of physical and mental numbness in her cell.

She was taken to a 'gloomy, thin and ageing' Gestapo captain who was under orders to offer her real coffee and a cigarette. Her 'mind was still a blank' as she was driven into 'the cold of freedom' and back to the Edouard VII, where she was warmed, and amazed, by a ration-busting breakfast of more coffee, warm rolls, sugar and butter. As she was eating, Borchers and 'three or four other people' entered. The 'tall and massive' man she had seen in the rue Villa Léandre the previous morning introduced himself. Hugo Bleicher's actions that day might have stemmed from a careful study of her psychology. He had worked out her role and the magnitude of Interallié from his overnight study of the seized documents; a tiny appointments book and a letter from de Rocquigny were in her handbag. He grasped what a masterful advantage it would be for the blunt instrument that was the Abwehr he disliked to turn a network back on itself and she was the key: if she could be persuaded to work for him, he would have a career-making asset. Hence his decision to offer his prisoner a slap-up breakfast and a deal. Roman, then in his own damp ground-floor cell in Fresnes, was later to comment, 'How great is the German psychological approach to women – comfort or death!'

Bleicher flattered Mathilde that she was 'far too intelligent and interesting to remain in prison'. His papers included the 'letters written in Polish by the agents in Marseilles (Tudor network) and Toulouse (Nestor network)', and the 'ongoing projects' and the 'drafts of all the messages' from the rue Villa Léandre; he had 'the industrial file ... concerning the materiel and products sent from France to Germany, agent reports and the general reports being prepared for London' from the rue Cortot; he had the radio set. It was clear that the Paris agents and sector heads dealt through her, and that she knew everything required 'to facilitate arrests'. If he was fast and she kept her meetings and her counsel, he might have his coup. And if his understanding of her diary was correct, she had an appointment on the Champs-Elysées in two hours.

He got straight to the point: he could have her 'shot several times over' for passing off an escaped Polish officer as her cousin and crossing the line illegally. She had 'practised espionage for more than a year'. He pointed out that her patriotism was worthless as 'England is doomed' and it was now up to her to 'save your own skin, Madame'. If she worked with him, she would be free that day; the alternative was immediate execution. He confused things by sweetening the offer without correcting his promise of freedom: she would be paid 6,000 francs* a month for her work, as the English didn't pay properly 'and always make other people work for them'. Bleicher had an intuitive understanding of the 'four mainsprings of spying' worked out by the NKVD in Russia over a much longer period than his few hours as a recruiter – money, ideology, coercion and ego – and was going for all except ideology, of which he personally had none.

Mathilde was 'numb'. She felt as if she had 'been hit by a sledgehammer'. Her spirit and drive collapsed in the face of something so much more powerful than her, and she became unable to take any responsibility or face the consequences of her actions. The survival instinct that had given her the opportunity to serve in Toulouse asserted itself again. She latched on to the word 'liberty' even as she knew it had to be a 'dirty trick'. Patriotism, as for so many spies, turned out not to be a prime motivator as abandonment loomed. The heroic fantasies that had driven her since childhood retreated. She was 'chilled to the marrow' by her choice. Bleicher 'did not wait for her to reply in any way', but took her arm and led her out to an unmarked black Citroën. They were driven the short distance to the Café Pam Pam just in time for her 11.00 appointment.

*

* Approximately £34; £1,880 at 2018 values.

Mathilde had been the go-between with a Deuxième Bureau network, Patrie. She traded information with one of their agents, Wirtz, or Duvernois as she called him, with whom she had her rendezvous that morning. The Pam Pam, once a chic hangout supplying hamburgers and jazz, was dingy in wartime. She had recovered enough of herself to point out that she too was filthy, that she looked like someone who had just spent the night in a cell, and asked to be allowed to visit the bathroom. Bleicher simply held her arm more tightly, said her appearance was 'of no importance' and led her to a table.

Mathilde's first betrayal was not of someone to whom she was close. But the detachment and the ease with which she played her role in her near-catatonia are striking. Bleicher took the lead and introduced himself to the Deuxième Bureau man as 'a friend' of La Chatte's. Wirtz was remarkably unobservant for a spy in occupied territory and was 'full of confidence' as he 'gave his message' to be passed to London 'in spite of the fact that [Mathilde] had no hat, no gloves and looked completely exhausted'; let alone that she was with a stranger whose eye she did not meet and whom she did not address. He even accepted a lift from Bleicher, who announced his identity in the car. Wirtz went white and gasped out that Mathilde was 'a total slut' before spilling 'all the information needed' to 'save his skin'. As he was taken into custody, he 'wept like a woman' in his terror and shame.

*

Bleicher realised that a successful agent-runner worked with the material at hand, and following the simple arrest of Wirtz, he now saw even greater possibilities for using Mathilde as a double agent. Borni had told him that Mathilde rang her mother daily, and he ordered her to make a call from the frayed lobby of the Edouard VII. Madame Belard had not spoken to her daughter for 'two or three days' and was 'in great agitation'. When Marchal reported that she had not shown up for lunch the previous day, Madame Belard feared Mathilde had been picked up by the Germans, and then Aubertin told her that Mathilde had been arrested for having 'false papers'.

Bleicher listened in to the anguished questions, and took command of the situation by making hand signals to his prisoner to 'tell her [she] was safe and sound'. Mathilde explained that she had been 'called away' for a couple of days but was back; she would ring Oncle Marco right away to 'set his mind at rest'; the same for René Aubertin. She wished afterwards that she had given some hint that she was speaking under duress, perhaps called her the unfamiliar 'Mère' rather than 'Maman' but was frozen into obedience to Bleicher. Her mother begged her to come to lunch, but Bleicher 'indicated that she should reply in the negative'. She did at least manage to say that she would come the following day. He 'reproached' her for making this plan as she put the telephone down. He knew he had to maintain full control of events to succeed.

Mathilde was moved forwards with 'terrifying activity' that gave no time for reflection and retreat. She had met Bleicher only a few hours earlier, and she was already his puppet as he made her ring Marchal, who was relieved to know that she was still at large. The trusting scientist wanted to see her, and made a date that evening for 6.00 at Chez Graff in Montmartre. Once again, she gave no clue that she was coerced. Bleicher was 'jubilant' when Marchal proposed bringing his friend Aubertin to the meeting. Aside from Roman, these were the two with whom she worked most closely, both men she had brought to the network and one of them her oldest friend.

Kieffer had already informed Bleicher that La Palette was used as a postbox, so he announced they were going to lunch there. The café's glory days of the 1920s, when it had been a haunt of Hemingway and F. Scott Fitzgerald, were long gone and the mirrors on the semi-circular wall that surrounded the red leather banquettes had grown even dustier in the past eighteen months. Most of the customers in the half-empty place were Germans in uniform or businessmen who had squared themselves off with the occupiers and now lunched with their own sort or with their girlfriends. A door in the middle of the long wall led to the basement domain of Madame Gaby, the lavatory attendant shopped by Kieffer in his treacherous petulance about the postbox. The old lady had 'never really understood what was going on' and regarded her visitors 'with terrified and puzzled eyes'.

Bleicher 'gobbled his food and paid no attention' to Mathilde. She had no appetite as she looked at her exhausted, crumpled reflection in the mirror behind him. At these moments of inactivity, shame washed over her; she was 'haunted' at what she was doing rather than fearful for herself. She felt 'totally dominated' by her captor. He saw her looking at her reflection and remarked that as they were going to the avenue Lamarck next, she would have time to 'attend to [her] toilet'. She realised with horror that she was going to have to confront her friend, staunch ally and protector.

Mireille Lejeune was in the concierge's room just inside the heavy double doors of her building. Mathilde could not look at her, and focused instead on the flowers from her flat. She introduced Bleicher as 'a friend' and saw the relief in Lejeune's face that she was 'free again'; Mireille confirmed that she had burnt the papers as requested. But lying broke Mathilde's 'great nervous tension' and she launched into a 'sudden silly argument' about the flowers. Both women were stunned by her outburst, and Mathilde collected herself to ask about money. Borni had told Bleicher that there were half a million francs in the flat but Mathilde had scornfully pointed out on the way over that if he had really read all the signals, he would know that they were constantly requesting cash from England and that they were down to 137,000 francs. Mireille fetched the tin box from a shelf in the lodge at the very moment Bleicher barked 'Where is your husband? Get him at once!', and the hideous truth of the situation became clear to her.

Bleicher sat between the two women in the back of the Citroën. Charles Lejeune was not at his police station. They drove around three or four other posts to which he might have been assigned, the fluttering hopes of the silent women dashed when they found him at the Petit Palais. The police chief gave away all he knew at the Hôtel Edouard VII. In his rage and fear, he even denounced Interallié as 'a monstrous spy organisation in which he had become involved, a hornet's nest from which he could not extricate himself'. His recantation did not help him, and he and Mireille never saw each other again. She 'remained proud and dignified' and betrayed nothing in her seven months in La Santé. She found it 'strange' that a woman in whom she 'had such confidence' had turned her and her husband in, but never spoke of Mathilde 'with hatred'; instead she expressed surprise and sadness that 'all the good which she did in life was washed out' by her actions in these days.

*

Bleicher carried on setting his brutal pace. He reinforced his dominance over Mathilde when he took her to Chez Madeleine in the 8th arrondissement and sat her at a table with Borchers and two others. Although she had little German, Borchers' raucous, self-congratulatory boasting was evident and she refused the foie gras and champagne he ordered in celebration. The food induced a 'moral nausea' which added to her 'feeling of annihilation'. She retreated into 'her senses', bereft of her 'reasoning power', unable to assimilate 'the cause of the shock and the suffering' that she was undergoing as the trauma came up on her 'like a sledgehammer' once again.

When Bleicher announced that they must move on to the meeting at Chez Graff, she prayed that Marchal and Aubertin would have a reason not to show up, but feared that their concern for her would guarantee their appearance. The call to her mother, a connecting link for this group of agents, had been a masterstroke by Bleicher. It was dark when they reached Chez Graff, whose red plush decor and revolving bar befitted its location near the Moulin Rouge. They parked around the corner on the rue Lepic and the Citroën was joined by two German military vehicles. She was ordered to enter the café alone, while Bleicher went to a separate table and four plain-clothes Gestapo hovered at the bar.

At six o'clock sharp, 'Oncle Marco, with the high-domed forehead and lively, smiling eyes' came in and 'threw up his arms' in delight at seeing his 'little Cat safe and sound'; he had even brought a gardening book with him that contained false identity cards for agents. He ordered cocktails and the familiar figure of René Aubertin entered. Aubertin was more circumspect as he had heard a rumour from Charles Lejeune that morning that the network had been betrayed. He had rung Marchal at the office to warn him that he had heard 'our friend is in trouble – she has a cold, has even had to be sent to hospital', but had been partially reassured by the scientist's confidence. He was, though, a soldier who disliked loose ends and still felt something wasn't right with his *petite princesse*, who looked simultaneously 'green with emotion' and 'positively livid'. Just as he had this thought, 'a number of people' approached him from behind, he felt two revolvers in his back and a voice said *Police allemande.* Don't move or we shall shoot you.' With characteristic phlegm, Aubertin knocked back all three cocktails before being taken away. As Elizabeth Marchal's birthday party was getting under way that evening, her father was being led into a cell.

*

Mathilde was 'deathly weary' but the day that had started with a lavish breakfast was still not over. Bleicher ordered the driver to take them back to avenue Lamarck, this time to the other postbox he knew about from Borni that was managed by Madame Hugentobler, whose husband Richard kept his ear open to German chatter in cafés and bars. The large, friendly woman was preparing supper for her husband, their fourteen-year-old daughter and infant baby as Bleicher placed the adults under arrest. She cried out that she could not leave the baby, to which Bleicher retorted that 'France will look after your children.' She was dragged away past her former friend and handler, who brokenly muttered *'Pardon.'* Richard Hugentobler did not resist arrest but remained silent through his imprisonment. Madame Hugentobler hanged herself in her cell that first night, unhinged by her separation from her baby. She was the first Interallié agent to die for the network.

*

Mathilde half-believed that Bleicher would keep his promise and leave her in Montmartre. But she found they were heading out of Paris and he told her that she would be safer if she stayed in Maisons-Laffitte. 'They' would be 'out for her blood' if it emerged that she had been present at the arrests; he also 'attached great importance … to obtaining her collaboration'. He presented her with the paradoxical arrangement that she was at liberty yet would live with him: she was to remain his prisoner beyond the shattering, pivotal thirty-six hours she had just endured.

When they got to the Baur house, Bleicher showed her to a room and, as she stood stupefied, began to undress himself. The day on which she had betrayed her friends, colleagues and country ended with her sleeping with her captor. For her, it was 'the greatest act of cowardice of my life' and 'the final smashing of my pride' as she tried to reconnect with human feelings through the 'warmth once more of a pair of arms'. All Joan of Arc fantasies were banished for good. However much she swore to herself next morning that she would turn the tables, Mathilde Carré was now a fully-fledged collaborator, wrung out and degraded. Animal fear and the instinct to survive had overcome her morals, alliances and dignity; sex represented safety and the life force in the midst of betrayal and terror. When she had had years to contemplate this night and the ones that were to follow and was asked at a critical moment about why she had gone to bed with Bleicher, Mathilde answered with a question of her own, one that was as central to her conduct as it was to that of many other Frenchwomen: 'Well, what else could I have done?'

She had further to fall before she could attempt to struggle back, but that night became the moral and judicial fulcrum on which her life and reputation were to balance.

8

Double Agent

Mathilde emerged from a comfortable room rather than from the freezing cell of the previous day. Her numbness was tempered by shock, exhaustion, distress, and, above all, crushing humiliation. A cold shower brought her to the reality of her situation. She 'hated [herself] for [her] weakness', and 'hated the Germans even more'. She felt 'tired and broken', caught in a trap, her pride 'smashed' but struggling to reassert itself as she vowed 'that one day [she] would make this German pay'.

The housekeeper served Mathilde, Bleicher and Borchers in the dining room, and the two Germans cheerfully called their silent house-guest 'their *Kätzchen*', their 'kitten'. The German diminutive of her code name emphasised their control over her. It was a relief to be left by the fire with two 'magnificent black Alsatian' dogs for company. Harry Baur's housekeeper was 'servile and amiable' to the German interlopers while her real employers were in prison. She was merely keeping her job and an eye on the house, whereas Mathilde was deep in questionable waters, most of all through 'the cardinal fault' of the previous evening. What the two women had in common was that they had no choice in the roles in which they now found themselves. Mathilde's great attribute of courage had failed her, initiating a self-savaging 'period of hate': how she dealt with that emotion and adapted to her circumstances over the ensuing days of relentless betrayal and shame would define her.

Her brief respite ended when Bleicher put her back in his car and, after another visit to La Palette to check on Madame Gaby, drove to her parents' flat in the avenue des Gobelins. On the way, her captor and lover made it plain that he knew about Jeanne

Belard's part in Interallié from Renée Borni, and her parents' survival accordingly depended upon her continued co-operation. He took the forthright approach on arrival to introduce himself as 'a Gestapo inspector' who had saved the life of 'their Lily' even though she deserved to be shot 'a dozen times over'. Madame Belard should at the very least be sent to prison, but instead would be 'allowed' to collaborate 'for the good of Europe and the world'. He belittled Mathilde as 'a foolish young idealist' who was now on the right path.

Mathilde's parents were 'flabbergasted'. Her father was too upset to speak but her mother, appalled by Bleicher's 'brutish face', contradicted everything he said and proclaimed her love of England even as 'he preached collaboration'. Bleicher filled their small flat for two hours, repeating that Jeanne could be arrested as a spy and mentioning some vague 'lists the Germans kept on their files' on which her husband Arsène's name could be found.

Mathilde said nothing. She was stricken that she held her parents' 'fate in [her] hands'. She observed again their 'conjugal felicity', the relationship to which she ascribed their inability to be close to her in her early years, yet now had to 'protect' through her own submission. Bleicher, whose 'indefinable character was impossible to read' for Madame Belard, had once again played his psychological cards with aplomb, driving his prisoner deeper into dependency with a mixture of logic and threats. Her mother was full of 'sorrow to think that [Mathilde] could have helped betray the French', while Mathilde was too ashamed to tell her 'the true facts', by which she presumably meant her capitulation the night before. Mother and daughter were only to meet 'three or four more times' before the end of the war, each encounter a repeat of this agony.

*

Bleicher knew of no blueprints or precedents for winding up networks or running double agents, and he had had no intelligence training; he was making it up as he went along, but understood speed was vital to turn Interallié to German advantage before the 'smashed' Mathilde could summon her spirit and courage. He had grasped the potential for a commanding double-cross operation, and left no time for reflection or warnings. He demanded to know Zarembski's Marseilles address which Mathilde was unable to supply. So the car and a truckful of Abwehr soldiers swept into the courtyard of Stanislaw Lach's building in the rue des Deux Ponts in search of the answer.

It was the first time that Mathilde had been to her courier's home. She went alone up the narrow stone staircase to the third floor, knocked and announced herself. Lach was eating lunch with his wife, and opened the door with a smile of greeting, only to be met by a desperate staccato outburst from Mathilde that she needed the address in Marseilles to send a message of warning to Tudor that 'things are not going too well with Armand'. The flummoxed Pole picked up on her note of panic and denied knowing anything about any Tudor or Armand just as Bleicher stormed in, revolver in hand. The room 'swam before her eyes' as Mathilde saw the Lachs' 'greatest distress'. It was only in the car that the courier's confusion cleared enough for him to realise that it was no coincidence that she and the Gestapo had arrived simultaneously.

Hugo Bleicher exuded satisfaction. He took his prisoner-lover back to La Santé to collect her few belongings, and on the way boasted about his success in turning Kieffer. After depositing her back at the Baur villa he went to look for the painter Arthault whose studio opposite the Cochin hospital had been Interallié's first base.

*

The first *Funkspiel** from occupied France was set up on the following morning, Friday 21st November, at a meeting in the Hôtel Edouard VII with Bleicher, Borchers and Lieutenant Kayser. Kayser, a lawyer from Mannheim in civilian life whom Mathilde thought 'looked like a Levantine trader', got straight to the point. They had two radio sets, one from the rue Villa Léandre and the

---

* Literally 'radio game'.

one just seized from Arthault's flat. They had the dictionary and the coding knowledge from Borni and the recent transmissions as guides to format, and were planning to keep Mathilde on the airwaves, but with disinformation. Max Desplaces had been arrested the previous evening and interrogated 'by two German technicians' about the mechanics of the radios but gave nothing away; he was 'astonished' that the sets could still be functioning as he assumed the quartz crystals that gave them their frequency would have been destroyed. They had three days to seal Mathilde's double-cross before the unsuspecting sector heads converged on La Palette on the 24th and realised her true situation.

The Abwehr men acknowledged Mathilde's unique status. She 'was the only one … in whom London, Marseilles and Vichy all have confidence'. The logic of Bleicher's order of arrest became plain to her as Kayser pointed out that 'nobody still at liberty will know that you are in our hands'. They had even identified the quarrelsome, banished François Tabet as a potential radio operator following Desplaces' refusal after Bleicher heard from Renée Borni that Tabet was 'a weak boy who likes money', the ideal turncoat.

Funkspiel was to become a standard intelligence weapon but at that stage of the war it was a breathtaking tactic. And the success of the gambit depended upon the fragile ego of Mathilde Carré. She, who had only days before been a proud and devoted Allied spy, would need to become a loyal servant of the Abwehr with total conviction whilst holding together the remnants of Interallié as cover. From her dazed co-operation over the previous days Bleicher believed that she would carry it off, and that he would be able to ensure she remained attached to him as his lover, his prisoner, his collaborator and his agent.

'La Chatte' would need a new code name to be 'plausible to London', and the Germans asked her what she would like: stressing that to them 'she would always be their little *Katze*'. Her choice, with its possible note of defiant loyalty to her country's cause, was 'accepted with acclamation': Mathilde Carré was to become 'Victoire' to fool London that she was fearlessly setting up on her own in their service.

*

The Abwehr could not afford to wait for Tabet to be rounded up before starting transmissions, and the first message went out the following afternoon: 'Following a German search have moved. Walenty probably arrested. I am working in peace with a radio in a new location. Awaiting instructions and money urgently. La Chatte.' The touch about money was deft, as London understood all too well the 'agents' perennial cry'. The only false note, which went unnoticed on receipt, was to write *allemande* for 'German' instead of the normal, dismissive 'Boche'. This word was to remain throughout the double-cross, and was either an attempt at a coded signal by Mathilde, or a polite shift from the Abwehr.

There was no immediate response from London, so the next message was more emphatic: 'We signalled that we have been hunted down by the Germans and forced to move. Awaiting instructions. Money urgent. We are moving again.' This elicited two replies: one asking for 'constant updates about Walenty' and the other saying that they were sending money to a Zarembski agent in the south and ordering that 'anyone threatened who cannot hide for a while in the occupied zone before getting back to work should get to the free zone'. *Funkspiel* was afoot.

*

After the main business of the day had been settled at the Edouard VII, the rest of the afternoon was more leisurely. Bleicher took Mathilde to Arthault's studio where the soldier on duty reported that all had been quiet, and then on to the rue Villa Léandre, where four armed Gestapo men stood guard and where Mathilde encountered Renée Borni for the first time since the anniversary celebration that now belonged in another life.

Mathilde was shocked to see her colleague and rival seated in her usual armchair, flanked by Borchers and Kayser. To be in that place without Roman, who had 'seen his life's work crumble', sparked her rage for the first time since she had entered her fugue state in the fog of Montmartre four days earlier. Now that their patchy veneer of professionalism had been dissolved by Bleicher, the two immediately started to fight. Borni told the Germans about payments to Dr Henri Collin, a bacteriologist friend of the Belard family whom she did not believe was an agent. Mathilde shouted that Borni 'lied with every breath and everybody knew it'. She was sure that 'the Germans believed [her] perfectly' in her struggle for superiority and need to apportion blame to Borni as she was led away.

After this bitter encounter, Bleicher took Mathilde out to a Saturday night such as any couple might enjoy in Paris, starting with supper at Weber's, a favourite haunt of the occupiers, and then on to a film before their return to the Baur villa. Her emotions had been kick-started in the release of jealousy and rage towards Renée, and she began to justify her day: she was 'convinced that one day she would take [her] revenge' and was using 'her feminine wiles' to get 'back into the stream'. 'In the eyes of men, particularly of the enemy', she had little to survive on as she became increasingly locked in by Bleicher's company and schemes. She could diminish her own treachery in her mind this way, but do little to salvage her always-flickering sense of herself.

*

Sunday brought the cruellest betrayal of all. Bleicher had found a note in her handbag from Lucien de Rocquigny, the slight pianist who scanned the newspapers and radio waves and felt a 'deep personal affection' for Mathilde. It confirmed a rendezvous as well as 'giving his new address'. Bleicher announced over breakfast that this was to be the first call of the day.

They were driven to de Rocquigny's *pension* near the boulevard Saint-Michel. Mathilde knocked, but nobody was at home. As they left, Bleicher spotted a barber's shop from the car and in one of the stranger intrusions of banal life into these hectic days asked the driver to stop so that he could have his hair cut. The driver asked if he too might be shorn, so both went in, leaving Mathilde in the car alone. It was a mark of their trust in the depth of her helplessness.

They moved on to Lejeune's *préfecture* building to arrest the colleagues he had given up, only to find that they had made use of their ample time to escape. Then it was back to the boulevard Saint-Michel and the dread moment. De Rocquigny flung open the door in a mixture of anxiety about the rumours he had heard and delight that she was safe, but before she could even attempt an acknowledgement of his greeting, Bleicher and two grey-uniformed men burst in. She retreated into the corridor. As de Rocquigny was led out in handcuffs, he 'smiled faintly' at her.

She later claimed, with justification, that the Abwehr would have found all the agents without her complicity thanks to the information they had seized. But she was never able to expiate the grief and shame she felt about de Rocquigny in particular, never even admitted to being present at his arrest, and barely ever mentioned the spy who loved her again.

*

Bleicher found a letter amongst de Rocquigny's papers from the exiled aristocrat and commercial artist Wladimir Lipski, and, after a quick lunch and further check with Madame Gaby in La Palette, they were on their way to Lipski's 'great crowded studio apartment' on the outskirts of Montmartre. A truckload of uniformed men was in position in the courtyard and the surrounding streets. Once again, Mathilde knocked while Bleicher lurked in the hallway. Lipski had not seen her since his recruitment a year earlier, but trustingly opened up to her. She asked for the 'documents and reports for Paul', de Rocquigny's code name, to which he replied, 'I don't know you, and I don't know Paul,' just as Bleicher charged through the door followed by his 'big strapping' henchmen to denounce him as 'L'Observateur'. Lipski knew the game was up for him and his daughter Lydia, the teenage agent 'Cipinka', his 'little chicken'. On the way to the Edouard VII, Mathilde even sat on one

5. — Le Creusot. - Usines Schneider. - Vue générale (côté Ouest).

Collection du Photo-Club. — Cl. Marcel Fèle, Le Creusot.

The factory town of Le Creusot, home of the Belard family when their daughter was born.
The Schneider works in the town became a key German armaments factory.

Mathilde Belard as a rural child
in the Haut Jura, 1911.

With Maurice Carré on one of their
summer holidays from Algeria in the 1930s.

Roman Czerniawski,
the patriotic Pole.

Czerniawski (*fourth from right*) with his regiment shortly before the Fall of France.

Toulouse, with its statue of Joan of Arc, was deep in the *Zone Nono* when thousands of refugees arrived from *La Débâcle* in the late summer of 1940.

The Champs-Elysées, Paris, under German occupation.

Lydia Lipski,
the teenage agent
code-named
'Little Chicken'.

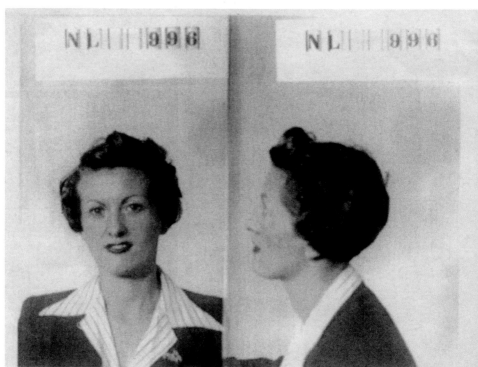

Monique Deschamps, the brave and mischievous Agent Moustique.

Interallié's headquarters at 8, rue Villa
Léandre. The radio was in the attic.

Roman's lover Renée Borni, Agent Violette,
whose life was to be inextricably
entwined with Mathilde Carré.

Roman Czerniawski was awarded his country's highest
military honour just before he was betrayed.

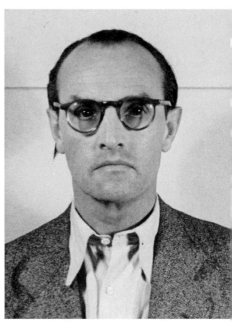

Hugo Bleicher, the interpreter and military policeman who went on to become one of the Abwehr's greatest spy-hunters and agent-runners.

Suzanne Laurent, the bar *patronne* who had a luxurious war as Bleicher's lover.

The corner of rue des Saules, Montmartre,
where Mathilde was arrested in the fog.

The dreaded La Santé prison.

of the German's, presumably Bleicher's, knee as there was so little space in the car.

Once again, Bleicher left no time for recovery or introspection. He decided to check again on the postboxes so headed for rue de la Michodière, and this time his luck was in. Franck, the head of F Sector who also helped the network change money on the black market, had left a note requesting a consultation with Mathilde that very day at 5 p.m. in the rue Villa Léandre. As F Sector included Boulogne and Calais, Franck knew that his appointments would be kept, and walked into the trap. He offered his unconditional co-operation to Bleicher, no doubt in part because otherwise his Jewishness would condemn him to dire imprisonment or death, and immediately gave up a key subagent.

*

Mathilde was given time to absorb the past days as the frenetic activity slowed by Sunday evening. 'Inner rage' washed through her, but she was 'powerless' to do anything except be 'ill-tempered' and 'idiotic' around her captors. She knew the possible consequences of direct confrontation and her emotions could only emerge in petty ways such as 'criticism of the soup'. She inwardly attacked the 'futilities' of her situation like a 'stupid, capricious worm'. Bleicher realised that he needed to pamper her to restore her equilibrium so ordered a car to take them, Borchers and Kayser out to dinner once more at Chez Madeleine. She was again made to feel important and needed, and noticed her appetite and her 'vitality returning' as the trauma started to recede. Her companions indulged in some heavy-handed teasing, 'making a joke of [her] arrest'; in an unsubtle reminder of her position, they asked her what her last wish would be if she were to be shot at dawn. Soothed by so much attention, she answered, 'to have a superb dinner, to make love, and to hear the Mozart Requiem'. She had referred to the Requiem ten years earlier to a friend, musing that she might like it to be played at her funeral, but this setting was very different. The words would come back to haunt her.

*

Collaboration was becoming normality as Mathilde was swept along by Bleicher's boastful success. All thoughts of honour and suicide had disappeared. Bleicher was cheered when they got back to Maisons-Laffitte to hear that Roman's former colleague Lieutenant Czyż was in their hands after he had paid an ill-advised visit to the rue Villa Léandre. It had been an outstanding haul for the new double-agent handler, but much still hinged on the meeting of the sector heads the next day. Bleicher was confident of her allegiance to him but wanted her to play a more active role in his strategy than merely observer and door-opener. He ordered her to make an appointment with René Legrand. Legrand was most often to be found at the Hôtel Majestic giving 'certain information about shipping and other matters' to anyone prepared to pay for it, and it was no surprise to Mathilde that he had come to the Abwehr's attention. She had been a frequent beneficiary of Legrand's information and black-market spoils but despised him as she believed him to be one of those who collaborated as well as resisted, 'a double agent' who 'simply wanted to run with the hare and hunt with the hounds'. She could not sense the irony in such thoughts – she needed to believe herself still to be on the side of the Allies, awaiting her revenge.

In the fluid confusion of loyalties, Bleicher was not aware that Legrand could be their man as well as their enemy, and came up with an incrimination scheme. Mathilde appeared at Legrand's office with her hand bandaged, supposedly from an accidental burn that prevented her from writing. So Legrand himself wrote down the details of cargo vessels leaving Casablanca for Bordeaux via South America, and the location of a German coal supply ship to fuel them, and his handwritten evidence was enough to ensure his detention. The ruse stemmed from Bleicher's desire to gather proof without physical violence if no confession was forthcoming, rare amongst his Abwehr or Gestapo colleagues. That evening there was 'an enormous party' at the Baur house supplied by the 'black-market provisions' seized from Legrand's store, with enough left over for the Germans 'to send presents back to their relations' at home.

*

While the frenetic dismantling of Interallié had been taking place in Paris, its chief radio operator had been working his way south to the Zone Nono. Włodarczyk arrived in Marseilles just before midnight on the same day as this Maisons-Laffitte blowout, and at 9 a.m. a telegram arrived in London from Zaremsbki stating that 'agents of Walenty escaped into the free zone … Walenty, his secretary and fourteen other agents as well as the postbox have been arrested by the Germans on the 18th November; all three W/T [wireless/telegraph] stations of Walenty as well as the codes are in German hands'. Zarembski requested 'cessation of W/T work in Paris' and lamented that 'Walenty was caught in bed with papers. Walenty was in the habit of writing down addresses'. He asked that the BBC broadcast 'La Famille Attention' three times daily in their messages personnels.

SIS refused the request. They 'considered it would be dangerous' to 'inform the Germans that we were aware of the incident'; to do so 'would give no hope for Walenty if the Germans had any doubt that they had not seized the whole of his papers and his organisation'. It was in part a humanitarian decision, but also a statement of their conviction that Victoire's contact had been genuine, that she had saved herself and could continue a semblance of the 'vital' network whose intelligence they desperately needed. Bleicher had won the first round through his innate, untrained skills as a spy. The speed with which La Chatte had been reimagined as Victoire and the deserved trust in which she was held in London had paid off for him.

*

Even though he was unaware of this vote of confidence in his double-cross from its victims, Bleicher was 'hopeful' of a good haul of the sector heads as he drove with Mathilde to La Palette on the morning of the 24th. She was briefed to send arrivals downstairs to leave their reports with Madame Gaby, where they would be arrested by one of the many Gestapo operatives packing the whole panelled, mirrored and extravagantly tiled pre-war artists' rendezvous.

Only one agent came in. Jacques Collardey was the spirited 'Paris ragamuffin' known as 'Coco' to whom Mathilde had taken such a shine. The sector heads had inevitably heard rumours, and collectively decided that it would be foolish to go in that day. But Collardey argued they needed certainty, and volunteered to go in 'lightly disguised' while the others, minus Kieffer, waited around the corner. The *maître d'hôtel*, Pierre Belle, claimed to know nothing about the 'German trap' about to be sprung in his establishment, and was on the first floor when Collardey came in. Collardey 'went up to [Mathilde] saying how delighted he was that she, at any rate, had escaped' and 'asked for news'. She sent him to the cloakroom to pick up a fictitious letter and a few minutes later he was on his way to the Edouard VII. Collardey was never heard from again, another favourite to whom she could not bear to refer in future.

The rest of that day followed a familiar pattern. Bleicher made her ring Tabet at the small hotel where he lodged on the boulevard des Batignolles and say she was on her way. Tabet was walking home when he spotted the unknown, bulky figure of Bleicher and fled; he was caught in the street by the back-up team. He had been so terrorised by Gane that he was convinced that this was somehow another murder attempt from him, and was almost relieved to realise that it was the official enemy that had found him. He too 'agreed at once to work for the Germans', and gave up a fellow agent, Kléber, without a qualm.

Thus Kléber was next: he denied knowledge 'of this spy organisation', but his mistress Jacqueline confessed in his place and offered to take Bleicher to another agent, known as Irenée II, who lived in Rambouillet. Jacqueline 'was terribly nervous' as they set off on their forty-kilometre journey and asked to stop at the Café des Sports near the Porte Maillot where many of Gane's crowd hung out, according to her. Bleicher was so confident in his agent-running abilities that he agreed. As soon as they were inside, Jacqueline went to the bathroom and slipped out of the back staircase, but too late to warn Irenée II, who was arrested just as his supper was being put on his table. He too confessed everything in his terror, including the identity of yet another agent, Isidore, who lived near the Odéon. They hurtled back to the city and caught up with Isidore as he walked home just before curfew. He started to tell Mathilde that Collardey had been caught that morning at La Palette and that there was going to be a further meeting of the agents at the Café Louis XIII on 6th December. This knowledge sealed his fate as Bleicher moved in. The domino effect of fear and instant capitulation continued.

Isidore told Mathilde that he had become a spy out of patriotism. He assumed she must be German to have turned as she had – he was unable to comprehend why anyone would otherwise betray their country. She admired him for his dignity, but his words seemed not to land with her. The vanity that was essential to prop up her fluctuating esteem then led her to reckon that she was 'the number one figure of this war' and that if she made a break for it the entire German police force would be mobilised. Bleicher had fed this side of her ego by emphasising that Interallié had been 'the greatest spy network' ever known.

*

Bleicher had bound Mathilde to him morally, physically, and practically, and now took care to tighten the knots. On the morning of the 25th, a week after her arrest, he announced the opening of La Chattière, known to his colleagues as Die Villa Katzensteg.* On some level he knew that without inner fulfilment she could still destroy his increasingly ambitious plans, and as well as the flattery of the new headquarters, he even went so far as to tell Mathilde on the morning of the move that his mistress, Suzanne Laurent, had

---

* Fittingly, 'the cat's web villa'.

committed suicide, so she need not feel jealous of any rival for his affections. Once again she believed herself to be the most important person in a crusader's life. Laurent had in fact been moved into a requisitioned apartment near the Bois de Boulogne whose owner, Monsieur Touche, registered 'two cases of Sèvres porcelain, a Persian carpet, 690 volumes of books, 18 drypoint prints etc.' missing between her moving-in date and August 1944.

La Chattière was La Petite Prieuré Villa in Saint-Germain-en-Laye, thirty kilometres from Montmartre. It was a handsome, Normandy-style house taken from a French banker and his wife. There was a large bay window at ground level and two half-timbered storeys above; the first floor had a spacious bedroom giving out on to a balcony that ran the width of the building and overlooked a well-stocked garden that was now running wild. This was to be Mathilde and Bleicher's room, with Borchers sleeping next door. On the top floor were the office and radio station, and the living quarters of the NCO, Propst. Renée Borni, 'much to her disgust', was moved in to this attic, in a room between Propst and the radio. Tabet, Tritche, Todt and Kayser drove in each day from the Maisons-Laffitte, Todt's main duty being to assist Tabet with the radio. This strange ménage was nominally under Borchers' command, but it was tacitly acknowledged that Bleicher 'was the executive' in control. Apart from anything else, Borchers was 'stupid and usually besotted by drink', whereas Bleicher was undeniably clever and teetotal.

Borni was seen as 'an amiable, if weak creature who was anxious to get on, if she could, with Victoire'. Any ally was better than none to her, even if to Mathilde she was still a threat and an irritant. Although she 'might have come in useful for catching some of the smaller fry', Bleicher knew that Roman was the great catch and was close to finalising a plan to use his girlfriend to bait him as a double agent. Borni was paid 3,000 francs* a month to code, and was kept to her attic as much as possible.

---

* Approximately £17; £940 at 2018 values.

When the two women met for the second time in the week since their capture, Borni was terrified by her situation, 'like an abandoned child', and begged to be able to work with Mathilde. But then she claimed that she had recently become engaged to Roman, who had made her swear that she would never work for the Germans, and she 'was to extract the same promise' from Mathilde, who 'merely shrugged her shoulders' at this. After the encounter, Mathilde poured her self-loathing out sideways again by making such 'a tremendous row' that the Germans 'had provided no flowers for her bedroom', that they 'never committed the error again' and made sure 'to try to humour her' from then on.

Interallié's paperwork – every transmission, all the maps, sketches and photographs so meticulously and carelessly kept by Mathilde and Roman – covered the sideboard in the dining room. Extra personnel came to the house to comb through it. Borchers and Kayser shuttled between La Chattière and Abwehr Saint-Germain with 'self-important demeanours and bulging important briefcases'. Many agents supplied information to several clients on an ad hoc basis and arrests and swift releases were commonplace, so it is hard to isolate the scale of his round-ups, but Bleicher – who behaved more and more like a 'dismissive tyrant', Mathilde thought – self-aggrandisingly noted that the cells of La Santé and Fresnes held about a hundred inmates more than the week before.

Kayser appeared one day looking 'like a malign fox', clutching the Abwehr file on the Deuxième's d'Harcourt. The fact that d'Harcourt had been apprehended in June with Mathilde's name on him gave Bleicher the idea of sending her to Vichy as his double agent: if she was seen by her contacts there, rumours that she had been captured would be dismissed, and she could be used as a penetration agent in the unoccupied zone. But Borchers, under whose remit such matters still ultimately fell, was sober enough to veto this risky strategy which could leave their triumphant double-cross in tatters. It was one of the only points at which Bleicher's untutored ambition outran his common sense.

*

Mathilde's capture had destroyed her family life as well as her dreams of resistance. She was repeatedly told that her co-operation was the price of her parents' freedom, and in her mortification found herself unable to discuss what she was doing with her mother. Bleicher was so confident in her collaboration that he allowed her to go to the avenue des Gobelins flat for lunch one day. Their daily telephone conversations had inevitably ceased, but on this occasion Madame Belard tried to talk to her daughter about 'working for the Germans' only to find her 'impenetrable' and be 'told not to ask any questions'. In turn, Mathilde was too full of shame to 'ask her advice' and left the 'frigid atmosphere' of this emotionally bleak scene as soon as she could. Her mother gave her 32,000 francs* as a desperate substitute for loving maternal counsel in the hope it would help her to escape.

Mathilde was drawn even further into Bleicher's scheme when he decided it was time to consider landing the big fish of Maître Brault. She had started divorce proceedings against Maurice Carré, and been to see her lawyer several times in the weeks before her arrest about that as well as intelligence matters, so had an excuse to re-establish contact.

The other betrayals to date had been of amateurs compared to the worldly, well-connected lawyer, but Mathilde had now fallen so completely into her role that she displayed neither nerves nor any desire to confess when she arrived in the avenue Georges V office in the early afternoon. She spoke to Brault for half an hour and confirmed that Roman had been arrested, weaving the improbable story that he had had a Polish secretary and mistress whom he had 'fired', following which the woman had gone off with another Pole who was probably a Gestapo agent. She quite possibly did not hear the echo of her own experiences in this farrago and seemed perfectly at home telling outright lies, including that he would be safe 'unless Armand talked', as well as that she too would be fine as she had moved with most of the reports. Which technically was true.

---

* About £180 (nearly £10,000 at 2018 values), presumably a substantial portion of their savings.

Brault urged her to go south, and she sent a *carte interzone* to Captain Achard in the first week of December announcing her 'intention to come to the Free Zone' and asking him to come to Paris. Achard verified her handwriting and registered the oddness of the request in the context of the rumours about Interallié, replying in a 'vague and anodyne' way without taking any further action.

Later, Brault was puzzled that Mathilde 'seemed so normal' despite the recent turmoil. But just as Mathilde never told Brault he was in danger or that she had been turned, nor did Bleicher follow up this charade with an immediate arrest. Others in Brault's circle, including the railway chief Boussel, were caught; Boussel had been useful to other networks, including that of the French–Spanish–Cuban Gabriel Picabia, SMH/Gloria.* Picabia escaped arrest on her next visit to Brault only by pretending she was there about a land deal. With fuller knowledge of Brault's reach, Bleicher had perhaps concluded that leaving him at large might lead to even greater riches than bringing him in. In this, he was shortly to be proved right: before the Gestapo eventually made their move, Brault was to introduce Mathilde Carré to the prize who was to inspire the third act of her war.

*

While Mathilde was in the lawyer's office, Renée Borni was being taken to her lover in Fresnes. There had been no particular need to interrogate Roman intensely as so much was known about his contacts, and Bleicher had calculated that if he could turn him now, his double-cross would be unassailable. His girlfriend would be the bait. Roman found Borni and Borchers waiting for him when he was taken to the 'prison office' on the afternoon of 27th November, nine days after his capture. Borni 'was very excited and was weeping so much' that neither he 'nor the captain was able to calm her

---

* 'SMH' was 'His Majesty's Service' backwards. Samuel Beckett worked for the network in Roussillon, and his experiences resound through *Waiting for Godot*.

for some time'. When she eventually subsided, Borchers left the room and Borni delivered Bleicher's proposal: the Abwehr wanted him to work for them 'on only technical matters'; he would not be questioned on anything 'concerning members' of intelligence organisations. Speaking in whispers, she said that she had come because she longed to see him and to tell him what had 'gone on so far' and that 'any resistance was useless because the Germans knew everything through La Chatte'. Mathilde had apparently even 'disgusted the Germans' by involving her mother. The couple had such little time together that Borni had included a list of those taken so far in a letter which she now slipped into his pocket. Roman found 'three-fourths of it filled with sentimental and personal matter' and most of the rest 'full of accusations against La Chatte'. The hysterical sentence 'all is lost, all people have been arrested' was repeated several times.

After Borni's departure, Borchers returned with four questions for Roman, whose answers were that 'General D' was indeed Duch (true); Interallié had no contact with other French organisations (untrue); it was working for the Polish army and not for the British (half-true); it did not have any contact with sabotage organisations (half-true more by chance than desire). In exchange for his answers and in the hope of his co-operation, Roman was transferred to the prison's drier fourth floor and provided with his 'overcoat, several changes of underwear, socks, a warm dressing gown and a muffler'. The benefits of harmless co-operation were plain, and they planted a seed in Roman's fertile mind that was to flourish into his most celebrated espionage success.

*

Borni was given the painful task of coding a message as soon as she returned from Fresnes. Once it had been checked for hidden appeals, Tabet transmitted it: 'We cannot give fuller details about Walenty. He was arrested with Violette. We suspect that the Germans have taken our documents, situation very grave, we must stop work for a certain time. We await your instructions urgently.

La Chatte.' This time the answer flashed back to 'stop work and disappear. Wire your suggestions regarding starting up wireless communication again ... Let us know what is necessary for you to carry on and what are the losses in the network.'

This gave the opening two days later for the beginning of a series of transmissions to make the double-cross complete. Message 1023 read: 'I am regaining courage. Have traced several agents ... We are installed in peace. Because of the theft of certain documents I am taking from now the name of Victoire and dropping Inter-alliée [*sic*]. The need of money is urgent.'

The Cattery knew there were still many gaps in their round-up, and they tried to cover for the potential exposure lurking in their ignorance of Fernand Gane and Monique Deschamps' whereabouts by transmitting over Mathilde's code name that she was 'worried about Moustique'; also that she did not know the whereabouts of de Rocquigny and Lipski. Daily messages were sent about how Kieffer was standing by to head south to pick up the money they needed, both in order to maintain the realism of the network and to allow Bleicher to hope that Kieffer would line his pockets. The supposed author of these concerned transmissions did not mention her emotions around the falsehoods when she was looking back over the events of these frantic days from the comparative calm of a few months later, nor when she could take a longer perspective on her actions.

The fake network was even stepped up to the point of repopulation. There were agents included in the reports sent to London who were now behind bars, including Collardey; others who were at liberty but far from their designated sectors, such as Kieffer. Less than a fortnight since the first arrests, they had apparently found agents for D, E, F, K and R sectors while many others were simply made up, including 'Pierre', a 'French journalist' who was in charge of Press. On 3rd December 'Victoire' bought some breathing space when she said that in spite of this activity, 'we will remain quiet until about 1st January'.

The month may have been quiet on the airwaves, but Mathilde's life remained spun on its axis. It had been just over a fortnight since her capture on the foggy Montmartre morning and the first meeting with the man she now worked for and lived with. She had gone in days from expecting a British medal to being present at the arrest of some of her bravest colleagues, as well as witnessing many of her countrymen turn with her to save themselves. She was habituated to her comfortable, degraded life with the enemy, and was no longer persuading herself that she was merely biding her time. Yet this next month of passive collaboration, out of contact with the Allies, was going to prove as momentous and defining as its predecessor.

9

Panther

The bitter winter of 1941 in which Interallié had been wound up mirrored the increasing harshness of the Occupation. Support was draining from Pétain's regime as further freedoms were curtailed and more laws passed to align France with Nazi ideology. Civilian executions were increasing from eight in 1940 to fifty-one in the first nine months of 1941 to over 500 in the ensuing six months. The 'Nacht und Nebel' decree of 7th December meant that political activists and civilian resisters could disappear into the 'Night and Fog', often never to be heard of again.

Food shortages were becoming acute as more agricultural produce was sent to the Fatherland and the deep-frozen Eastern Front. Coffee had vanished altogether to be replaced by an emetic liquid; barely edible black bread was on ration to replace croissants and baguettes; cafés no longer offered sugar; people carried little boxes in which to put cigarette ends to be reconstituted. Those who had enough to eat were either under Nazi protection, farmers breaking the rules, rich, ingenious or crooked, and the country was becoming the most malnourished of the western occupied nations. In Paris, 'Wanted' posters were proliferating, and German notices in the Métro and on walls boasted about their executions. These were defaced each night in defiance of the curfew by 'V for Victory' signs. Wehrmacht soldiers were not allowed to patrol alone after dusk. To survive meant collaborating to some extent: as Sartre put it, 'Everything we did was equivocal. We never quite knew whether we were doing right or wrong; a subtle poison corrupted even our best actions.' 'Système D', after *se débrouiller* (to unravel or disentangle), became the order of the day in a world where norms were becoming meaningless and the only essential was to stay out of trouble.

There was a desperate need for slave labour in German factories and Vichy mendaciously promised 'good food, good pay, concerts and free holidays' to their citizens to fill the jobs. Even so, numbers fell short of requirements and secret round-ups in target cities were ordered: Marseilles had to send 300 workers or 'it would be forced to bundle its own policemen on the trains going east instead'. After America entered the war in December, it put pressure on Vichy to prevent Germany using French facilities in the Caribbean; they were unable to comply as their freedom to take independent decisions was so diminished. By November 1942, the unoccupied zone had ceased to exist as the whole country came under German control following the Allied invasion of North Africa. Laval hailed the removal of the demarcation line as a benefit of the French collaborationist policy, and used the police and army to crush resistance as the remaining two-fifths of the population discovered the exigencies of living under an occupying power.

Britain was facing a bleak outlook. From late 1941 until the summer of 1942 the Russians were on the verge of defeat and the Americans cancelled much-needed deliveries of aircraft to the RAF as they entered the war. The day after Pearl Harbor, the Japanese had attacked the Philippines, Malaya and Hong Kong, a week later they entered Burma, and the British began their 900-mile retreat to India. On 15th February 1942, 85,000 men surrendered Singapore to an attacking force of 30,000 Japanese. Malta, the key to the Mediterranean, was under constant bombardment by the Luftwaffe.

It was against this backdrop of defeat and complicity that the chance of redemption offered itself to Mathilde Carré in the guise of an idealist attached to the emerging Special Operations Executive in London. It was a rich opportunity, but one even more fraught with peril than what she had lived through in the past two years, and one which she was unable to seize until after the most damaging deception of all had been perpetrated over her name.

*

London needed to believe in Mathilde. They were desperate for her intelligence to the point that they squandered a significant victory at a time when success was in short supply. The rotund Gilbert Renault, known as 'Colonel Rémy', had recently become a prime source in the occupied zone; he was reckoned to 'emit more heat than light', but his reports on the German warships and U-boat activity on the Atlantic coast were widely respected. His agents kept a close eye on the harbours used by the 26,000-ton battle cruisers, *Scharnhorst* and *Gneisenau*, and their escort ship *Prinz Eugen* that were the glories of the Kriegsmarine. In the winter of 1941, the ships were under repair in Brest. The repeated RAF bombings had failed to put the dockyards out of commission, and it was dangerous to enforce a blockade of the escape lanes within range of German attack. Inside knowledge of any movement of the battle cruisers was required.

Rémy's gallant Lieutenant Philippon sent a message from the naval base on 6th December warning that the ships were 'preparing to leave', as the 'preparations of the big docks 8 and 9 indicate that departure possible between 1st and 15th January for a naval operation possibly combined with the *Tirpitz*'. Bombing was stepped up but Rémy's agents reported 'that the attacks had been largely ineffective'. The warnings became increasingly urgent as 1942 got under way: on 1st February the ships were 'in condition for action' and that departure was 'likely to take place around eleven one evening or midnight during the next period of the new moon'. Six days later they warned 'Departure absolutely imminent. Pay special attention to the period of the new moon.' Meanwhile, the Cattery was sending out contradictory messages that the ships were 'quite unable to put to sea' owing to bomb damage and that 'in any case most of the crew had now gone ashore'.

London knew that 'the shipping information supplied by Interallié had been exceptionally good' in the past and took the easy path at a time when almost no reliable news was coming out of

Paris; 'the Admiralty preferred to accept these comfortable and reassuring messages rather than believe the urgent warnings being sent by "Colonel Rémy's agent"', as the frustrated British spies later complained. When the *Scharnhorst, Gneisenau* and *Prinz Eugen* did make their dash up the Channel in the early hours of 12th February, there was, as the Rémy reports had estimated, very little moon showing. But nor was there enough Royal Navy activity on the coast, although in England one motor torpedo boat was being prepared for despatch to Brittany to carry a strange group back over the Channel, summoned by Mathilde on behalf of her newest colleagues.

*

SOE came under the Ministry of Economic Warfare, whose minister, Hugh Dalton, insisted that he needed a free hand 'to use many different methods, including industrial and military sabotage, labour agitation and strikes, continuous propaganda, terrorist acts against traitors and German leaders, boycotts and riots'. Independence from both the War Office and the intelligence services would be essential to the unit's freedom of action: it was run from a 1930s building in Baker Street reached from a side entrance discreetly marked 'Inter-Service Research Bureau', and those who came to it from the War Office in Whitehall and elsewhere were surprised both by its dinginess and that uniforms had been replaced by open-necked shirts.

F (for French) Section was born on the night of 10th May 1941 when its first group leader, Pierre de Vomécourt, was parachuted into Châteauroux, in the centre of the country. His brief was to assess the strength of resistance to see if it was 'sufficiently coherent and vigorous to justify the risk of Britain sending aircraft and precious munitions to revitalise and support their efforts'. He travelled around, meeting those 'declaring in private their hostility to the Nazis' and weighing up their 'probable future worth to SOE'. London recognised that 'within a short time [he] had laid the foundations of a powerful movement which covered the greater part of occupied France [and] gradually assumed leadership of other spontaneous organisations'. He was the scout and spearhead for the largest underground civilian militia ever seen.

De Vomécourt knew that even in a few months the British would find it 'hard to arrange priority clearance for equipping the French' and that to succeed he could not 'run any extra risk of detection' or involve himself in any 'unusual or unacceptable activity by normal standards'. The alliance between him and Mathilde Carré that began at the end of 1941 was certainly unusual and would have been impossible had he known the truth about her from the start. Yet each would become the saviour of the other.

*

Betrayal begat betrayal in the first weeks of December, each one habituating Mathilde further to life as a decoy and guide. Yet despite Bleicher's concomitant successes, he was still a mere Feldwebel in rank, which became 'a very sore point' as it was clear to him that he was 'quite obviously the brains behind' the Abwehr's success. A British intelligence officer on his case heard that the 'extremely efficient' Bleicher was even 'on more than one occasion seen to snatch a telephone from a senior officer in the middle of a conversation and continue the conversation himself'.

On the 6th, he found the gathering at the Café Louis XIII that Isidore had given away. Mathilde went in first again, and 'two more agents' were taken. In his trusting ignorance, one of them, Robert Gorriot, told her about his contact with a former minister for industry, Guy Chaumet; the other, the B Sector head, gave away two of his subagents. Despite the three weeks since her own arrest, the situation in Paris was so fluid, and the intelligence-gatherers were so used to colleagues being arrested and then released, that one of these was 'overjoyed to see her because he had feared she had been taken'.

Gorriot also worked for another Resistance group in Brittany, Overcloud, and had compromising documents stitched into his clothing. He too turned to protect himself and his family to become a *double* and penetrate Overcloud. He became the first example of the Abwehr's 'new tactic of inserting "sheep" into all the organisations, to get to know them well and then at the appointed hour when they knew enough the Boche would initiate mass arrests', as Mathilde bluntly summed it up.

On Chaumet's return home, he found his wife giving tea to Mathilde and Bleicher. Before he realised what was going on, he volunteered 'the vital information' that his fellow agent and black marketeer Théophile Burlot would be coming to see him the next morning. Burlot himself 'gave away everything', including the real name and address of Roman's favourite fisherman César, as well as many others 'working in the underground'. The craven man went so far as to offer to 'set up a Gestapo office at Rennes' but Bleicher was now adept at judging the cascade of collaboration that had stemmed from his first meeting with the drunken Lemeur and concluded that his prisoner was not 'trustworthy'.

*

Mathilde's encounter with Kieffer was inevitably emotionally complicated. It triggered internal questions around her own guilt and whether her arrest had been inevitable once he had started the whole train of betrayals, and whether she was now as double-died a traitor as him. Kieffer was entirely at ease in the world of deceit, and was running a lucrative black-market business in 'food and clothing coupons, cigarettes, spirits etc.', sharing the proceeds with Bleicher. He had apparently 'accepted his new job' as Bleicher's roaming mole if 'he was not used against airmen, for those fellows were sacred to him', as he put it to Mathilde in one of the nuanced but meaningless conditions used to save face in the world of treachery.

Bleicher let his two prime double agents have an hour together, and Mathilde was struck at once that Kieffer was still wearing his same leather jacket, as if becoming a turncoat would have led to a wardrobe change, and that he retained his 'sassiness'. He recounted the chain of events that led to the arrest of Roman, maintaining that he 'had done everything I could to save you, but I couldn't do any more ... They were too strong for me and wouldn't let it go ... ' She admitted that she 'had no right to judge anyone', although was unable to resist the poisonous addition of 'apart from Violette', which enabled Kieffer to claim that in his own case Charlotte Buffet was to blame. Mathilde pointed out that he was much more 'free' than she was as she was 'always with [the Germans] ... living with them ... sleeping with them ... was a part of their community'. In the distinctions between traitors who had caved in so fast, having a degree of self-determination and agency, even living in one's own home, counted in her mind as well as in practical terms.

Kieffer later used that freedom to pursue his double-dealing without apparent remorse. He was sent to Caen by Bleicher to run a fictitious network and funnel information and resisters into German hands. The British realised late in the war that 'all these people were convinced they were working for the Allies' as Kieffer's agents in turn informed on any *résistants* in their district; but even though other members of the Abwehr acted decisively and mur-derously, Bleicher himself distrusted the traitor who had handed him his first coup so thoroughly by then that he 'took no action' on his information.

*

Mathilde feared that Bleicher would try to rope her into whatever he had planned next for Kieffer, but 'another, far more important episode' was already in train just out of her sight. Ironically, it was a tribute to the esteem in which Bleicher was held, and decisions he had taken in recent days, that enabled her to make the most of it – once she had got through her Christmas in German hands.

Bleicher's career in Paris was thriving and Suzanne Laurent was ensconced in comfort, so he went to Cherbourg on leave to tidy up his affairs there in the third week of December. He had shown the 'well-satisfied officers' of the Abwehr who were 'living extremely well ... at a leisurely pace' a more effective way of carrying out counter-espionage in only a month. Borchers took advantage of his absence to ask Mathilde to dinner 'like two old soldier pals' at the Grande Restaurant in the Gare Saint-Germain-en-Laye. Borchers drank 'aperitifs, wines with his food, brandy and more brandy' while complaining about how nobody understood him, how he had not heard from his son on the Russian Front for three months now, how his work was 'not important enough for someone like him', and how he was going to demand a transfer to Istanbul for 'interesting times' now that 'France was finished'; she should come 'on this splendid mission' as his secretary. Mathilde had managed to remain comparatively abstemious through this inebriated onslaught, but could barely breathe in the claustrophobic atmosphere of the restaurant and asked to be taken back.

As Borchers 'tottered' homewards, he spotted a bar that was still open and went in to have 'a bottle or two for the road', inviting all the German NCOs in the place to join him and insisting the terrified proprietor remain open long after the curfew. He was so far gone that he even toasted Mathilde as '*la plus grande espionne internationale de cette guerre*' before grabbing three bottles of champagne and demanding the NCOs come back to La Chattière, where he finally passed out at four o'clock in the morning. Next day, she swore that she would keep quiet, but the episode helped her 'regain her confidence' for whatever lay ahead.

Bleicher was ringing in daily and heard about the 'scandalous chain of events', which he passed up to Commandant Eschig. Borchers was noted down as an operational security risk while Mathilde's discretion and failure to abscond 'created confidence' in her in turn; she was now allowed to go out unchaperoned, edging closer to the freedom given to the detested Kieffer. The incident brought about another immediate change in the Cattery in that a new chief arrived from Maisons-Laffitte: Mathilde was very taken by the Austrian Commandant Ische, a 'large, strong, handsome colonel, typically Viennese in his beauty, charm and gallantry'.

Communication with London was sporadic through December as forewarned. Transmissions mainly involved demands for money and further reassurances that the network had been repopulated. But by the 14th, nothing had arrived and there was fresh concern that they had been rumbled. The messages took on a bold, threatening tone: 'We are surprised by your silence. Yes or no, do you want to help us in our future work? We are not at all disturbed at present and have found a sufficient number of agents, especially on the whole of the coast sectors B, C, D, E and F. In connection with Pétain–Göring negotiations work promises to be most interesting. Sabotage and subversion activities are increasing in strength, this is not the right time to abandon our aims.'

To the relief of La Chattière and the Abwehr, this brought an instant reply: 'Further to your W/T message ... we have sent the money. At present we are looking for ways and means to transfer the money to France.' And two days later an acknowledgement that anything coming out of the Pétain–Göring meeting was certainly of interest. That the meeting in question, to cement Franco-German co-operation, had taken place in the Yonne over two weeks earlier, indicates just how little information was still crossing the Channel, and how much Interallié was missed. Admiral Darlan's declaration after the summit that the choice of 'collaboration' was made to protect France's interests 'to live and to remain a great power' was the most telling public acknowledgement to date of the enhanced subservience of the Republic to the Reich.

*

Borchers decided to throw a Christmas party at the Madeleine before he went on leave. Once again, he drank himself insensible, and had to be helped on to his train home. This time, Ische saw to it 'that he was sacked and sent to the Russian Front', which he survived to become a surgical-bandage salesman post-war. There was a further celebration at the villa on Christmas Day itself, but Bleicher decided that he and Mathilde should stay away from that, much to his fury when he heard that his colleagues had 'distributed all the good things they had taken off the French agents who had been arrested' and saved nothing for him, the prime originator of such largesse. His lowly position was emphasised when he was offered 'a sum of money' by Eschig 'in connection with his break-up of the Interallié affair', an 'insult' which left him 'furious'.

Bleicher's anger changed to anticipation when Maître Brault set aside his suspicions and asked Mathilde to ring him on Boxing Day, ostensibly to discuss her divorce. On the call he told her that he had been 'at a very important meeting' the day before at which he had come across 'a young chief who, having returned from England, is going to co-ordinate all the organisations' of resistance. This figure wanted to have lunch with her that day. She waited with her shadow at the Café Georges V on the Champs-Elysées, but Brault and his contact did not show. Bleicher, fearful of a great coup slipping away, ordered her to ring the lawyer from the café. Brault apologised that the 'young man in question' had been unable to join them, so could they try again at seven o'clock?

She and Bleicher were back in position in good time. Bleicher was 'reading *Paris-Soir* quietly and, as always, lying in wait' when Brault arrived and presented 'Monsieur Pierre de Vomécourt, or, more exactly, "Lucas"' to her. But even before she had time to react, Brault, who had on 'his usual hunted-spy demeanour, looking to the left, to the right and behind him', hissed that they could not talk openly as the 'Gestapo would certainly be there'. He was 'in a great state of nerves' and did 'not like the faces of the people sitting at an adjoining table'. He alluded again to de Vomécourt's arrival from England, and commended her own 'glorious career' as a spy to him before they made a plan for her to go to 'Lucas's office at eleven o'clock the next morning'. Bleicher's researches that evening suggested that de Vomécourt was a 'small-time political agitator' which was enough in itself to give him 'indescribable joy' but the next days' events were to more than justify his strategic forbearance in leaving Brault at liberty earlier in the year.

*

Edouard Pierre Fourrier de Crévoisier de Vomécourt was about to turn thirty-six. He was a slightly built five feet seven inches, with short, chestnut curly hair, alert and intelligent eyes and a wide smile. In many ways he was similar to Roman Czerniawski, 'vigorous, talkative … a good shot, a fast thinker, full of energy and enthusiasm'. Mathilde came to appreciate his 'great willpower, icy courage' and, in another similarity with Roman, the animated 'gestures of over-keen men'. He was the youngest of three brothers from a Lorraine family with a tradition of military service that started with their great-grandfather, who had been tortured and killed by the Prussians in 1870. They had come to live in Hove, on the south coast of England, when Pierre was two years old. Their father had volunteered for army service in 1914, even though at the age of fifty-one he was exempt, and was killed early in 1917. The oldest boy, Jean, lied about his age to join the Royal Air Force, was shot down, wounded and drew a war pension for the rest of his life. The family returned to France with their mother in 1920 and when Pierre had finished school and his *service militaire*, he went into business in Paris.

At the outbreak of war, he joined the British Expeditionary Force as Anglo-French liaison officer to the 7th Cameronians, and on 17th June 1940 was in Cherbourg with orders to find his way to Bordeaux and on to North Africa. As he was pondering this, Marshal Pétain's 'broken voice' came over the radio 'telling the country that an armistice had been signed and the fighting was over'. With no intention of becoming a prisoner of war, de Vomécourt rushed to the docks and caught the last ship out. He landed in England on a perfect summer's day that contrasted with 'the tumult' he had left behind, along with his wife and children. Some weeks later, he heard that two boys had been executed in Nantes for cutting telephone wires and resolved that 'if such courage and patriotic devotion still existed in France, what else could be done to hinder the German war effort?'

De Vomécourt was convinced that practically the entire country remained at war with Germany 'in their hearts', which inspired him to get in touch with Major de Châteauvieux, the

Deuxième Bureau chief in London, to explain some of his 'ideas for sabotage'. Châteauvieux 'expressed interest' and said he would be in touch on his return from a short trip to France, but the 'gallant, friendly' major was captured and executed. De Vomécourt then contacted de Gaulle's right-hand man, Colonel Gaston Palewski, who decided de Vomécourt would be of most use as political representative of the Free French in Vichy. This did not appeal to the man of action, who was also 'troubled' to find at the Free French headquarters in Carlton Gardens Terrace 'a certain number of officers who were mainly interested in what their salary would be'. So he diverted to the embryonic SOE to propose that they 'send men like me back to France, to teach the people how to fight the Germans. To teach other boys like those at Nantes how to hit the Germans effectively and, if possible, not to get caught or be killed.'

After a brief and ragged period of training in the New Forest in which they did not even have blank ammunition for their Sten guns, de Vomécourt made his May 1941 jump into his homeland at the head of a unit that soon included Roger Cottin ('Roger'), the former managing director of the London branch of the luxury soap-maker Roger et Gallet, and the Lancashire-born oil engineer Major Benjamin Cowburn ('Benoît'). Their papers, carefully forged in a grey stucco house on the Kingston bypass, identified them as commercial travellers. Alongside his brief to assess and co-ordinate the potential for organised resistance, de Vomécourt was to investigate the possibilities of destroying 'railway communications, petrol dumps, ammunition dumps and especially aerodromes'.

In early June he called for two containers of 'warlike stores' to be dropped close to his brother Philippe's chateau near Limoges. Philippe was working as a railway inspector and ensured that as much of the fruit and vegetables going by train to Germany was swapped with the rotting produce intended for his countrymen. He and his gardener's son-in-law fended off the suspicions of the local gendarmerie and hid the 'tommy guns, fighting knives, plastic explosive, and limpet mines with delay fuses' in the shrub-bery. Jean meanwhile was sabotaging canal locks in the waterways around Mathilde's birthplace of Le Creusot, whose belching facto-ries were now manufacturing armaments for the Wehrmacht.

Pierre was lucky to escape when his radio man, Georges Bégué, following whom all SOE operators were code-named 'Georges', was informed on to the Marseilles police. That operator's successor was Jewish and denounced as such by a prying neighbour in Paris and executed without trial. De Vomécourt had no means of com-munication to London, a disaster as he could now 'call on the services of something like 10,000 resisters'* in a network he planned to call Autogiro. Amongst his agents was a well-connected valet and former head waiter from the Dorchester hotel in Park Lane called Noël Burdeyron who introduced de Vomécourt to Michel Brault, who in turn told him that the Interallié radio was still oper-ational and under the control of Mathilde Carré.

*

Bleicher ordered Mathilde to listen carefully, 'not to lose a single mouthful', to ask as many questions as she could, and to 'give him advice' based on her experience when she met the Frenchman that evening. He was in his most conceited humour, and told her that she should act as de Vomécourt's superior as 'he looked more like a little novice than like a spy or saboteur'. Above all, she should remember everything and offer him whatever he wanted: false papers, agents, messages to London. And then once again 'his old song' emerged, that if she 'tried any "dirty tricks"', immediate death would follow'. He would be waiting in his car a few metres from de Vomécourt's office and would storm in if she had not emerged by midday.

---

* In early 1942, a further SOE calculation increased this number to 23,500–24,000 resisters when smaller, existing organisations were brought together under de Vomécourt's leadership.

Mathilde took to de Vomécourt immediately. He struck her as 'essentially likeable … a clean man, solid, idealistic, full of good ideas'. But he was also someone she could take in hand as he lacked 'the right stature to lead his Organisation, didn't have the physical stamina of a great resister and had no knowledge of military matters'. Overall, he 'lacked the necessary drive' which she, in her best moments, had to spare. She chose to forget that she belonged to the Abwehr when she decided he represented 'excellent soil to cultivate and perfect', someone to whom she could attach herself and mould, as she had Roman in less complicated days.

De Vomécourt trusted her because Brault had recommended her, because of her history with the outstanding *réseau* Interallié, because she was his only option to extricate himself from his operational isolation, and because he liked her. He 'explained everything', giving away classified information in his hope and relief. He was in a hurry, so much so that he needed to get to London the next day if possible. She knew this was a 'fantasy, as he had no detailed plans, no news and no money' but he was intending to spend the next night on a 'secret airfield' near Chartres in the hope of being picked up by a Lysander from England. If he did not succeed in getting away, she told him to be in touch with her again on Monday, and they would meet to put in hand '*une collaboration complète*'. It was a telling phrase after an encounter that left her feeling 'magnificently joyful', sure that she had now found her 'revenge' on the Germans, even if it was not clear how to carry that out.

As with the most successful double agents, Mathilde was doubly trusted. The new operation to take de Vomécourt and his contacts was christened 'Nobel' by Bleicher, and she was code-named 'Baghera'. It was a promotion from 'La Chatte' to the Hindi word for a black panther. She wasted no time in exercising her new leverage and demanded that she leave the Cattery, with its underlying stench of constant betrayal and Borni's misery, and return to Paris. Bleicher put the wheels in motion: he was convinced of her loyalty, and was himself keen to spend more time with Suzanne Laurent in her well-appointed apartment.

Just before the meeting, two transmissions had been sent to London, the first of which announced Mathilde's new identity, while the second threatened to cut off contact altogether: 'If on 10th January I am still without money I will abandon you and will pass with my agents to another organisation for the liberation of my country.' This produced the speedy reply that 'if you do not think the Boche can decode your message', 50,000 francs* would come her way, a sum that showed London's ongoing faith in her new network.

*

De Vomécourt's exfiltration from Chartres did not happen, so Mathilde's radio became crucial to get him to England. His key allies, Roger Cottin and Ben Cowburn, had arrived in Paris to become members of what the Englishman called 'the Paris Secret Agents' Club'. Cottin was forty, and had also joined SOE after his evacuation from Dunkirk to England. Cowburn was in his early thirties, stocky, 'fair-haired, clean-shaven, with a pleasant smile and a very pronounced scar on his left temple' as well as a tooth-brush moustache; he spoke English with a trace of a Lancashire accent, and immaculate French after working in the oil industry in Paris. His speciality was to utilise his engineering know-how to calculate the most impactful place to plant a bomb on a train, and to organise the sabotage of the closely guarded oil depots and refin-eries that kept the Luftwaffe operational. He used to cross the demarcation line lying just above the rails in the two-foot-high, slatted recess under the water tank of the Bordeaux–Marseilles Express which he climbed in and out of at Montauban. Feldwebel Bleicher, until recently a lowly military police interpreter in Cherbourg, now had this intrepid man, the rest of the Paris Secret Agents' Club, and the wider thousands of resisters tantalisingly within range.

---

* Approximately £300; £16,500 at 2018 values.

*

On the last day of 1941 a transmission to London with dual author-
ship struck a very different tone to the evasions about Roman and
demands for money:

> Please give the following message to Room 055 War Office*
> urgently ... Send LYS [a Lysander] to fetch me 3rd, 4th or 5th
> January on the ground used for the departure of Walenty ...
> Send one wireless operator, two W/T sets and important
> funds. If LYS impossible, send by man on the landing ground
> at Vaas near le Mans with one wireless operator, funds, a con-
> tainer ... If operation impossible send me money by the US
> military attaché at Vichy ... I am fusing all healthy organisa-
> tions in both zones, counting on you. Reply urgently ... if you
> are sending Lysander or by man or money to Vichy ... Lucas.
> Victoire.

Bleicher was delighted that he had landed someone who could
summon Lysanders, wirelesses, money and senior diplomats as the
telegram left La Chattière. For Mathilde, de Vomécourt held the
possibility of salvation, powerful enough to save her from her current degraded state, but she needed to tread carefully and weigh
her options. She continued to play the game, although she seemed
able to push thoughts of extrication aside: she had a dinner with
Bleicher and Kieffer which was 'full of jokes about the end of
England and about working together, the excitement of that
moment when nothing could put those men off their stride'.

In the same week she was lionised by the other side as well. De
Vomécourt arranged a lunch in 'a deluxe black-market restaurant'
for Cowburn and Cottin to meet the 'helpful Madame Carré'.
Cowburn found her 'slim and pleasant' but 'very short-sighted' as
she 'constantly peered at us from puckered eyelids'. Mathilde

---

* The secret address for MI5.

recounted the 'catastrophe' of Interallié, from which she had been lucky to escape and how she 'rejoiced' at being called Victoire. She appreciated the Lancastrian's 'collection of blue funny stories', and felt thoroughly at home in their company, seemingly oblivious in the moment that she was betraying them with every boast.

Her contradictory nature was standing her in good stead as she was able to display loyalty to both of her new allies without showing the strain. The wrong move as the keeper of secrets could lead to death from either of them, but for now she felt the elation of safety in double indispensability, without any clear idea how she would act in whatever might follow. If she felt threatened, she did not show it, yet the entertaining company she kept and the meals she was bought heralded her period of greatest jeopardy.

10

Bait and Switchback

Major Ben Cowburn was permanently on his guard against 'the swarm of spies and informers' lurking to destroy SOE's fledgling operations in France. He had also had the experience of waiting for three days on either side of the full moon in early November 1941 for the 'kind of experimental operation' of a supply drop by parachute at Vaas, halfway between Le Mans and Tours. The nervous 'reception committee' in Paris had huddled over the radio at eight o'clock each night to listen to the BBC, hoping for 'Pierre is well', meaning the operation would go ahead. The one time the broadcast was followed by the 'drone of a plane', they turned on the three small red lights as a guide but the aircraft circled several miles away for half an hour before heading back home. On the other nights it was 'Pierre sends greetings' – the flight was abandoned. To stand by for a further twenty-four hours for a drop that might easily be postponed for meteorological reasons or lack of British aeroplanes or someone's blunder was known in SOE parlance as 'being crucified'.

There was nothing scheduled for the December moon as adverse weather conditions were predicted. De Vomécourt was keen that an aeroplane in early January should not only pick him up and bring the vital weapons, but be a test of the drop-off and pick-up systems. It was a relief for Cowburn when a message came via the 'Polish radio link' on the 5th that SOE was 'hoping to send you money and wireless operator' as well as a question for Victoire about where her cash should be delivered; he did not suspect 'spies or informers' for a moment. De Vomécourt even added that Madame Carré had introduced 'another survivor' from Interallié, 'a Belgian businessman who had managed to procure a permit to drive a car', to take the three of them the 200 kilometres to the drop point. If the radio had been 'a godsend', a car in an organisation that was more used to bicycle transport seemed close to a miracle. Cowburn hoped this was the turning point that would enable F Section to 'become active', while Mathilde was wondering how this expedition might turn her strange, doubly compromised situation to her advantage.

*

Roger Cottin, de Vomécourt's 'assistant', sometimes called 'Roger des cheveux blancs' owing to his prematurely white hair, had gone ahead to Vaas on 6th January. De Vomécourt, Mathilde and her 'Belgian businessman' friend, Jean Castel, met at a café near the church of Saint-Germain-des-Prés at five o'clock. The 'Belgian' was Hugo Bleicher, who had adopted the nationality to explain any guttural inflections. Surprisingly for a travelling salesman in civilian life, he was unable to drive so he had brought one of his German colleagues 'disguised as a French chauffeur' for back-up, as well as a picnic supper. He wanted to infiltrate de Vomécourt's world thoroughly to maximise his catch and would have a quiet word should a curious patrol flag them down. De Vomécourt did not detect anything untoward in the party.

They were met at the field that was to serve as a landing ground at nine o'clock by Cottin and the local schoolmaster, but heard nothing for so long that they decided to leave one man on watch while the others retired to eat the 'sandwiches issued by the German counter-espionage service'. As they sat around the fire in the cottage of 'a friendly peasant nearby who had been nominated to bury the containers in his garden', they praised the brave patriot and 'indulged in anti-German propaganda', initiated by Bleicher. He was enjoying the chance to run down the Third Reich and soon he and his driver were relaxed enough to fall asleep in their chairs.

Mathilde realised that she had Bleicher 'entirely in her power', yet did nothing. There was no knowing what de Vomécourt's reaction might be if she told him the truth. In his desperate situation, he probably would kill her as well as the two Germans and flee. She had no strategy in that unlikely, paralysed moment, and decided to keep her counsel.

They gave up the vigil before dawn, and the unlikely car-load of a German soldier pretending to be a French chauffeur, an Abwehr officer posing as a Belgian businessman, and in the back seat an SOE officer next to a woman he believed was on his side but who had just betrayed members of a major intelligence network, headed back to Paris. Apart from the non-appearance of the containers, each had reason to feel pleased enough with the night's work and optimistic about their espionage future. De Vomécourt was back in touch with England; Mathilde was in the thick of the war again; and Bleicher had a hold on the Resistance movement.

The travellers got back in the early morning. Mathilde had been given a list of flats 'requisitioned' by the German High Command in Paris that had belonged to 'Britishers or Jews' and had chosen 'a magnificent one' in the rue de la Faisanderie, a short walk from the place Victor Hugo. It had belonged to an 'Italian Jew' who had made his way to South America leaving behind his beautiful furniture and photographs, and, coincidentally before him, had been the home of the playwright François de Curel, de Vomécourt's uncle. Since the outbreak of the war its occupants had been a German captain, his lover and their maid: the officer had been posted to the Eastern Front, the lover was asked to make way for Mathilde, and the maid, Marguerite, stayed on.

The move preserved de Vomécourt's illusion of Mathilde's independence but Bleicher was not going to let her totally escape his supervision, so he moved in with her under his alias of Jean Castel. Since Mathilde was 'not subject to the restrictions of rationing' and keen on luxury, as Madame Castel she made sure fresh flowers and other comforts were delivered. A 'large stove that was kept alight night and day' was installed and the bedroom's three radiators were permanently on; she was grateful that 'the Army of Occupation were allowed to do whatever they wanted' in a city where fuel was in acute shortage and which was currently 'suffering appalling

weather, snow and ice'. Bleicher was able to spend more time with
Suzanne Laurent now that he lived in the centre of town, so it was
not much of a hardship for him when Mathilde pretended to be ill
to 'withstand [his] advances'.

*

SIS had put the wheels in motion to get the 50,000 francs to her via
an agent in the Felix network who deposited the cash with the concierge at a house in the boulevard Malesherbes to await collection.
Bleicher gave her 10,000 francs* (which she hung on to for the rest of
her war) and pocketed the rest, telling Ische that only 10,000 had
been sent, which he had given to her as a present. Although she
was keen on money herself and did not seem to mind its origins,
Mathilde took a high-minded view of Bleicher's self-enrichment and
considered that 'the financial impropriety of these men is shocking'.

To maintain authenticity as well as to maximise their income,
the Abwehr radioed back over her name that it was 'absolutely
impossible to work with 50,000 francs', that she would need 'at least
20,000 francs per sector and moreover all the expenses of rents,
radio etc.' On Mathilde's behalf, they totted it all up to 'a minimum
of 300,000 francs'† if she was not to find 'all work impossible'. A
week later, when nothing more had been heard on the subject,
another stern message was sent claiming that 'agents are already on
the point of passing on to another organisation; lack of money
becoming lack of confidence'. In the middle of the month, de
Vomécourt managed to get 2 million francs‡ parachuted to him in
Vichy and smuggled back over the demarcation line. He was asked
to give 200,000 to Mathilde to keep her largely fictitious network
afloat, but by the time this order came through, everything had
changed. He had to find a way to appease her that would keep himself and the hopes of the resistance movement alive.

---

* Approximately £60; £3,300 at 2018 values.
† Approximately £1,800; nearly £100,000 at 2018 values.
‡ Approximately £11,500; over £600,000 at 2018 values.

*

Mathilde had to escape her double-dealing dilemma, and took a daring risk in exposing it. The bacteriologist Henri Collin had been a subject of interest when his name cropped up in the account book immediately after her arrest, but her statement that he was just an acquaintance had been accepted. Bleicher now wanted to reassess him. Collin was 'an intimate friend' of Major André Achard of the Deuxième Bureau who thought of him as 'a man in whom one could have confidence but at the same time extremely timorous and at times imprudent', which made him a questionable repository for Mathilde's inner turmoil. Nevertheless, she rushed to Collin's laboratory just after his return from Spain and Vichy in January 1942. She had had five days since the Vaas trip to turn her options over and needed to share them with someone who might give the objective advice of the scientist. On the one hand, she was very comfortably set up; on the other, she had seen an as yet not fully formed possibility of salvation with de Vomécourt, whose character, passion and loyalty were far more attractive than Bleicher's controlling cynicism. Maybe the fact that the Germans still seemed likely to be victorious was a weight on the scales.

Collin looked 'as impressive as ever' in his white laboratory coat and listened to her 'calmly' as she told him that she 'had been arrested by the Germans ... and was now under close surveillance at all times'; she had been made to go to meetings with agents who were then captured. She 'confessed' everything, unpacking her fear, guilt and tension to his judgement. Collin said that in Vichy there had been 'doubts about Duvernois' arrest after he never came back from the appointment with you at the Pam Pam' and Achard was 'truly anxious'. This pushed Mathilde to the crux of her dilemma: she was working for the Germans but had been 'put into a different organisation' which she would 'have to betray at a given moment'; she 'absolutely did not want to do that'.

The gamble was a tribute to her desperate state. And, as often when risks are given voice, she got a powerfully unexpected reply. Collin thought his 'poor little Lily' was 'completely mad' and he trusted her because she 'had done her duty more than anyone else would have done for over a year'. She had had the 'outrageous good fortune' to come out of Interallié alive and should now 'keep quiet' around the Germans and 'not do anything silly'. This statement of faith gave her the courage to say that her visit had another purpose: Bleicher wanted to meet him for dinner.

In the Aux Vignes de Seigneur restaurant a few nights later, Mathilde introduced Bleicher as 'Jean', and her controller proceeded to 'interrogate' Collin about his 'Spanish trips and the people [he] saw there'. Collin gave nothing away and took care of the bill in order to establish a modicum of dominance. This meant that there had to be a retaliatory meal on the Abwehr a few days later at which Collin again neither incriminated himself nor confirmed any suspicions about Mathilde's Vichy connections.

*

De Vomécourt had spent most of his own funds on Autogiro. He and Cowburn had parachuted in with only 20,000 francs each and even after the arrival of the 2 million he bore a grudge against his paymasters as he, like Bleicher, felt 'the English at that time weren't very generous'. SOE reassured him that he 'could communicate totally securely on the Interallié radio, that is to say via M. Carré'. But just as these cross-Channel transmissions were being tapped out, their lead agent's money worries were swept aside as he arrived at the horrifying realisation of Mathilde's double-dealing.

His suspicions had first been awakened when she showed him a message from London asking for information about Saint-Nazaire's coastal defences. The town was the home of the Normandie Dock, the only Atlantic mooring large enough to service the newest addition to the Nazi fleet and the most powerful warship in the world, the 52,600-ton *Tirpitz*. If the heavily defended leviathan were loose in the Atlantic, she would 'wreak havoc on convoys already suffering massive losses from German U-boats'. But she would not be risked at sea if the dock was unavailable as the only alternative for repairs would be to head up the Channel to Germany, with attendant exposure to British attack. Churchill wrote a memorandum to his chiefs of staff that January declaring, 'No other target is comparable to it. The whole strategy of the war turns at this period on this ship.' He asked for schemes for its 'destruction or even crippling', and SOE demanded information from de Vomécourt.

Cottin came back from an exploratory trip to say that it was 'practically impossible to go into Saint-Nazaire without a residential or work permit'. When de Vomécourt made an 'apparently innocent remark' to Mathilde about this, she replied that 'her network' had had no trouble with access and information-gathering – which he realised might mean that the Germans had seen the SOE signal, and had had time to seal the town before Cottin could get there. Even though the occupiers were fully aware that the dock would be first an intelligence and then a military target and would have taken such steps anyway, the seed was planted in de Vomécourt's jumpy imagination.*

It took root thanks to one of Bleicher's few mistakes. On the evening of 16th January, Mathilde gave de Vomécourt the false identity papers that he believed she had conjured up for his *bande* through her Interallié connections. They were not strictly speaking forgeries at all, but officially produced documents complete with actual Wehrmacht stamps and signatures, a long way from Roman's hectographic stamps, and far too good to be forgeries. De Vomécourt's suspicions were now making him hyper-alert, but he thanked her calmly for the papers; she replied that they were 'nothing to what she could be doing' for Autogiro.

*

---

* The Normandie Dock was destroyed in SOE's most audacious success. A redundant battleship, HMS *Campbeltown*, laden with explosive and manned by hundreds of commandos, was coasted at the right tidal moment at the dock gates on the night of 29th March. An estimated 400 Germans were killed, most the day after the ramming when they were looking over the ship and the time-delayed explosions detonated; 169 British died, with a further 215 taken prisoner; five Victoria Crosses were awarded.

The following evening, Bleicher announced that he was planning to arrest Brault at dawn because Brault knew too much about her affairs, including the arrests of Roman, the Dampierres and Coulomb, and above all her involvement with de Vomécourt. In order to protect her and the possibilities she represented, the well-connected lawyer had to go.

Michel Brault was always prepared for the dawn raid. This time, his luck was in as he had returned from Vichy on the previous evening, and rushed straight from the station to the theatre before returning home late, so that his concierge could truthfully say when the thundering on the door started that she had not seen him come in. Brault pulled on his dressing gown, in the pocket of which was a key to the door to the servants' staircase beyond the kitchen, a Parisian architectural feature unknown to the Gestapo. His wife quickly hung up his clothes and made his side of the bed so that she too could deny that he had been there. Somewhat at a loss and hoping that he might reappear, the Germans hung around the house all morning, but allowed Brault's sixteen-year-old daughter to leave to go to school. As soon as she got to a call box, she rang the telephone numbers she had memorised.

The maid was released when she complained that she needed to start working; she took Brault 'clothes, bread and black coffee all hidden in her shopping bag'. After six hours pondering in the attic and on the roof, he was able to come down the service staircase again and disappear into the city. Later that day his nephew brought a note to de Vomécourt that 'he had escaped arrest and that he must not trust anything to do with M. Carré'. A few more hours of brooding passed before the nephew came by again with a countermanding message that 'M. Carré was not implicated in any way.'

De Vomécourt managed a clandestine meeting with the lawyer next day at which Brault 'confirmed that he did not believe her to be responsible for his failed arrest'. He still had faith in the strength Mathilde had shown over the previous year, and was aware that there 'were numerous other people who had been arrested' and who could have shopped him. For de Vomécourt, though, the perfect identity cards, questions she had asked about his people's real names which was 'never done by people who are doing this sort of work', Saint-Nazaire, and the Interallié arrests added up to enough doubt. His superiors would have ordered him to 'vanish at once, not even pausing to assassinate her if her death was going to complicate his escape', but he could not contemplate that. His life and his dreams of resistance were in her hands, and for the latter's sake at least he had to decide his strategy alone.

Bleicher was furious when he telephoned the Hôtel Edouard VII from the rue de la Faisanderie to find that Brault was not waiting for him. He railed against the incompetence of the Gestapo and regaled Mathilde with stories from his Cherbourg posting: how on one occasion a man had asked if he might go next door to kiss his dying wife goodbye, only to return with a machine-gun, kill three of the arresting party and never be seen again. 'The people at Abwehr headquarters were very clumsy' and anyone about to be arrested had 'a fifty-fifty chance of escaping', he reckoned. He instructed her to ring Brault's office, but his secretary Ginette said he was not there and Mathilde had better stay away as Ginette had a terrible cold. This conversation and its easily decoded warning sent Bleicher into a 'new rage' in which he must have wondered if his protégée's cover was holding and whether de Vomécourt was still in play.

*

De Vomécourt had a rendezvous with Mathilde at four o'clock, and had decided to 'gamble' on his suspicions. He could not dissemble when everything hung in the balance. It was 'a game which had been started', and now 'all [he] could do was get on with it and hope for the best'. He 'taxed her directly' that he thought her 'responsible for the attempted arrest' of Brault, but considered her reaction 'perfectly natural ... She was horrified at such a suggestion and stated categorically that she had nothing to do with the affair.'

Then Mathilde took her own risk. Perhaps the desperate reaction of her parents to her collaboration was always in her head. The shock of her arrest and early days with Bleicher had receded. She saw in front of her a figure of nobility and destiny to whom she could nail her own hopes, desire for accomplishment, and esteem. With him she might start to make amends for her actions of the last seven weeks. She confessed, unheeding of the consequences in her relief.

She began with her arrest and the choice offered by Bleicher of death or betrayal. Once she was 'compromised', she had to agree with her captors that it was 'useless to struggle against them' as they were 'too strong for her'. Although she had 'accepted that she would work for them in an instant', she was certain that she would 'get her revenge at the right moment', which could be now.

De Vomécourt had to think fast. It would have been 'easy to liquidate her right away', but if she suddenly disappeared the Gestapo, 'who obviously knew her well', would be swift in retribution. He would have about three hours in which to warn some of his colleagues, but everyone he knew would be under suspicion, and his urgent mission, and occupied France, set back for months or years. All the 'chiefs of the Resistance movement' he had been cultivating would be threatened.

He 'decided to play an obviously highly dangerous game'. He would get word to London that the 'Polish radio was in German hands' and then use that same radio to 'deceive the Germans' and thus, somehow, 'save many lives'. He had to follow his instinct that he could re-turn Mathilde and double-cross the double-crossers. He told her he believed her, and talked in the language of honour that appealed to her: it was 'now in her power to redeem herself' and together they could 'perform great deeds'. He was unwittingly echoing Roman's recruitment of her, and once again she found herself stirring at the invitation to be a key part of a great enterprise.

She should return to Bleicher and tell him that she had been taken further into de Vomécourt's confidence: he had let on that when he was back from England he was going to gather every Resistance leader for a meeting, so the Abwehr would have the opportunity '*décapiter toute la Résistance*' in one fell swoop, a strategic masterstroke. To feign being a double agent whilst becoming a triple agent would strain the most accomplished of actors, and de

Vomécourt could only hope that she could carry out this perilous subterfuge.

Time was up. She had professed loyalty, but the outcome was most uncertain. She came away believing he had 'unlimited confidence' in her and they could do 'fine work' together. His day, which had already included a conversation with the fugitive Brault and a confrontation with the woman who had his life in her hands, now held dinner with Cowburn and Cottin, whom he had to fill in on their situation.

As she had when a nurse, when she was in Toulouse after her meal at La Frégate, and again when she and Roman moved to Paris, Mathilde felt that she 'was living again', trusted on the intoxicating level where the 'least mistake … would have involved a major catastrophe' for herself and others. Her 'responsibility was enormous' as she 'had to play the German game with the maximum of cunning' and to 'camouflage Lucas's organisation' to avert disaster. She was treading her most dangerous path yet. De Vomécourt might flee 'that night with his friends and warn the British', condemning her to imprisonment or death as a traitor to the Abwehr. Neither the brazen jokiness of her British accent in Brest nor the numb insouciance she had shown at the arrest of her colleagues would help her now if she were to give either side cause to doubt her loyalty.

De Vomécourt was not as naturally psychologically adept as Bleicher, but he had handled Mathilde superbly. Bleicher was overjoyed by what she told him: to bring off such a coup against the Resistance would surely get him the promotion he craved as well as shore up the Occupation. She felt powerful and necessary again, aware of her responsibility. If she were to wobble once the fear and excitement of the day had subsided, or arouse Bleicher's curiosity, it would be over for her, de Vomécourt and his followers, and a massive blow to her country's hopes. She was resolute in the latest great challenge the war had thrown at her, determined that she and de Vomécourt should have 'the last laugh'.

*

Roger Cottin and Benjamin Cowburn were adroit, brave, and used to calculating degrees of danger, but were nevertheless stunned when de Vomécourt told them his 'very, very bad news' at dinner. Cowburn was so shocked that where he should have felt 'a tingling of the scalp, a quickening of the pulse, a sickness in the pit of the stomach', he was completely dazed, and found himself 'stuffing another forkful of *pommes de terre à l'huile*' into his mouth. He was appalled that he had spent the evening at Vaas in the company of an Abwehr official.* Their contacts could be blown, any forthcoming drops by air or sea would be at the mercy of the Germans, and their own lives were in jeopardy. As far as he was concerned, they had walked into a trap.

They had only two options: to 'disappear at once' or to 'try to deceive the Germans while trying to let London know quickly'. De Vomécourt was convinced that 'her repentance was sincere' and if his flattery that she could be 'the greatest of all "treble" agents' had hit home, the situation could be turned to their advantage. By the time pudding arrived, Cowburn had had the bright idea of using Mathilde to trap and kill Bleicher. De Vomécourt suggested a more subtle approach and started to explain his half-formed plan, which they embellished with gusto and substantial quantities of wine. The party dispersed into a snowstorm, full of uncertainty, and Cowburn lay awake wondering how this 'intrigue straight out of a cheap spy-thriller' could possibly play out. With his Lancastrian pragmatism, he thought that if they were not arrested that very night, Carré was probably playing straight with them, and he would approve the plan on SOE's behalf.

De Vomécourt asked his brother Philippe, who as a railway man had a much-prized pass to cross the demarcation line, to come to Paris urgently. He explained the inevitability of 'a general arrest' unless he succeeded in 'turning the tables' on the Germans. If de

---

* When Cowburn next met Bleicher, the German was pretending to be an officer. The sartorially conscious English major was not fooled for a moment: nobody who wore such cheap shoes could have high rank.

Vomécourt disappeared, Philippe was to pass on the news to London via the US military attaché in Vichy so that his network would have a chance to disperse, but otherwise he was not to breathe a word. Philippe was set up at a neighbouring table in the café on the rue Marboeuf where he and Cowburn had made an assignation to meet Mathilde so that he could 'observe', watch for an ambush, signal if anything went awry and even try to take surreptitious photographs so that if she 'changed sides again' there would be proof of her treachery.

Cowburn found de Vomécourt 'calm and serious' and Mathilde 'anxious' that he might have absconded in the night and suspicion fallen on her. Cottin was watching closely from one nearby table, Philippe from another. Mathilde stressed Bleicher's hatred of the British which gave Cowburn pause for thought, and made him glad that he had practised rolling his 'r's so assiduously to reinforce his disguise as a native Frenchman; she also reported that his ambitions had grown, and that he had decided to let Autogiro become a 'big group and then take everybody at once'; 'for one agent he managed to arrest' there might be 'a hundred he would never catch' so he wanted to keep the person at the top firmly in his sights and bide his time.

After she had spoken, Cowburn signalled that de Vomécourt was to continue with the 'great plan' they had embroidered: to dangle 'the promise of a success that exceeded their wildest dreams' so that German greed would outweigh rational doubt. They would let on that the Resistance circuits were 'far more numerous' and 'far more active than the Germans imagined'. They even invented a senior British general who would be attending the leaders' conference 'to spend a day or so giving personal directives on co-ordination', and she should announce that the main purpose of de Vomécourt's journey to London was to 'prepare the general's trip'.

The 'fantastic plan' had one more element added to it that night: Mathilde would accompany de Vomécourt, sit in on the 'Secret Service meetings' and return with him by parachute. She would, they decided, use 'Radio-Bleicher' to transmit false information from London so that he could drop back unheralded. A healthy degree of optimism is essential to protagonists of an underground war, and what Cowburn called this 'Machiavellian plan to transform disaster into success' was that optimism's boldest expression.

*

Philippe de Vomécourt immediately set off for Vichy to report to the Deuxième Bureau on events in Paris, even though Pierre knew that it would take 'ages for the message to reach Britain via Geneva and Washington' in the diplomatic pouches. He considered asking Cowburn to leave under the Bordeaux–Marseilles Express, cross France, over the Pyrenees to Spain and on to England as a quicker route, but a pre-emptive message came from London asking him to suggest a landing place for a fast boat on the Brittany coast between Saint- Brieuc and L'Aber Wrac'h or between Raz and Quiberon. He pointed out that these beaches were part of the *zone interdite* and were bound to be heavily patrolled against just this type of incursion, but would come up with another place for a sea exfiltration.

The next day de Vomécourt was fully expecting a 'welcome party with the Gestapo' as he could not believe Bleicher had swallowed the plot. But once again Mathilde came alone and said her German controller had looked 'favourably on the idea', had got near-unanimous clearance to proceed from the Service Centrale de Paris, and hoped to get permission from Abwehr head office in Berlin within the next forty-eight hours. It was a good thing that they had no idea that the Gestapo, 'surly with enmity against the Abwehr', were 'bluntly opposed' to the notion of letting de Vomécourt out of their sight, and would have preferred that he 'and his friends should be arrested and shot'.

*

On Thursday 22nd January, Mathilde demanded that some former agents be released from Fresnes; brought back Bleicher's approval for the dual departure – characterised by Cowburn as the Germans 'licking their chops in anticipation of the glorious catch' – and went to bed with Pierre de Vomécourt for the first time.

She had power over both de Vomécourt, who knew of her triple status, and Bleicher, who did not. Bleicher would need liaison with Autogiro and as Roger Cottin courageously agreed to stay on after his chief's departure, she saw an opportunity to have René Aubertin freed from Fresnes to fill a parallel role for the Abwehr. Her guilt and residual sense of loyalty superseded her strategic thinking in that Aubertin was also related to Brault, connected to the Deuxième Bureau, a former soldier and an unbending patriot. Bleicher accordingly refused, and instead suggested Claude Jouffret, one of the select few at the Interallié anniversary celebration. Jouffret did not hesitate to go over to the Nazis for 4,000 francs* per month, justifying his switch on the grounds that he was needed to look after his parents who were both in a 'defective state of health', as well as an honest 'desire to get out of prison'.

Mathilde came to 'the little bachelor flat' de Vomécourt had rented in the rue Villaret la Joyeuse to report Berlin's approval. She was elated at being key to an Allied deception and inspired by her new partner's vitality and patriotic fortitude. He was carried along by her attractive excitement, by relief that he had found a way out of his near-fatal dilemma, and maybe by the less worthy thought that to forge a physical bond would bind her loyalty more tightly to him. In a potent balance of attraction, need, relief of tension and tactical calculation, Mathilde Carré and Pierre de Vomécourt became lovers.

*

The next few days passed slowly enough. De Vomécourt spent them working out a survival plan for his organisation should everything go wrong. He 'singled out' anyone who might be known to Mathilde or Bleicher. He was sure that his followers 'in the provinces, in Normandy, Brittany, the East, the South-East and

---

* Approximately £23; £1,200 at 2018 values.

elsewhere' were safe as he had not divulged their identities to
Mathilde, and they became part of what he called 'the parallel network'; he even rented another office to conceal this outfit. Although
he felt secure in her alliance and in 'her passionate love for him', he
obviously 'could not forget that it was thanks to her that the
Germans knew about' him and it was an 'elementary precaution' to
'reorganise outside her knowledge'. Hundreds of lives could be
saved by his foresight.

He found he had to put an unexpected twist to the deceit he was
perpetrating on the Wehrmacht. The rumours in Vichy about La
Chatte's treachery were gathering pace and he made a quick *aller et
retour* to quash them as well as to pick up money. The irony of his
journey to deny what was true – that he was in league with someone who was also working for the Abwehr – was lost on him in his
urgency. He could not trace Brault, so instead told the truth to his
friends Lieutenant Colonel de Souzy and Achard. All he could say
was that he knew 'perfectly well what [he] was doing', that he was
'playing a dangerous game', but his eyes were open. 'At all costs',
any talk about La Chatte was 'to be avoided'; the important thing
was that he 'had confidence in her' and would tell them what was
going on 'in due course'. The whole of Vichy was so riddled by all
sorts of intrigue that his puzzling statements, seen by Achard as
'highly evasive', were not probed.

Brault had actually holed up in Cannes. Twenty-four hours after
the lawyer had hidden in his attic, an informer in the Hôtel Lutetia
in Saint-Germain-des-Prés had identified him. Bleicher decided
not to pounce until Brault joined what he assumed would be a train
from the Gare de Lyon heading south, as a move in the capital ran
the risk of 'burning Mathilde'. A few days later, he learnt that Brault
had dyed his hair and obtained new identity papers, and asked his
superior Commandant Schaefer for 'two or three agents' to follow
him on to the train. Bleicher was appalled when he arrived at the
station himself to find three men from his old service, the GFP,
who 'felt totally German at a hundred paces, and did not speak a
word of French'. But now, in the often-paradoxical circularity of
espionage, it had become important to Bleicher as well as to de

Vomécourt that Michel Brault kept anything quiet about Mathilde that might disrupt the new plans, so Bleicher had 'decided to let him go' rather than run the risk 'of giving the Vomécourt game away'.

*

By mid-January de Vomécourt was on the knife-edge of exposure. His exfiltration had taken on a new urgency since Bleicher had full knowledge of it and he could leave no time for a change of mind. When he dismissed the heavily guarded Brittany beaches for a pick-up, he suggested other coastal locations before an airlift was proposed at Estrées-Saint-Denis near Compiègne, from where Roger Mitchell had been safely taken the previous November. The moon period was 29th January until 5th February, and Mathilde, de Vomécourt, Cowburn and Cottin went the short distance to the landing grounds on the 30th. De Vomécourt had added a condition that the 'plane should take two passengers, small and of light weight', and repeated 'Two passengers essential condition.' Cowburn never could accept that Mathilde might not be double-crossing them and she was aware of that. Their 'particular antipathy to each other' made all their encounters uncomfortable, but he kept himself in check out of operational necessity.

Once again, 'everything went wrong', as London put it, and despite 'day-to-day news of Lucas's movements' being sent over Victoire's signature, on the 31st a communication arrived to say that 'it would be practically impossible to have the air operation during the January moon on account of the very bad climatic conditions'. Another month's delay threatened disaster: either the Nazis might change their minds, or rumours from the south might lead to Mathilde's exposure.

De Vomécourt was ever more dependent on his lover's strength of purpose and ability to dissemble. He kept the Abwehr in play by giving Mathilde enough crumbs to pass back: sometimes obvious meetings 'with well-known Frenchmen in Paris at restaurants and cafés', sometimes 'the odd false bits of information' such as 'the importing of a Corsican murderer into occupied France'. He was also aware that in consorting with a known collaborator he was breaking every rule: 'it was never worth underestimating the intelligence services' in London, who might either be appalled by his actions or applaud him for removing a dangerous double agent from Nazi control.

Bleicher was also uneasy. He spent the first few days of February taking in more members of the Felix and Overcloud organisations, and each arrest made the exposure of Mathilde more likely as she remained a notable survivor of the round-ups. When London went suspiciously quiet on the airwaves, they were nudged in a transmission in which she said she 'must ask you to come up on the air at given times' as 'when my operator listens in vain as during the last three days ... this attracts the attention of the Boche and we are seriously in danger without usefulness or result'. It was the first use of the word 'Boche' since she had gone over to Bleicher, possibly a subtle indication of her realignment. The next day brought a more aggressive message that London was 'starting to treat [them] as a joke' and that if there was no reply by the 12th Victoire would 'abandon [them] with [her] machinery for another serious organisation'.

She maintained her poise. She told de Vomécourt about the Overcloud operation, and he was desperate to send a message to London to warn its leaders who were being briefed there to stay away but could not. After their return to France, they spent the rest of the war in camps, including Dachau and Bergen-Belsen. However, she did succeed in using her inside knowledge to keep some agents at large by allowing de Vomécourt to warn them, including the 'probably English and probably military intelligence' Jean Stockmans. On the other side of the coin, she became an Abwehr celebrity, and 'a colonel about to leave for the Eastern Front came to see her because ... everybody was interested in La Chatte'. This 'displeased her so much' that she complained to Ische about the dangers such sightseeing presented to their plans.

Mathilde was given strength by her dual role. She was needed more than ever by both Bleicher and de Vomécourt, who were in the strange position of wanting a successful exfiltration for dia-metrically opposed reasons. With her newly regained esteem and energy, she did not stop to question what would actually happen to her if she made it across the Channel. How to get her there was puzzle enough for all of them. After a brief period of control, she was back at the mercy of the war.

11

Operation Waterworks

The failed pick-up at Estrées-Saint-Denis was a setback. De Vomécourt had now been frustrated for two months by the weather and the RAF, and could not wait until the next moon. The Abwehr was not known for its patience and with the British gearing up to invade North Africa and Stalin determined to 'deny the Germans breathing space', there was added pressure for successful operations. De Vomécourt believed that Mathilde was onside, but appreciated the thin threads by which his freedom hung.

A sea exfiltration across the Channel was less vulnerable to climatic and lunar variations than an air operation, and de Vomécourt asked Cowburn to see if he could fix a landing in Brittany, something he had dismissed before. Cowburn approached an agent who came up with 'a patriotic friend' with a villa near Moulin-de-la-Rive and a 'motor-lorry' to transport any incoming supplies. Cowburn felt bucked for the first time in a month, and hoped this adventure might 'be as good as the tame locomotive at Montauban'. As any landings would be watched by the Germans, he suggested a plan to enable him to escape and Cottin to appear ignorant of any prior knowledge. To reinforce the Abwehr's assumption that the SOE men did not know that Mathilde's radio had been turned, a signal went requesting that the motor torpedo boat (MTB) bring two more agents for employment in France; but when it came to it, these men would climb back aboard and return to England alongside Cowburn, Mathilde and de Vomécourt. On arrival, a message would be sent to Cottin: 'Arrived safely Stop Regret Benoît and two agents embarked with us account suspicious movements on beach suggesting discovery and ambush', to preserve his cover of innocence.

Cottin was fully aware of his jeopardy but 'with a great deal of fear accepted the risks associated with this agent of the Gestapo', Bleicher, as Cottin's continued presence in the capital would reassure the Abwehr of their successful double-cross. He had been introduced to Jouffret by Mathilde, and the two men would meet twice a week for Cottin to hand over the London traffic intended to triple-cross the Germans. Cottin was to 'vanish when the order to do so was given through another channel'. Cowburn was 'inclined to be incredulous' that they could fool the Abwehr with their plot, each plank of which made the whole structure more precarious, until he had an epiphany: those who deal in lies are more likely to believe other lies; the 'queer mental kink' necessary to be a master of deception cannot easily be switched off when 'words which have no foundation in truth or fact' come the other way.

*

Operation Waterworks was a humorous entr'acte for Mathilde that repeatedly highlighted the poised precariousness of her situation. It was scheduled to take place on Friday 13th February, with a backup the following night. London took five anxiety-inducing days to confirm Moulin-de-la-Rive as the venue, during which de Vomécourt continued to make his 'parallel network' as safe and effective as possible, briefed Cottin on the precautions he should take, and, above all, kept Mathilde up to the mark. She was displaying 'qualities of courage, physical endurance and good humour' in days of 'suspense, danger and discomfort'. He appreciated how her spirit was nourished by the prospect of perilous action, and launched a campaign to lift her sense of herself.

He shared some 'rich possibilities of the future' with her: they would 'help the RAF' conduct an air raid on Fresnes that would cause enough chaos and panic to 'make possible the escape of the Gestapo's prisoners there', including Roman and other former colleagues. They would blow up the Abwehr headquarters at

Maisons-Laffitte and the Hôtel Edouard VII and 'become the leaders of the underground war'. Mathilde was so carried away by these heroic fantasies the she threw in further ideas which more seasoned spies decided 'smacked too much of a gangster film to be put into effect'. They would arrive back on a Friday and Bleicher would be so pleased with her for arranging the 'enormous meeting' of the Resistance organisations that he would be bound to give her 'an enormous dinner' the following night. She would poison him then, and he would not be missed on a Sunday so she would have time to 'destroy all his records'. After a period in the unoccupied zone, they would return to Paris with fresh identities and 'build up a new organisation'.

Bleicher too was feeding her sense of importance, as well as allowing his own naïve espionage ego to preen. He instructed her to come back from London with 'as many names as possible of British intelligence officers'; she was to 'adopt any measures' to find out what the plans were for 'military operations against the continent' and gather propaganda material 'giving particulars of the morale/population, food situation, bomb damage, the chief political personalities and their rivalries'. He told her she should write a book, *Fifteen Days in London Under the Eyes of the British Secret Service*. As Mathilde packed her small suitcase on her last afternoon, he had yet another idea: he had bought her a new dress with some of the SOE funds which she must take 'to show the British that France was still the leader in fashion'. He suggested that after the great Resistance round-up, she should go to Tangier and 'set up an office' in that nest of spies. As an afterthought, he threw in an order for a box of cigars from Fox's of St James's.

Nevertheless, the pressure started to threaten Mathilde's psychological stability. Cowburn was unable to come to a meeting with her and de Vomécourt one day, which caused her to panic that he no longer trusted her, that 'the whole scheme would collapse and she would lose her life'. She was thrown off-kilter when she heard from Bleicher that the Gestapo had found the whole plot 'too clever to be feasible' and 'were pressing' for the immediate arrest of the Resistance men. Cottin and Cowburn, by contrast, diverted their fear into phlegmatic humour, chuckling when they passed a roadblock that they could say they were under Gestapo protection if challenged.

London too had good reason to be anxious. The same day they gave the go-ahead for Operation Waterworks, a message arrived from SIS in Geneva. Michel Brault had had time to ponder his attempted arrest, the collapse of Interallié and Mathilde's fortuitous escape with the radio. When he got to Vichy, he went to air his doubts to Simoneau, who let on that he was now almost certain that Mathilde was behind the arrest of his *agent de liaison* Duvernois, just as Collin had warned her. Brault was aghast when he realised the peril in which he had placed de Vomécourt by his introduction, and sent an urgent message to London: 'Every effort should be made to send instructions by some other means other than Lili repeat Lili ... She was arrested end November and released again after promising to act as informer.' Luckily for all concerned, the arrival of this warning was not joined up with the confirmation of SOE and the Navy's agreement to send the fast MTB to Brittany two nights later.

*

The Belards had not heard from their daughter since a letter 'full of banal news' at the end of December, but Mathilde took her new lover to visit them. Her mother had no idea if de Vomécourt 'knew the real situation my daughter was in', and assumed that she was still collaborating. When Mathilde told her she was on her way to England, the small figure 'did not inspire confidence'. She asked her father to 'kiss her goodbye', and her mother's parting words in wartime were that she 'would rather weep on your grave than know that you were working for the Germans'.

As the party climbed aboard the Paris–Brest Express on the night of Wednesday the 11th, Bleicher and Sonderführer Eckert, the Abwehr IIIF officer-in-command, were elsewhere on the train. Mathilde was wearing her trademark 'dazzlingly red hat' despite de Vomécourt's objection that it made the party so conspicuous; he soon worked out that its very purpose was to make them obvious to 'the paternal and benevolent eye of the Gestapo'. A message had been sent to the beach area the day before instructing the local authorities not to 'disturb a group of two men and a woman with a red hat'.

Another order had gone from General Stülpnagel, military commander of occupied France, to Generaladmiral Otto Schulze, Commander-in-Chief Naval Forces Brest, to ensure 'no night patrols were to be carried out along the coast of Brittany between Perros Guirec and Locquirec', a distance of over thirty miles. As the *Scharnhorst* and *Gneisenau* had already steamed up the Channel from Brest that day, Schulze could be quite relaxed in obeying.

De Vomécourt and Mathilde sat in a different carriage to Cowburn. The so-called 'Express' arrived at Guingamp in the early hours of the morning of the 12th, and the three travellers met up in the station buffet for coffee; Mathilde had brought real sugar from German supplies as well as sandwiches. Their final stop on the local train was Plouigneau, where they began their fifteen-mile 'march to the coast'. Their German escort had got off the train at Morlaix and was continuing by car.

They felt liberated after the anxious, mistrustful claustrophobia of Paris and talked openly, the two men carrying Mathilde's suitcase in turn. They used British agent slang to agree they were 'contaminated' now they were under the eye of the occupiers. Albert Camus, later to become the editor of the Resistance newspaper *Combat*, used a deadly rat-born disease in the Algerian port of Oran (from where Maurice Carré had embarked for Syria) as a similar metaphor for the Nazi occupation in his parable *The Plague*. In the novel, each person responds individually to the disease: some 'suppressed their value judgements' and accepted everything 'as it came' to carry on with life as best as possible; some blamed others and looked for personal revenge; only a very few worked together to root out the pestilence.

After two hours, they reached the village of Lanmeur and stopped in a small hotel for a lunch of onion soup, omelette and rabbit pâté (the last brought by Mathilde from her well-stocked larder) and quantities of red wine. A couple of gendarmes – who either had not got the message to stay back from the distinctive trio or were actively checking up on them – asked a few loose questions before the walkers headed on through the last of the melting snow.

The hamlet of Moulin-de-la-Rive was set into a rocky bay with numerous coves and headlands, a few houses and a barracks. The sea was calm and they walked around the breakwater to get the lie of the land. In Locquirec, they ate supper in an otherwise empty dining room 'and watched a magnificent sunset' before setting off back to the beach at ten o'clock. They nearly bumped into two uniformed Germans in the road, and had the strange experience of the soldiers going to the verge and then turning their backs on them. They 'fumbled their way' over the rocks to the beach and lay down on the shingle behind a ridge of stones as protection from the chilly breeze on the 'cold and miserable night'.

Cowburn was to shine a light over the incoming tide from midnight, flashing it at intervals. A gold pencil-case fell out of his pocket as he reached for his torch and was lost on the shingle. It crossed his mind that this was not a good omen on what was by this point Friday the 13th, but he pushed superstition away to keep the torch trained.

Some time between half-past midnight and one in the morning, he became aware of a 'black form by the water's edge'. He went forward until he could make out a figure in gumboots to whom he whispered 'Hallo, Maurice.' The arrival replied 'OK, Edouard,' and told him the MTB was anchored in the bay, and the boat which he, Lieutenant Abbott, had rowed in was along the shingle. Another dinghy was bringing the wireless operator, Lieutenant Redding, the radio and the weapons. Neither lieutenant had a clue that they were under enemy eyes, nor that they were about to be ordered back on board and to England.

By the time they spotted the silhouette of the second boat, 'the tiny craft was bobbing up and down' as the sea had become 'quite choppy'. They waded into the surf to help beach it. It was manned

by an oarsman and alongside Redding was a uniformed Royal
Australian Navy sub lieutenant named Black. The newcomers
'floundered ashore', only to be told of the change of plans. All of
them should get back into the boats and immediately row back to
the MTB where the redoubtable Major Bodington, a pre-war *Daily
Express* journalist and now F Section's second-in-command, had
remained watching from the bows in his distinguishing white duffel coat. That would make a party of four more than expected for
the Channel crossing on a craft which had a draft of only just over
a metre in rough seas; the arrivals had planned on swapping Abbott
and Redding for de Vomécourt alone for a speedy journey to safety,
and were surprised by the new instructions, the presence of
Cowburn and most of all to be transporting a civilian Frenchwoman
with a red hat and a suitcase.

But they jumped to and called Mathilde forward, suitcase balanced on her head, to start loading the 'pram-dinghies', as the little
boats were not very encouragingly nicknamed. They held the near-
est one as steady as possible, threw her suitcase in and pushed and
lifted her, in her sodden fur coat, after it. When Mathilde had one
leg over the side, a wave capsized the pitching boat and although
her case was caught, a quantity of weaponry and radio equipment
disappeared into the surf. She was dragged under by the weight of
her coat, a 'horrible sensation' from which she emerged coughing
and clinging to de Vomécourt until she could once again feel the
seabed under her feet. They righted the dinghy and de Vomécourt
tried to persuade Cowburn at least to save himself but by now 'the
state of the sea and the boat' itself made even that impossible. All of
them were 'struggling in the foam' while the breakers were 'roaring
and pounding' around them.

Black had a small torch which he used to signal to the MTB,
while the two men who had rowed the dinghies, by now designated by the forthright Cowburn as 'about as seaworthy as an
upturned umbrella', swam back to the MTB using the capsized
hull of one of them as a float. Black advised them 'if they could not
do anything, to scram'. The rest struggled, exhausted and frozen,
back to the beach.

A short while later, they 'discerned a large black shape being tossed up and down' and waded back into the sea to meet the MTB's lifeboat being rowed towards them. Cowburn continued until the water was at shoulder level, but the boat was still some thirty feet away, its bows rising out of the sea as each wave came in. The crew were 'handling it with amazing skill' but clearly if it came any closer it would founder on the shore. Cowburn retreated, cursing that they had not brought this sturdier craft in the first place, at which point Black slapped him down by saying it was against naval regulations that it had been launched at all on such a mission.

Operation Waterworks, its name now darkly ironic, was abandoned. The MTB headed home, leaving six: Abbott, Redding, Black, the 'furious and dripping' Mathilde, and the more outwardly sanguine yet equally perturbed and sodden de Vomécourt and Cowburn. De Vomécourt advised the two agents to hide in the woods as strangers 'might prove too great a temptation for any Germans who didn't understand the importance of the instructions from Paris and might arrest them', and thereafter to take their chances. Black left them as he was in uniform so could expect to be fairly dealt with as a prisoner of war if caught.

The dejected travellers trudged the five kilometres back to Locquirec in their salty, waterlogged clothes to sit outside the hotel until it opened. Cowburn tried to lighten the moment by cracking a joke that 'as the party consisted of a German agent, a British agent and a French agent, it only needed the OGPU* to make the party complete', but all three agents were intensely aware that if the Germans discovered they had been tricked at this late stage, de Vomécourt would be harshly punished and Cowburn possibly shot that day anyway. If Mathilde could 'no longer play on the credulity' of Bleicher and his associates, her usefulness would come to an end in a welter of recrimination and reprisal.

They would have to rely on her to get them out of this alive and unshackled. Abbott had hissed in the surf 'that the Victoire transmitter was suspected of being blown', which raised the possibility

---

* The USSR's secret police, which had become the NKVD in 1934.

that the night's farcical events might bring the Germans to their usual ruthlessly pragmatic senses to abandon the whole deception. They could only hope that conditions would be better that night.

Abbott and Redding, both French-speakers who had been travel agents before the war, were taken that morning. 'Poor staff work' in London meant that Abbott had not been told where they were going to land, and Redding had been given only 'a glance at a Michelin road map of the neighbourhood' before they had set off. They 'stumbled through the darkness' until they found an isolated barn in which to hole up, only to be sold to the local police by the farmer in the morning. The two men were sent first to Fresnes and then to Colditz Castle; a few months later, they would have been shot. Their only contact with the Autogiro network they had been sent to support was their meeting in the surf with its leader.

While de Vomécourt and Cowburn were in the hotel, the bedraggled Mathilde walked to the barracks to telephone through her report. She got through to Eckert and lectured him about 'the noise made by the German guards' the night before. Eckert, under orders to keep her on side at all costs, meekly told her that this would never happen again and 'congratulated her on the way she had behaved'. He even said that he regretted the arrest of Black, but that they had no other option.

While Mathilde was delivering her complaints, a Feldwebel sat himself down next to de Vomécourt and Cowburn. He got out photographs of his wife, children and motor car, and told them how much he was missing home, and 'was tired of the war'. When Mathilde returned he departed 'with much smiling and saluting', and the men realised that his errand had been to stop them making a run for it. On the positive side, their double subterfuge seemed intact as she reported that the Germans were 'quite thrilled' about the night's events and 'keen' to have another go.

The hotel let them dry their clothes in the kitchen and gave them dinner; the staff knew better than to ask questions about oddly assorted, damp and marine-smelling guests. They made their way to the beach again at about eleven, and at midnight Cowburn started flashing his torch. They 'waited and waited', but 'nothing, absolutely nothing happened', possibly because London had decided the operation had now been blown and everyone would be captured. They left the beach chilled, tired and dispirited in the early hours of the morning of 14th February to trudge back along the now-familiar path.

*

Mathilde, de Vomécourt and Cowburn got on the early bus for Morlaix where they were soon joined by an NCO shadow. They read the newspapers, which carried the story about the *Scharnhorst* and *Gneisenau* breakout, beside which Cowburn felt their 'own little catastrophe paled into insignificance', although, still smarting from the 'cockle-shell pram-dinghies', he was incensed anew by the shortcomings of the Royal Navy. It was no consolation when Bleicher told Mathilde later that they had provided 'a wonderful experience' for the watchers.

In Le Mans, the three stayed in separate hotels. Mathilde mourned her suitcase's inundation, and that 'much of the linen was missing and the dresses completely destroyed'. The next morning Cowburn slipped on to the 'painfully slow' train to Tours while the others headed for Paris. In Tours, he bought a ticket on the Bordeaux Express to throw any watchers off his trail, but instead got on the stopping train to Montmoreau, where he caught a bus and later crossed the demarcation line on foot. He then took another bus to Périgueux and after a late lunch in the station buffet of a tin of foie gras and an entire bottle of wine, and an ensuing stomach ache that felt like 'being crushed under a rock', he hopped on and off several more buses to arrive in Limoges.

Three days after he had first flickered his torch into the Bréton night, Major Cowburn arrived in Vichy. He was unshaven, his shoes stained, his clothes salt-stiffened as he 'dashed past the Gestapo surveillance team into the now-skeleton American Embassy' and begged them to wire London with de Vomécourt's messages. He looked more like a tramp than a British officer as he ran out again and caught a train to Lyons where, 'half-starved with exhaustion', he collapsed into the flat of Virginia Hall, his fearless American colleague whose wooden leg did not prevent her escaping on foot over the snowbound Pyrenees the following winter.

A few days later, Cowburn started his journey to England. He, Mathilde and de Vomécourt had agreed that the Abwehr would be told that he had got fed up of waiting for boats and aeroplanes and had gone to explore a land route through Spain for them all. As he pointed out, it would be 'no more fantastic than some of the other nonsense' which the inexperienced Bleicher had swallowed so far.

Cowburn's transmission did not arrive in London until 25th February after wending its way to War Office Room 055, where it caused bafflement and concern. After its report that 'both boats capsized' and 'officer captured' on the 13th, it went on to warn 'Be cautious all messages via Victoire', and then the near-contradictory 'Send all instructions re departure via Victoire but for rest keep to generalities and questions on which you wish to appear to require information.' De Vomécourt stressed that it was 'vital for informer and self be in London by March 1st', and that 'if not I may be a fatal casualty'. 'Benoît', on his way to Spain, would have 'all information in case of accident to self'; if he made it, 'Greatest coup may be scored and many lives saved'. None of this helped them to work out whether they were meant to trust Victoire or not. They did not even know her real name or how she had come into their soldiers' lives.

Major Bodington from the MTB was able to report after his cross-Channel round-trip that 'the Victoire line of communication is working under enemy duress'; what was puzzling, though, was that it was 'surely unreasonable to believe, had the enemy been in full possession of the details of this operation, that he would not have taken advantage of capturing all the people collected on the shore in addition to a fully equipped MTB with outside personnel on board ... which could not escape from the somewhat perilous neighbourhood except at most at half-speed'. Even though whatever was going on in France was unfathomable to London, Mathilde and de Vomécourt's secret had paradoxically held good because of, rather than despite, the soggy failure of Waterworks.

*

By the time all this was being discussed, there had been yet another exfiltration fiasco. A signal arrived on 16th February from London ordering a further sea operation on the night of the 20th from the rocky promontory of Pointe de Bihit, near Morlaix. The lovers again left Paris on the Brest train, alighted at Morlaix and got on the local bus to Lannion. Mathilde travelled light as Bleicher did not seem inclined to replace her wardrobe. As before, they were kept under close observation at the station and visually checked when a Luftwaffe officer pulled the bus over. They set off for the point after supper, but got lost and only just made it in time; even so, they were not entirely sure of their location. At dawn they gave up and caught the milk train back to Paris, where Mathilde was told that the German watchers on the cliffs had seen a boat signalling about four kilometres away. The British, ignoring the fact that they had Admiralty charts while their passengers would have at best a tourist road map to guide them, tartly commented later that the enemy 'appeared to have managed the watching of the operation very much better' than the would-be escapees.

The dunking at Moulin-de-la-Rive and then the two nights' wait in the February cold was enough discomfort for Mathilde. She pointed out the toll the operation was taking on her clothes, belongings and health, and the Abwehr must 'see that she had proper accommodation in future'. Eckert agreed that if they had to wait again, there would be a room laid on. She was relieved by the commitment and excited when the message came through that yet another pick-up would be attempted at Bihit Point on the night of 26th February, two months since Brault had first mentioned de Vomécourt to her.

The moon would be practically, dangerously full that night, but Whitehall and Baker Street judged that every day de Vomécourt was not in England was potentially costly. And just as Moulin-de-la-Rive had helped the British conclude that Mathilde was not a threat to the exfiltration, the repeated failures had actually increased the German desire to see things through. They 'could not believe that she would renounce her beautiful flat and flowers etc.' and repeatedly put herself through these experiences 'to work for the English again'. She would 'not even [be] paid that much'. De Vomécourt had been fearful that this last 'aborted pick-up' would make the Abwehr 'give up their plan to let me go to England' but it turned out that they were 'impressed' that the enemy were prepared to risk a boat four times. He was obviously every bit as important as they believed.

De Vomécourt's transmission from his last trip south arrived after this new plan was laid: after its tortuous journey via Lisbon, it predated Cowburn's hard-fought message by only four days. In it, he reinforced his desperation about the risk of the exposure of Mathilde's status. The urgency he felt was in the unmilitary opening phrase, as he launched in with 'For God's sake resume at once messages via Victoire', and continued that he was 'fully aware of the real situation'. It was vital to 'arrange my trip to England via Victoire earliest possible' as there was undoubtedly 'danger if trip delayed'. He dangled the unnecessary incentive that he was 'preparing finest coup yet' if he was brought out, but 'must come to England for detail'. It was 'deadly danger' if the British 'do not immediately resume Victoire for real instructions my trip and harmless general topics' but when he was in England he needed another route to his people in France 'for secret communications'. He ended with the same exhortation as he had begun: 'For God's sake do not take any action against Victoire until I say so'. They could not be more aware that something was very much up with the mysterious Victoire but increasingly baffled as to exactly what that might be.

*

The 'wandering couple' and their unseen watchers took the familiar route to Morlaix and Lannion where they met their 'faithful servant', the talkative, family-minded Feldwebel. They dined at Trebeurden before setting off on the fourteen-kilometre trek along the rocky paths to Bihit Point. De Vomécourt started signalling at midnight, and an hour later gave a shout. He urged her to put on her glasses for the next bit and they scrambled down a rocky escarpment to jump into a cockleshell boat manned by a lieutenant and a rating. At last they, the MTB and the weather had coincided and they were on their way.

*

The spy who four months before had been sending invaluable intelligence to England and who had seamlessly switched to being a double agent was now returning physically to the British under the eyes of and with the blessing of the Third Reich. Both sides had taken substantial risks and shown confidence in her loyalty to them, and she had played her parts with aplomb. Hugo Bleicher was so sure that she would be finally on course this time that he had decided to take Suzanne Laurent on holiday to Hamburg rather than attend the departure of his primary agent.

As Mathilde looked back over the calm sea, she saw a light in an abandoned house just below a concrete pillbox where Eckert was watching the proceedings disguised as a Luftwaffe sergeant. She felt triumphant as the dawn broke 'rose-pink' on the south coast of England. By the time they landed in Dartmouth, Devon was 'gleaming in the early sun' to welcome her on her first visit to the country that was at first 'astonished to find [her] in the party at all' and thereafter was to remain charmed, enraged, frustrated, guilty and generally confused by her.

12

London Surprise

Major Nicholas Bodington of Special Operations Executive was English politeness personified to Mathilde Carré, whatever his inward alarm, after de Vomécourt had hissed a brief introduction about his heavily scented companion in the fur coat as he clambered aboard the MTB. The Royal Navy laid on a handsome breakfast for them in Dartmouth where she met the head of F Section, former Ford Motor Company executive Colonel Maurice Buckmaster. The party then went on by car to London, stopping for lunch at Paignton where Bodington, by now affectionately known to Mathilde as 'Le Père Blanc' on account of his white duffel coat, rang ahead. By the time they arrived, a young woman from the Auxiliary Territorial Service called Valerie had been to Selfridges to purchase 'bedroom slippers, a nightdress, underwear, soap, toothpaste and even a box of face powder', and some last-minute modifications had begun on the flat prepared for de Vomécourt.

That first night Bodington put them up in his Mayfair house, and threw a dinner party for his star operative. Mathilde was at one table, de Vomécourt the other, and throughout the evening 'they were always exchanging glances and he paid her every possible attention'. Among the guests were Buckmaster himself; the newly promoted Squadron Leader Philipson who had greeted Roman on his arrival in England; MI6's Tom Greene, a tall, reassuring figure described by Mathilde as 'a real wardrobe of a man', who had been deputy head of station in Paris until 1940 and was now working with A4 Section dealing with the Free French and Polish government-in-exile; the scholarly intelligence officer Lewis Gielgud, brother of the actor John; and the thirty-year-old, French-speaking

Christopher Harmer of MI5, who had just been anointed her handler.

Harmer had been a solicitor in Birmingham before the war and was 'witty, intuitive and glintingly clever', which qualities would need to be at their sharpest as he studied the newly arrived enigma. His first impression was of a 'sensual, sensitive and highly intelligent woman who would be capable of great loyalty in proper hands, likes flattery and would be capable of extreme jealousy'. It was an astute summing-up of the person who was to consume so much of his time, thought and energy for the rest of the war.

For now, all conversation was strictly 'only of general matters' until the soldiers and spies could assess the altered situation. To the British, Mathilde carried 'all the glamour of one who had been "in the field" for a long time', made the more appealing as she was travelling 'under the protection of a great Resistance leader'. It was a top-grade welcome, although she was 'so tired' and up-ended by her journey that she did not remember much of 'what happened that first evening' except that her initial impression of London was of its 'legendary fog'.

*

The next morning, Mathilde went with Valerie to see her and de Vomécourt's new home. Porchester Gate was a large Edwardian apartment block on the Bayswater Road; number 39 had a view just above the treetops of Hyde Park. It consisted of a hall, a large sitting room, one big and one small bedroom, and an up-to-date kitchen and bathroom. It was one of the best billets available, fit for one of de Vomécourt's eminence. That day the place was filled with workmen making it 'lousy with microphones' for her on Bodington's instructions; Valerie hurried her charge downstairs for a cup of tea while muttering about how slow the electricians were to make the lights work. A message was on its way to Colonel Allen of the Post Office asking for any mail to be intercepted as 'the man' staying there 'has as his mistress a woman who is known to have been in direct contact with the German espionage organisation in France'

and 'a close watch on their contacts and activities' was needed. A
Special Branch detective inspector, Louis Gale, was detailed to live
in. These measures were both an indicator of both how, as Dick
White (later the only man to head both MI5 and MI6) put it, this
was 'an important affair', and how little command Mathilde would
have of her own destiny. It was to become the central paradox of
the next few months.

Christopher Harmer arrived in the afternoon. He was a member
of MI5's B1a Section, the Double Cross team that reported up to the
punningly named XX (Twenty) Committee created and chaired by
the Oxford don, Wimbledon tennis player, member of the Olympic
hockey team and cricket fanatic J. C. Masterman. Masterman was
keenly aware of the potential of double agents, and his rigorously
managed department was already proving its worth: Dušan Popov,
a Yugoslav working for the Abwehr, had been turned in December
1940 and code-named Agent Tricycle, after his fondness for three-
somes in bed; he was running scores of imaginary and diversionary
subagents. A few weeks after Mathilde's arrival, the failed Spanish
chicken farmer Juan Pujol Garcia was in Lisbon but pretending to
be in Britain. Garcia, code name Garbo, put out misinformation
about troop and naval movements with the help of various guide-
books and a Portuguese primer called *The British Fleet* from
the public library. The Abwehr treated his intelligence with near-
reverence and did not question any of its detail, such as that
Glasgow dockers would 'do anything for a litre of wine'. They lav-
ished praise on him, particularly when he too recruited fictitious
subagents. Both men had considerable tactical roles to play in
Double Cross, thanks to their creative handling by B1a, who were
nevertheless currently flummoxed that a self-confessed German
agent 'had been sent over to this country'.

Below Masterman, the outfit's operational head was Thomas
Argyll Robertson, known as 'Tar' after his initials. He was a cheer-
ful, easy-going Scot in his early thirties who wore tartan trews in
MI5's St James's Street office and as a result was nicknamed 'Passion
Pants'. Next in the hierarchy was John Marriott, another civilian
solicitor whose rather more analytic style complemented Robertson's

enthusiasm and ebullience. The other officers included Billy Luke, a rich Glasgow industrialist with a taste for high living, Cyril Mills of the circus family, Hugh Astor, son of the proprietor of *The Times*, and Harmer himself. The office was full of high jinks and cricketing metaphors. They were, according to Harmer, a group of 'overgrown schoolboys playing games of derring-do absorbed from reading schoolboy books and adventure stories'. The only woman present offset this jolly atmosphere: Gisela Ashley, who went by the name of Susan Barton, was German-born, 'vigorously anti-Nazi' and deadly serious about her work. A fellow female agent in a very male world, Susan Barton was to be one of Mathilde's sternest companions and harshest judges.

Neither Harmer nor MI6's Tom Greene had had much time to prepare for their encounter, but did know that in Mathilde's role 'as an SIS agent' at Interallié she had 'done remarkably good work', and that she had recently been 'playing with the Germans' to whom she could have given away 'other parts of the Walenty organisation'. Her personality 'created a favourable impression', and she came across as 'sincere and telling the truth' as she unloaded the betrayal of the Big Network, her own arrest and 'collaboration with the Gestapo', the arrival of de Vomécourt and their subsequent escape. She held nothing back as she recounted her suspicious resentment towards Gane and Deschamps, the round-up of Interallié colleagues, the plans for the bombardment of Fresnes and Gestapo headquarters and the assassination of Bleicher. For all that she felt 'physically and mentally exhausted', she quickened at the chance to impress and serve again during the hours-long interrogation.

Bleicher had briefed her with a list of Interallié agents who were 'supposed to have been saved and to be still working' for the Allies, which included Kieffer, Jouffret, Aubertin, Tabet and Collardey, but she stated each man's current situation. Her interrogators knew that Collardey was in prison and asked her what her answer would have been 'if she had been taxed with this fact'; she replied that she would have said the man to which their list was referring 'was a different Coco'. Bleicher had also supplied an intelligence report

which would 'show her capacities and capability' to make her cred-
ible to the British, but she admitted that much of this information
was unconvincing propaganda based on the first transmission
after her arrest; notably that the 'effectiveness of troops in all
regions' was 'actually 1/6th of what had appeared in the original
report'. Other than this document, she had arrived without any
steers about disinformation as 'it had been left to her to invent a
suitable story'. The anxiety of Masterman's team about the person
SOE had brought to the country was allayed to an extent by this
interview. It was now their turn to think fast about whether to turn
her again. A message was sent on the Interallié frequency that read
'Arrived safely. Everything OK. Remember 1500 Hours Tuesday.
Lucas. Victoire.'

*

At the same time as Mathilde Carré was making 'a remarkably
good impression', Pierre de Vomécourt was discussing her with
SOE and MI5 in the person of Tar Robertson, who needed more
detail about their recent weeks of working under Abwehr oversight
before they could get on to the critical business of the mobilisation
of the Resistance. He went to the SOE flat in Orchard Court,
Portman Square, an ocean liner of a 1930s mansion block where the
door was opened by a man 'in butler's uniform, who welcomed
him with a butler's smile'. Arthur Park was a reassuring presence to
the arrivals and departures on Special Operations business, a
speaker of perfect French as a result of his pre-war work as a messenger for Barclay's bank in Paris. He had a prodigious memory,
knew every agent by real name and all pseudonyms, and was adept
at spiriting them from room to room before they encountered one
another. De Vomécourt's narrative chimed in every detail with
Mathilde's on his urgent debriefing and his real work could begin.
    Foreign Secretary Anthony Eden wrote to Winston Churchill
about the 'head organiser' in France who had over '20,000 men at
his disposal'. Eden considered bringing them together to feed the
prime minister's love of unconventional warfare. But in the end,

the manner of de Vomécourt's arrival militated against this: any conspicuous behaviour might compromise others, as well as make him 'a marked man' on his return. It is also possible that Eden did not want to introduce anyone associated with the taint of collaboration to Churchill. It was a stigma Mathilde was desperate to overcome.

*

She had gained in confidence and authority when she was interviewed again a couple of days later. She reiterated that the Germans had considered her 'clever enough to answer any questions put to her' and that her mission was to bring back any information on how the 'Polish and British services worked', as well as on 'the life of the civilians and their reactions'. She even suggested that MI5 give her 'a plan' for *Fifteen Days in London*, 'a kind of timetable, what day I did so-and-so, what day I did this and that' so she could simply transcribe the manuscript.

MI5 were even more surprised by Bleicher's gullibility when she told them that she was to 'persuade' the British and Polish spy organisations 'to send someone to France to replace Walenty' and to 'reconstruct the organisation', helping them along the way by asking for London to produce a plan of their ideal network so that they could 'fit it in with what was left of the old' set-up. The Germans might have been naïve in going along with the plan thus far, but they were not so foolish as to believe that the British 'would not hesitate to send someone else' back with her. She herself understood her own usefulness would last only until de Vomécourt was taken, which by her reckoning was two or three weeks after their return. She assumed she would then be on her way to Tangier, as she and Bleicher had already discussed, to join the treachery of spies there.

But a few minutes later, after being taken once again through her first encounter with de Vomécourt and whether the Germans had 'got the wind up', Mathilde suddenly changed tack in her eagerness to impress on the British her true allegiance. She announced that she and her lover would be escaping to the unoccupied zone where they would 'change our identity, dye our hair and set up a new organisation', the 'sources and agents' for which the couple were keeping secret for now, not least because Bleicher was skilled at inserting his own people, such as Kieffer, into such outfits. It was the first time since her arrival that she had needed to aggrandise herself to cover up her uncertainty, as well as a warning to them about the depth of her attachment to de Vomécourt. Her interrogators let the fantasy drift away and moved on to discuss Collin, the money they had sent and the different wireless operators to reassure themselves again that they could 'certainly accept her as genuine'.

*

Colonel Stanisław Gano, head of the Polish Deuxième Bureau, was a tough, cynical career soldier who had seen service in the Russian army in the First World War. He needed to assess Mathilde's credibility after her part in the betrayals of their network as well. He found parts of her story, including the 'puerile way the escape was organised' and 'small details', such as those concerning Bleicher's fashion purchases and the 'projects for the future on their return to France' hard to swallow even when told of the Feldwebel's inexperience and the laziness of his Abwehr colleagues. But he concluded that Mathilde was 'calm, intelligent and logical and generally gave the impression of speaking the truth'. Although 'she should not be assumed to be absolutely reliable' as no collaborator ever could, he too gave her a clean-enough bill of security health for her at least to remain at large.

Gano and Commander Wilfred 'Biffy' Dunderdale of SIS, the liaison between his organisation and the Poles, conferred with Greene, Harmer and Robertson, and Brigadier Gubbins and majors Keswick and Buckmaster of SOE. Gano and Dunderdale pronounced that they were 'no longer interested in the case of Victoire', because 'as soon as a source of information was tainted' they had to 'wash their hands of the case'. The SOE men were much more gung-ho, verging on irresponsible, when they announced that they were 'asking themselves what could be lost if the Lucas/Victoire plan' of liberating Fresnes and murdering Bleicher was put into action, even though they accepted that monitoring 'the Paris transmitter' was pointless. The best soldier-spy minds in the country agreed that a quadruple-cross was a turn too far, and they had better things to do while 'the time spent in determining what was true and what was false in the messages received would outweigh any usefulness derived from the set-up'.

The only person in London who had seen Interallié up close was Roger Mitchell, the frequent visitor to the rue Villa Léandre in its last, personality-ridden weeks. Mitchell had been dropped into France on a few occasions since his last sighting of Mathilde in the first week of November, and had heard 'contradictory reports' of her fate that veered between imprisonment and 'living in good style'. It did not occur to him that both were possible. Furthermore, Mitchell did not believe his star-struck acolyte Kieffer was 'the sort of man to work for the Germans', which made him 'cast doubt' on Mathilde's story of the collapse. He spent some time extolling Renée Borni's 'extremely attractive' virtues and thought it 'suspicious' that she was coding as the Germans 'could very well have done it themselves'. If anyone had been treacherous within Interallié, Mitchell thought, it would have been Gane and Deschamps as he had witnessed their alleged intrigues during Roman's absence. Mitchell's testimony emphasised the swirls of rumour and intrigue around all espionage and Resistance operations in France; how each observer could read something different into motives and outcomes, and none be sure about anything.

*

Cowburn finally arrived from Lisbon to give 'overwhelming evidence that Lucas at least is genuine', and provide blunt reassurance that there could be no 'conspiracy' between de Vomécourt, Mathilde and the Germans: as Cowburn was 'an Englishman whose loyalties are unquestioned' this was the final confirmation of her allegiance. Even the sinuous imaginations of the Double Cross team could not work out 'what advantage could accrue to the Germans by sending Lucas back with an agent who had instructions to admit that she was controlled'. Furthermore, if it was a proper German operation it had been carried out with a high degree of 'incompetence', which the British attributed to 'an affair of this magnitude' being 'apparently handled by relatively junior members of the Gestapo'. In fact, it exhibited an almost insulting lack of professionalism.

They were keen to keep Mathilde close, to get every last detail of her knowledge of the Abwehr and to guard against the 'minute' chance that the two arrivals were being watched by the Germans, but the greater priority was to protect the Resistance, which meant she had to return with de Vomécourt. The enthusiastic Robertson was looking forward to 'concocting an extremely good document for her to take back' to the Abwehr based on the 'personalities of [his] organisation, the food conditions, morale and general information about the opinions of members of the Cabinet, together with a small amount of military information'.

As far as Mathilde was concerned, she was still being stalled and mistrusted and her position and skills ignored. Her frustration at being led again through her past rather than concocting a future legend spilled over when she was next interviewed in Bayswater. She was taken back over her story, which now had some new flourishes, such as that her former dinner date Oscar Steininger was 'a very great enemy to the Nazi regime' and should be recruited. In her enthusiasm to impress, it seemed not to occur to her that Marc Marchal, who had introduced her to Steininger, had not been heard from since she had confirmed his role to the Abwehr. Although this conversation was mainly to give descriptions of Ische, Bleicher, Eckert, Kayser, Propst and every other German she had come across, she could not resist asserting that Borni had become the mistress of both Propst and Borchers. When the focus turned to handling her return, she 'gave vent', in the unemphatic words of an English handler, 'to a certain amount of dissatisfaction with her position'.

It was the sort of situation she found intolerable. She was simultaneously supported by all this high-level attention for her
courageous, unexpected part in de Vomécourt's essential exfiltration, and exasperated at not being valued. The 'dissatisfaction'
stemmed from not being at the centre of things, considererd
important enough to be involved in 'Lucas's projects'. She 'was
linked up entirely with him' and 'should be in on all the discussions'. She accepted that she had 'no formal training' in espionage
and would very much appreciate 'instruction' so that she might
give of her best. She highlighted their central dilemma: how to
make use of her, and how to do so in relation to de Vomécourt. And
what to do about her if they could not, as the lovers were the
enmeshed protector of each other. It was a knot that needed unravelling for the sake of France and the war.

*

SOE were less trusting and gung-ho than their compatriots in MI5
about Mathilde's return with disinformation, as she would also be
able to report back on their activities in Occupied France and
endanger lives should she turn again. Brigadier Colin Gubbins,
director of operations, Western and Central Europe was given the
thankless task of telling de Vomécourt 'that in no circumstance'
should Mathilde accompany him back. He had 'a long talk' with
him on the subject, and came away thinking that the Frenchman
'would be prepared to work without Victoire'; above all because,
'whether he should grow a beard and disguise himself under his
old identity' or reappear 'in a new identity', it was essential that his
officer 'make another appearance in France to keep up the morale'
of his followers and to 'try and save' his mission. The schemes to
blow up the Gestapo building and murder Bleicher were simply
'not worth the risk'; the 'one and only real objective' of the whole
fraught operation was to build up the Resistance, and Mathilde
could play no part in that. De Vomécourt's pragmatic understanding was essential and welcome, but then came the question of his

lover: to SOE she was a problematic pawn in a much bigger game, but still needed to be kept onside.

It only took 'a little discussion' between the SIS, SOE and MI5 men to recognise that to intern her would 'antagonise' de Vomécourt. They did not pause to consider the questionable morality of taking such action against someone who had been an outstanding agent. Yet to have her 'run around in London without any job to do' was 'obviously undesirable'. Dick White proposed that he arrange for her to be spirited away to the country; de Vomécourt might be less bound up with her if he did not see her daily. Buckmaster went further in 'tentatively' suggesting that she might be got right out of the way of F Section and 'work among the Arabs', just as Bleicher had implied. Dunderdale read her better and pointed out that it was 'necessary to give her some definite work to do', to 'flatter [her into] thinking she was undertaking something very important'. Harmer lent her a typewriter and suggested that writing 'a complete account of her experiences' might occupy her to an extent, and might even include useful intelligence nuggets.

There was also the urgent, linked issue of what to do about the 'Walenty transmitter'. MI6's counter-espionage Section V had analysed the traffic following the break-up, and ran through the possibilities: if de Vomécourt was to go back without Mathilde, 'the Germans will have to assume that we have swallowed a very improbable story' about her authenticity, as on her being 'examined thoroughly' on her arrival, it would be clear to any espionage organisation that there were inconsistencies in the messages sent over her name after Roman's arrest, including about the receipt of British money; if de Vomécourt were to return alone and in disguise, the Abwehr would believe that she had turned back to the Allies, which might play very badly for the trusting Cottin and others unless he too were to 'disappear'; a faked aeroplane crash in which they both perished would give de Vomécourt freedom to operate but might also condemn Cottin and in turn wreck the whole Autogiro scheme. The needs and possibilities for the spies and SOE seemed to be pulling in different directions.

The Double Cross unit was confident that there were no unturned Nazi agents inside their networks and could afford to be bold. They would convince the Germans that Victoire had succeeded in persuading them that she was loyal to the Allies, and that the reason for the extension of the stay beyond the planned fifteen days of her future bestseller was that de Vomécourt was building up an 'even greater' organisation than originally conceived. Those left behind might be safe if the Germans believed that patience now would reap still greater rewards later. Which would not be until the April moon, to give de Vomécourt time to perfect 'the magnitude of the projects in view'.

They would use her transmitter to tell the Abwehr that de Vomécourt would be parachuted into the unoccupied zone then before making his way to the north. Cottin and other key figures would go to meet him 'to get them out of the way' of the occupiers before the announcement of Mathilde's re-entry accompanied by 'several W/T operators, agents, arms, explosives etc.' But just before her dynamic arrival, de Vomécourt would disappear and 'urgent messages' that 'Victoire's operation is all keyed up and ready to start' would be unable to produce him. They would never hear from him again, at which point the Germans would be told that 'the project has collapsed' and has to 'be completely reorganised'. The transmitter could then be used as and when it was useful to do so, and Mathilde's continued presence in London explained in isolation from de Vomécourt. The intelligence services saw no reason why the hitherto credulous Germans would not fall for this. Once SOE had signed the plan off, two of the three issues – de Vomécourt's unseen return separate to Mathilde, and the future of the transmitter – would be solved. The third, how to keep Victoire undercover while still making the most of her identity, remained.

*

Evelyn Grist was a powerful figure with a predilection for hats, necklaces and shawls. She had been with MI5 almost from its first day, was fanatically devoted to its founder, Vernon Kell, and thought that everything that had happened since he was sacked in 1940 had been to its detriment. She was currently in charge of A5, 'the listeners' at the Security Service's building in Mayfair; a post she would hold as world war moved into Cold War and the era of the Atom Spies and the Cambridge Five. 'Mrs Grist's girls' reported from the microphones in Porchester Gate that de Vomécourt had told Mathilde that it looked as if he would be going back without her. This had led to a 'quarrel' in which she had said 'that she would go her own way and he would go his', and that 'he irritated her and she did not like his manners'. She huffed out to a party before a late, 'drunk and penitent' return. The row awakened the protector in de Vomécourt and he put pen to paper. His 'flowery style' could not soften his 'strong criticism' of the 'British intelligence services' treatment of Victoire' who was being 'neglected'. The strain of her uncertainty was getting to them both, and was threatening disruption of the grand plan.

When Harmer next visited his charge, she had apparently accepted that she would be parted from de Vomécourt, and that 'she could not show her face in Paris for some considerable time'. But she was also 'boiling up for a real complaint'. She was resentful that she had been billed for two new dresses after the ruin of her suitcase in the sea at Moulin-de-la-Rive, and furious that 'Lucas and his department' had not 'taken her into their confidence' earlier. She offered her view that the Allies 'could not win in this war' since they seemed incapable of dealing with 'women agents' who had played a notable part in the victory of the 'last war'. As her dreams of being in the tiny pantheon of female spies alongside Mata Hari faded, her vulnerability and grief spilled over into anger.

Harmer was keen to pass on the increasingly vexed issue of Mathilde and told Bodington that whether or not she went back to France was entirely up to SOE, as MI5 had no interest in her once they had used the transmitter for long enough 'to enable Lucas and all his organisation to disappear' and re-emerge incognito. If SOE did not want her, they owed it to her to tell her themselves. Bodington was thrown: de Vomécourt was a 'personal case' he had recruited and 'coached' from the start, but much as he found

himself liking Mathilde, he was personally ill-equipped to handle
her. Rather than address her directly, he even came up with a
scheme whereby a doctor would 'advise her that her heart is weak
and that she must stay quiet for an extended period and avoid all
strain', including getting upset about de Vomécourt's departure,
and she could not leave as she would be unlikely to survive a parachute drop. He overcame his concern about the chosen doctor's
assistant's 'very Left Wing, pacifist views' to make an appointment
for Mathilde to visit him in Clerkenwell, but their proper qualms
about the plan meant it was dropped as events took their course.

*

A message from Mathilde was sent on 10th March: 'After a week of
tiredness and lack of rest I am starting work. Date for return not
yet decided.' A few days earlier, Bomber Command had dropped
450 tons of explosive on the Renault factory, now making 18,000
lorries a year for the German army, at Boulogne-Billancourt in the
western suburbs of Paris.* The largest raid of the war so far was a
military success with only one Wellington bomber lost, but at a
cost of nearly 700 civilians killed. While Mathilde's personal situation was still eating into their time, it was a good moment to start
transmissions on her wavelength.

An enquiry about the raid was duly sent to encourage the belief
that the triple-cross was still alive and successful. The German reply
had to keep their side of the pretence plausible and gave the undeni-
able news that 'reconstruction would take several months'; but at the
same time pride required the addition of some clumsy propaganda:

---

* Louis Renault was arrested in 1944 for aiding the Germans by upping production in his factories at their direction, and his shares in his company were
seized by the state. It has been debated whether his fatal haemorrhage in captivity in October 1944, before he could stand trial, was the result of a beating in
Fresnes or, as his death certificate reads, natural 'cerebral complications of
vascular origin'. His defence would probably have been that his collaboration
protected his workers.

they were unable to resist quoting Fernand de Brinon, who had just set up the 'Groupe Collaboration' to forge closer cultural ties between occupier and occupied. De Brinon claimed that 'Britain had abandoned France in her most tragic hour and now has bombed the civil population.' The Abwehr could not have chosen a less persuasive source to inform enemy intelligence about the success of their raid, but the 'Walenty transmitter' in London acknowledged that the information was 'very much appreciated', asked for news of the bombardment of the 'Matford [Ford] works at Poissy', and instructed Cottin to 'prepare propaganda tract to justify recent bomb raids'. The Germans were receiving information and requests that chimed with their own desires and ideology, and failed to observe one of the cardinal rules of double-cross espionage: to analyse and reanalyse every transmission with a cynical mindset.

By the time of this exchange, Mathilde's allotted fortnight was up and Bleicher was starting to show anxiety: 'agents are starting to come back from their sectors' and they would like her to 'indicate approximate date of return'. Four days later, the British replied over her name that she was 'working hard', and that her 'date of return not yet fixed'. As a proof of her loyalty and a distraction that spoke to German greed, she was also 'making efforts to send money so that work can continue'.

The blandness of this holding transmission disguised the ongoing, circular debate about how to handle her in these crucial days before the April moon dictated de Vomécourt's drop. Bodington decided that his agent should have the job of telling her definitively that he was leaving, but de Vomécourt was perfectly aware of how this would be received and 'refused point-blank'. He pointed out it was 'a matter for the British Intelligence Service' whose charge she was – he would stand by whatever the spies decided, but was not going to be the messenger. Once again, she was being handed around like an unwanted parcel.

The delicate task eventually landed with 'Uncle Tom' Greene, as Mathilde was fond of him. Greene decided to inform her that it was a 'decision of the chiefs of the British Intelligence Service' and that there would be 'considerable difficulty' if she refused to accept it.

But after a sleepless night 'worrying', he rang Harmer first thing in the morning with 'a load of trouble'. He had come to the conclusion that it was 'absolutely impossible for him' to deliver the message as he 'had no background' in the relationship and was keen to 'see Lucas to find out exactly what his attitude was'. Harmer relayed this to Keswick who pointed out that 'the only result' of that would be 'a very stern rebuke about the way Victoire had been treated since her arrival'. Harmer rang Greene back to point out that 'another Service', SOE, should not be blamed for what had become the 'perpetually embarrassing subject' of 'agents and their grievances' and they should get together.

Harmer spent an hour and a half stiffening Greene's backbone over a drink at his club and they concocted a script: after many discussions, a high-level operation had been set up in which de Vomécourt would go back to France while they 'covered the position by radio', which necessitated Mathilde remaining hidden in England. De Vomécourt would come back after two months or so, at which point they would 'set about getting her back to France or to Tangier'. Greene had a date with her the next day, but had a further wobble on the grounds that he did not want to be thought 'to have invited her to lunch merely to break the bad news'. Harmer rather testily said she had to be told within the next twenty-four hours and suggested that 'U35' should join them and 'throw out an invitation to her' to stay with him in Gloucestershire as a sop to her feelings. 'U35' was Jona von Ustinov, a man Dick White credited as 'the best and most ingenious operator' he had 'the honour to work with'. He, if anyone, could charm and distract the increasingly fractious Mathilde.

After Greene's anguish, Mathilde 'completely nonplussed' him and Ustinov the next day when she told them at lunch that de Vomécourt had informed her that she would not 'be going back' with him; she 'seemed delighted with this decision', it appeared in the belief that she was being kept back as a prelude to a period of usefulness in her own right. The Englishmen were caught off-guard by her agreeable reaction and blustered that they would 'have to go back to the office for instructions' before saying anything more.

Mathilde remained at her most agreeable when Harmer and Greene came to call the following evening, 20th March. She would give 'her full collaboration', and suggested messages that could be sent out, including further offers of money to protect Cottin and keep the Germans happy. She was beginning to think of herself as an agent again rather than as an encumbrance and requested 'an apartment to herself' without 'restraint', as she had had in Paris.

De Vomécourt backed her up. He ran through his grievances about 'the treatment meted out to Victoire', which Harmer and Greene sidestepped by claiming his earlier complaints had never reached them. He then seized the agenda by telling the room that 'the General Staff' had decided that other 'matters must take precedence' over the plans to 'blow up the Gestapo and so on', but he was only going on condition that she was 'properly treated in this country' and that when she arrived back in a couple of months she must set up 'an information bureau', as befitted her skills. Mathilde interjected that this venture would consist of only four or five agents, nothing like the scale of Interallié, while the British refrained from comment. Harmer's appreciation of Mathilde 'increased as a result of the evening's talk', and her sense of her possible value restored her spirits to the point where she even disarmed the British handlers by self-deprecatingly acknowledging that the British must agree that she 'was an impossible woman'.

Harmer's departing promise that he would discuss how best she might be utilised was disingenuous, born out of relief that she seemed so much more amenable now that she had come round to her lover's departure. But to Mathilde it was an invitation to hope that ramped up her expectations to a cruel degree. When Harmer next came to Porchester Gate three days later, she was ready to start work at once, and had given thought not only to what questions to send to 'her agents' in France but also to what sort of sums of money would be needed: 200,000 francs* per month sounded right. Harmer diplomatically replied that he would 'go into the question of sending the money immediately' before taking her

* Approximately £1,200; £66,000 at 2018 values.

back to the first meetings with de Vomécourt and their exfiltration. He grasped the need to 'create the illusion that she was a free woman' and to run through these moments of intrigue and success to sustain her morale at a point of such delicacy that she was not even permitted to buy a stamp or make a telephone call.

She would need papers and another name once she was on her own. She had loathed 'Denise Martin', which was on her ration book, as that was more suitable for a 'French servant girl' than for someone of her importance. After some internal debate between the considerably grander 'Marguerite de Trevise' and 'Marguerite de Roche', she chose the latter. Susan Barton had rented a flat for her in Stratford Court, Oxford Street, for eight guineas per week from May and she was allocated a ready-tapped telephone number. Meantime she would be put up in Rugby Mansions, Hammersmith. Susan Barton would 'mind' her there and Harmer allowed her to have a transistor radio as a distraction 'in spite of its effects on Mrs Grist's activities'. In a little over eighteen months, she had moved through near-suicide in Toulouse to becoming the 'colonel' of Interallié, German collaborator and double agent, and then triple agent for the Allies, and soon would be in watched comfort as Madame de Roche.

*

As the moon waxed and de Vomécourt's departure got closer, the deceit that would buy him at least six weeks' cover was laid down. On 24th March, a series of transmissions was sent to Paris: Jouffret was told 'because of change of tasks [Mathilde and de Vomécourt] have been taken into the English organisation' and would need to stay 'for another month to receive directives'. He was instructed to find a landing field for their false joint arrival in mid-May. A follow-up announced that money was on its way, and yet another told Cottin to make his way to Vichy, which he would understand to mean his boss would arrive imminently for real. Once de Vomécourt had been dropped safely, Jouffret would signal that Cowburn 'had been taken prisoner on the Spanish frontier' and

Cottin was to return to Paris to 'warn ... the other agents what was the true position' before returning to the unoccupied zone where both men would lie low. Further plans would be announced at the start of May around 'the imminent return of Victoire and Lucas'.

That last week of March saw hectic traffic between Victoire and Jouffret. As well as scouting out landing fields, Jouffret was asked to analyse the success of the latest raids on Saint-Nazaire and to give more detail on the Renault and Poissy bombings; to establish if Roman Czerniawski could be bought out of Fresnes; and to have reports prepared by all agents on the 'exact position of all stores of munitions, fuel, oil, food and equipment' as well as 'new fortifications and railways being used'. The Double Cross team were enjoying themselves as they provided de Vomécourt's smoke-screen, and could only hope that the deception would not be passed up to echelons above Bleicher, as they realised 'that any intelligent enquiry into the case must make them extremely suspicious as to what the real position is'.

*

Harmer arrived in Porchester Gate for the last time on April Fool's Day to be present when Buckmaster and Bodington came to take de Vomécourt to his final briefing. De Vomécourt, who had stopped shaving his moustache and had his hair dyed black as a rather sketchy disguise, was issued with 'a phial of potassium cyanide' against the moment when he decided the better option to torture was suicide. That night he was to be parachuted to within a few hundred yards of his brother Philippe's house to re-emerge as 'Sylvain'.

Mathilde was 'not particularly friendly' to her lover at the moment of farewell as she steeled herself psychologically for his absence. She wept briefly once he was gone before rounding on his 'many faults ... his insignificant and rather ugly appearance' and 'his lack of manners'. His presence had provided security and status for her, and now she had to haul on her carapace of independence to keep fear at bay. She was only to see Pierre de Vomécourt once more in her life.

Her minders were pleased that they had lined up Ustinov to calm her emotional turmoil. He was a cosmopolitan figure who, despite his small stature at five feet two inches, stood out in MI5. He had been born in 1892 in Jaffa, to a Russian father and a mother who was the daughter of the royal armourer to the Ethiopian king, a Polish–Jewish convert to Christianity. The family became naturalised citizens of the German kingdom of Württemberg and Ustinov was awarded the Iron Cross, First Class, and the Knight's Cross and bar in the First World War. He had become a journalist in the Netherlands and married a Russian, with whom he came to England in 1935 rather than prove he had no Jewish ancestry; shortly afterwards he began to work for the Security Service. He was a flamboyant showman and superb mimic, equally at home imitating chorus girls and prime ministers, gifts he passed on to his son Peter. Jona von Ustinov detested his first name with its Old Testament resonance, and had been known from a very early age as 'Klop', after the Russian word for 'bedbug', fittingly for a diminutive man most often to be found in other people's beds.

Mathilde went to Gloucestershire over the Easter weekend but it was far from balm. Ustinov, whose hatred of anyone who had aided the Nazi regime, mistrusted, even loathed her. Sex was a great motivator for him, and he did not feel attracted to what he saw as her 'rather *faisandé*** charm', which led him to cast doubt on whether Bleicher could possibly have had an affair with her as 'every German officer in Paris had the opportunity to "write on better paper" (as they so delicately say in German)'. Ustinov's reverse sexual logic took him to the argument that she must have insinuated herself into working for Bleicher before her arrest, and therefore Mathilde had betrayed Borni, not the other way around. The theatrically minded agent could not believe that the Abwehr would have been taken in by someone whose 'technique, like her acting, is rather crude and more suited for provincial audiences', and therefore must be in England as an inept Trojan Horse. He did

---

* Gamey, like a well-hung pheasant.

at least credit her 'high intelligence, physical courage and sang-froid'. He spotted her need for flattery and her love of money, phrased as 'the dance around the Golden Calf', but was unable to account for either Czerniawski's or de Vomécourt's trust in her despite the success she had brought both of them. The latter was, in his opinion, 'a doomed man': she was 'like the shirt of Nessus that inevitably kills the man who wears it'. Even her stated desire to see her mother again was suspect to Ustinov: he concluded that 'like Voltaire's God, one would have to invent [Madame Belard] if she did not exist' as a reason to go back to Paris and 'depart from our hospitable shores'. It was a splenetic and devastating indictment, and a one-sided assessment so far removed from that of his more thoughtful colleagues that it served to highlight the impossibility of any understanding coming to Mathilde from some quarters for her actions before and after her collaboration.

She herself was in the benumbed state that followed powerful emotional events for her. Her fate was out of her hands once more. That Easter, 'when the daffodils were in flower' she turned away from spies, soldiers, dissembling and notions of her own heroism, back to the childhood fantasies of living peacefully in a rural setting. She took more pleasure in the company of Nadia von Ustinov than the worldly Klop, soothed by the painter's 'love of nature coupled with a sweet innocence and an open, frank simplicity'. They went for walks with Nadia's dog Ophelia, and as the winter of betrayal, a frozen immersion in the Channel and desperately repeated justifications gave way to an English spring, the exhaustion of the war started to lift a little – even if her essential presence in London was about to become ever more of a challenge to Harmer and his colleagues.

13

Spies' Conundrum

April 1942 saw both sides employing Mathilde Carré and her self-created code name for their own hopeful ends: the British to deceive the Germans and buy Pierre de Vomécourt time to galvanise the Resistance, the Germans to double-cross SOE and MI5, and thereby stymie it. The most important link in the twisted chain, the unlikely agent on whom the stability of the houses of cards depended, found her own fantasies of becoming 'the most important spy in the war' frustrated. She realised she was exhausted and 'drank far too much', but was able to 'admit, believe it or not', that she 'was almost happy' now that her 'nightmare was behind' her. As long as she remained in a mirror world of collaboration, double and triple agents, her strengths counted for little but her weaknesses could be disastrous. The next few weeks brought high living, confusion, scheming, espionage and counter-espionage, resistance, arrests and deadly peril in London and Paris in an intense mixture as the protagonists fought their corners.

*

De Vomécourt got to work right away. At the end of 1941 he had rented 'a warehouse' from a 'front man' and obtained a number of blank permits intended for 'movement of German goods' so that when his resisters were gathered, they and their weapons could be ferried around in the lorries he now set about acquiring. A Belgian named Léon Wolters, 'an engineer of the highest quality', was 'in charge of the transport company'.

The transmitter in London kept up a barrage of requests to sustain the impression of his domicile in London with Mathilde. On 4th April six questions needed an urgent response, including what was happening at the Renault works, and what was being manufactured in the explosives factory, the Pouderie Nationale de Sevran-Livry. Mathilde saw the messages before they were sent, and occasionally offered a more idiosyncratic turn of phrase but otherwise was redundant for espionage purposes. Yet she needed to be kept onside for psychological and operational reasons: the British could never categorically rule out that she was not playing a deeper game than they believed and would find a way of signalling to Bleicher that de Vomécourt had surreptitiously returned. Above all through the dealings of the past few weeks, they were alert to her unpredictability, reinforced by Ustinov's derogatory analysis. B1a knew that she had to be kept out of the way for their triple-cross to succeed, but were simultaneously concerned to maintain her spirits as she moved to Rugby Mansions under the watchful eye of Mrs Barton.

Susan Barton had every reason to mistrust Mathilde: she herself had left Germany in the 1920s, appalled by the rise of fascism. She had joined MI5 after a short-lived marriage to a British homosexual and now lived with another intelligence officer. She had been a valuable spy as secretary to the German naval attaché in The Hague until the Venlo Incident of November 1939, in which two MI6 agents were arrested on the Dutch border in a Nazi sting operation. Her name was on a list the agents carried and she had to flee. As 'a most formidable intelligence operative' who had stood by her beliefs at the cost of her upbringing and family (her brother was a serving U-boat captain), she was ambivalent about Mathilde: she found her 'exceedingly charming' but sensed that charm was only a 'thin veneer'; 'she can be very amusing' yet 'her sense of humour is at times almost infantile'. In her own easier certainties in the war, Barton did not try to understand why Mathilde might make 'offensive remarks' about 'unfortunate Free French officers' who had not seen their countrymen's recent struggles at first hand.

Mrs Barton eventually came down against Mathilde, concluding that she could be 'an exceedingly dangerous woman' who would turn against her protectors 'vindictively' if she ceased to be 'amused' in her exile. She could not be expected to understand that her charge was hollowed out and unfulfilled, and that her search for 'amusement' and 'luxury', and 'her interest in men' filled that void. Harmer recognised well enough that 'sooner or later' things would go badly for them when they had little use for her and 'could not carry out her wishes', but for now Mrs Barton was credited for having 'skilfully brought [Mathilde] round into a more reasonable frame of mind' following her lover's departure.

Mathilde had no influence over her living arrangements, her finances or the war, and little to do once the debriefings had ceased. She had told MI5 everything and her lover had now returned to the scene of the action. She took up Harmer's suggestion that she might write an account of her adventures so far and began *Mémoires d'une Chatte* on the day she moved to Rugby Mansions. Her manuscript had taken on a very different tone by its completion, but for now it was a chance to recreate her recently past glories and firmly fix her loyalties to the Allies to sustain her self-esteem. She chose to begin it with Maurice Carré's departure from Oran on 18th September 1940, a moment that held 'no anxiety' for her, the beginning of her life of the past thirty months. This project was to occupy her little free time as she determined to make the most of the strange, scrutinised freedom which she still believed had only a month to run.

*

Post-Blitz London was a chance for her to return to the high living she had briefly seen and despised during the *drôle de guerre*. She went to 'the hairdresser's, to beauty parlours and to dress shops'. MI5 had given her one hundred extra clothing coupons on top of her 'salary' of £50* per month, which she used to have dresses made

---

* Approximately £2,750 at 2018 values.

by Madame Leach in Green Park, Mayfair. Her love of music was reawakened: she went to hear the St John Passion in the Albert Hall, to the cinema and to the Russian ballet; she heard Denis Matthews on the piano, whom she found 'delightful', as well as Benno Moiseiwitsch, who was 'more of a virtuoso than an artiste'. She frequented the restaurants of Piccadilly and Knightsbridge, including the Berkeley Buttery, where delicious food appeared in the converted stables of the hotel, and the haute cuisine Ecu de France in Jermyn Street, where she took against the 'too cocksure' Free French officers. One day in Harvey Nichols she bought herself and Valerie, her Auxiliary Territorial Service minder, matching black velvet neckbands with crimson flowers; Valerie found it 'a rather macabre thing' but kept it long after the war as a souvenir of their association.

This lifestyle did not come cheap. Even before Susan Barton's time and the rent for Rugby Mansions, Mathilde's cost to MI5 and SOE, who split the bill two-thirds to one-third, came to £140.15s.3d.* for April alone. Most of this was incurred in housekeeping and entertainment: both Harmer and Mrs Barton reclaimed about £35 each. But from Harmer's point of view, 'these fabulous sums of money' were worth spending to head off the possibility of 'an interminable stream of complaints' as he juggled his idiosyncratic agents.

The woman who had lived her adult life until the war as a teacher in Paris and then in Algeria, and who had spent the end of the previous year collaborating with the Abwehr, once again tried to reinvent herself while liberated by Harmer and his colleagues' licence – this time as an international woman of mystery. Charles Mackintosh was introduced to the Geneva-born 'Madame de Roche' by Captain Anthony Gillson, 'a nightclubbing playboy and racehorse owner who transferred to SOE' from his regiment. A few nights later, Mackintosh called at Rugby Mansions just after eleven o'clock to take her to the 400 Club in Leicester Square. In the nightclub, where an eighteen-piece orchestra played to dinner-jacketed

---

* Approximately £7,700 at 2018 values.

dancers, Mathilde told Mackintosh that her father was Turkish, her mother Swiss, and she had been brought up in Lausanne but had been in England for two years. Yet she was ignorant of the Brasserie Montbenon, one of the most famous restaurants in Lausanne, and when asked why her English was so poor, simply replied, 'Because I'm stupid.'

Mackintosh challenged her, at which point she dropped her grand cover to claim that she was part of 'a French sabotage organisation in collaboration with "Pierre"', had worked for the Germans for a time and had come to London under their auspices; she had 'offered to return to France' as a British agent, and 'expected to return there at the end of May'. She gave away so much that Mackintosh thought it his duty to file a full account of his night out with John Bingham* of MI5. Such an episode ran the risk of exposing a vital and complex operation for Harmer and his colleagues, but given their desire not to antagonise her, she was not even reprimanded.

In the middle of April, Mathilde saw Roger Mitchell. Harmer had not mentioned Mitchell was in town but perhaps it was inevitable that they would run into one other. She was lunching at the Mayfair Hotel with Vera Atkins of SOE, a Romanian–German with perfect French who had been detailed to keep her entertained that day. Mitchell approached her, and they discussed 'the break-up of the Walenty organisation', but their recriminations were 'fairly inoffensive'. Mathilde had the grace to say that 'although she had never liked [Mitchell] and had considered him to be a not very courageous man, she was nevertheless very pleased to see him in London'. She treasured kindred spirits who reminded her of her previous life.

She spoke most mornings to Henri Wotitski, a Czech friend of de Vomécourt's from pre-war Paris. The men had met frequently in March at Chez Victor and the Cumberland Hotel, and Wotitski kept his promise to de Vomécourt to check up on his girlfriend. He rang

---

* Best remembered today as being, not least in his physique, a model for John le Carré's George Smiley.

to gossip about the night before, and they lunched at the Café Royal in Regent Street or its less gilded neighbour Oddendino's, where he told her about his love entanglements. She confided that the real difference between them was that he was not forced 'to live in an unreal world', and that she was spending her inner time once again divorced from reality and 'in a world of dreams – imagination'.

In the middle of April, Wotitski took her to a concert given in aid of the Free French which inevitably provoked her to become quarrelsome: she denigrated 'the woman he was going about with' as beneath him socially and intellectually. Her comments in her unsettled state carried shades of the period when Roman had gone to London and she had undermined Renée Borni on the same grounds. Borni herself had by now been deemed 'more trouble than she was worth' by Bleicher as Propst was handling the coding and Kayser was distracted by 'making love to her'. She had been blackmailed into silence and sent back to Lunéville.

Wotitski was an habitué of gambling clubs, procured bottles of whisky and brandy on request, and was a constant source of irritation to the watchers and listeners tied up in her affairs, which involved 'activities on the fringes of the black market' as well as his fruitless attempts to try 'to get himself recruited as a police informer'. Mrs Barton was 'very concerned' when he took Mathilde to 'a very peculiar German refugee club', which in turn made Mathilde suspicious enough to ask that Gale, the Special Branch officer, should 'go along there with them and make notes', but nothing came of it.

Harmer recognised the importance of the detective inspector to her, and had planned that Gale should 'see her periodically and entertain her occasionally' after she had left Porchester Gate. He even suggested Gale might go round for a daily French lesson with her 'to keep her occupied'. Gale's superiors did not consider this a good use of an officer who had 'a great deal of other work on hand', which Mathilde 'took very badly', claiming that 'the British had broken the first promise that they had made to her': that she would teach Gale French so he could 'look after security' for Autogiro. For her, this was a breach of trust and a diminishment of her operational possibilities; for Harmer, it was another reminder of how carefully he needed to tread to keep her contained to protect their main mission. And how they had to work out what to do when the Abwehr expected her back in a month.

*

Mathilde's sybaritic existence kept her uncertainties about her future at bay, just as her memoirs could help her relive her triumphant past. De Vomécourt would return soon, and the two of them would be dropped back in the eleven-day period around the May moon. He was protected by the only tool the British had, her radio wavelength. They put out messages that made clear he was still in London, such as one about his visit to Cottin's old friend Peggy, who 'sends you many greetings'; they demanded more information about specific factories and troop numbers to keep the enemy tied up to protect what they believed was a successful ongoing operation. As Mathilde checked this correspondence under Harmer's watchful eye she must have recalled the danger and excitement of her real intelligence-gathering of the previous year.

The fictitious de Vomécourt bought himself time off-air just after his departure as he was 'leaving for about two weeks for special training far from the capital'. Another week on and a message came the other way that 'Benoît was arrested at the Spanish frontier ... a fortnight or three weeks ago', the code that meant Cowburn and Cottin had met up. It was a moment of 'triumph' for London, marred by a signal from the Abwehr that was a reminder of how short time was: 'I await your return at the end of the month. Please tell me immediately if return will be delayed.' The British replied vaguely that 'the exact date of our return' could not be settled until Lucas was back from his 'special training', and dangled the promise that everyone should be 'more and more careful as we are about to become the largest English organisation'.

In a move designed to entice Mathilde back and to extort more money, Bleicher now decided to throw Czerniawski into the mix. Jouffret had announced on 24th March that he was in negotiation 'with a Polish lawyer' to get Roman out of Fresnes and wanted instructions. The British replied that that was 'very interesting' and that Victoire was 'discussing subject with competent author-ities'. The Poles in London, who lacked the optimism of the Double Cross men, had heard a rumour that Roman had been shot in mid-April and wanted no part of any of this. Jouffret came back on the airwaves to say the lawyer, Dr de Kosseki, needed 250,000 francs* to spring his client, plus a further 10,000 for him-self, payable in advance. Some weeks later, he insisted that for de Kosseki to do his job, he needed to know Walenty's real name, 'place and date of birth'. Bleicher, in his nervousness, was setting a test for Mathilde to be sure it was she on the other end of the transmissions.

*

The moon started to wax again without Mathilde's appearance by parachute. Whatever happened to her next was not discussed with her by Harmer and his colleagues even as the moment approached when they would have to sell a decision to the Germans. De Vomécourt's success as he worked under strict radio blackout was critical to her.

Everything changed on 25th April. Long messages were sent over her name asking for 'the source of power, A[nti-]A[ircraft] defence and morale of workers' in no fewer than nine factories, a request put in by the Poles who were growing anxious about the extent of the subterfuge on their transmitter for fear that it could somehow lead to the exposure of Zarembski and his Tudor network; about 'new armoured formations' and the names of 'senior Boche offic-ers'; all questions to take up time in return for a sprinkling of intelligence. But when it was Jouffret's turn to come on air, he was curt and to the point: 'Roger arrested ... Danger for us not immi-nent as Roger and his agents do not know our organisation. I await next Tuesday your instructions.'

---

* Approximately £1,400; £77,000 at 2018 values.

This was a bombshell and a puzzle combined. If the loyal Cottin had been arrested, what had happened to de Vomécourt? They knew from the pre-arranged Benoît message that the men had met as planned, and that Cottin had received the money. Mathilde posited that if Cottin had been arrested by the Gestapo as opposed to the police, they would not have announced it because 'if they knew her to be double-crossing them … there was a danger that Roger might betray her under interrogation and [she and de Vomécourt] therefore probably would not return'. She thought it much more likely that he 'had got himself arrested for a trivial misdemeanour' such as when Cottin had stayed out all night at a club and been reprimanded by de Vomécourt as his papers were not foolproof and he had far too much money for 'a man with no occupation in Paris'. If the Abwehr had really got Cottin and found out that she had been turned back, she believed they would assume that she and de Vomécourt would both be 'kept in London for their own personal safety'.

On another hand, Harmer wondered if de Vomécourt had ordered Cottin to 'go underground', and consequently the Germans were alarmed that 'Lucas' had 'found out the real position' he was in, double-crossed by her on their behalf; this could be 'their way of warning Victoire that he has fled, so that she can take steps to arrange her return'. To Harmer's way of thinking, if Cottin had really been arrested, the Abwehr would not have announced it. He hoped that they would get a message confirming this theory in the next day or so; if he did not, de Vomécourt and the whole elaborate operation, potentially the Resistance network itself, was in jeopardy.

The next transmission from the British attempted to get at the truth. 'Victoire' asked Jouffret how he had found out about Cottin, and blew a little smoke in the eyes of the Germans by pointing out that 'since Lucas organisation dormant' without its leader, Cottin 'can only have been arrested for a trifling offence and should be soon released'. She would 'await Lucas return here this evening' from his mythical absence on training and would tell him about Cottin when they let her know further details. These were needed fast as 'we must decide about our return this week'. The deception had somehow held good for three months, but now they needed to extract urgent information from the Abwehr.

*

Autogiro had indeed been close to standstill in de Vomécourt's absence. Noël Burdeyron had derailed a train carrying soldiers on leave in central Normandy by dint of removing a rail, but this was 'a slow, noisy and cumbersome expedient' that resulted in only four deaths. De Vomécourt had arrived back with no explosives and no wireless after the thirty-fifth 'Georges' had 'gone to ground'. He stayed a fortnight in the unoccupied zone and went to Paris on 16th April, where he found Cottin 'suffering from nervous tension created by life under Gestapo surveillance and under threat of arrest, without the hope of escaping if the least thing went wrong', and therefore extremely relieved to see him. Cottin would not have long to wait now until he could disappear after his lengthy limbo, and his replacement, Jack Fincken, was already being trained up.

De Vomécourt had to get messages back to London about 'a dropping operation' on 4th May and concluded that his best route was through a pair of couriers to Virginia Hall in Lyons, and for the wooden-legged Texan to forward them on in the diplomatic pouch via Switzerland. He dispatched one of these couriers with details of 'landing grounds where no parachutists would be spotted, next to woods where the lorries would be hidden to transport the weapons'.

Micheline de Vomécourt had no idea about her husband's movements and was surprised to get a call from him. They lunched together on 22nd April and he came straight out with a request for a divorce to which she 'amicably' agreed. It was as if he felt the need to sort out his affairs as he entered a perilous period. He moved straight on to a rendezvous with Cottin, who was due to see Jouffret, 'the agent for the so-called Polish service', the following evening at six o'clock.

Cottin did not return from the encounter. Fincken was sent to the bar 'to find out if there had been any trouble there' but apparently the two men had left together amicably. De Vomécourt could not believe that anything could have gone awry as surely the Germans were 'waiting for his own return before interfering'. He reckoned that if Cottin had been taken, it would be as part of a scattergun 'police raid' he would be able to talk his way out of. De Vomécourt nevertheless took safety precautions and went that afternoon to tidy out his office above the Lido cabaret on the Champs-Elysées, leaving only 'a few maps' scattered about to give the impression that he would be back soon. He gave his papers to Fincken before going to his room in a flat that belonged to the trusted Wolters.

*

De Vomécourt put his 6.35 mm revolver in his pocket and slipped out at four o'clock the following morning. He edged his way from house to house along the curfewed street until he reached its cor-ner, where he pulled himself into a doorway, looked back and waited. At 4.30, a car pulled up and several figures rushed into his building. He moved fast, and telephoned word to Wolters from a call box that Wolters was on no account to go back to the Champs-Elysées office, nor to the escape office on the boulevard des Italiens. He would run through some 'technical questions' about the trans-port operations later and, most importantly, introduce Fincken to him as he would be running the show on the ground from now on. Next he sent an agent, Daisy, to Virginia Hall with a handwritten message to say that 'Roger had disappeared and it was feared had been arrested by the Germans'. Daisy had verbal instructions to 'bring back a W/T operator at all costs'.

At midday, de Vomécourt and Fincken were waiting opposite the Café des Palmiers to meet Wolters. They watched him enter and 'as far as they could see, he was not followed' so they crossed the road and joined him. A minute or so later, four men entered, stopped in front of their table, trained their guns on them and ordered them to raise their hands. De Vomécourt dared not reach for his revolver with those odds. The three Frenchmen were 'marched out of the

café' and driven to the 'Gestapo centre' at the Hôtel des Terrasses. It
was a crushingly swift unravelling of Pierre de Vomécourt's dreams
of resistance less than a year since he had first been dropped into
France by SOE, and four months after his first meeting with
Mathilde and the start of their adventures together.

*

A few days later Madame de Vomécourt was telephoned by a
German officer who informed her that her husband wanted to see
her in Fresnes. A man who introduced himself as 'Colonel Henri'
came to her flat, and took her away from her 'two or three children'
and their 'young, very brave nanny' to question her in the car
before driving her to Fresnes. She said that she was 'more or less up
to speed with her husband's activities' but for 'several months had
not heard a word about him' and had 'never had anything to do
with his business'. When they arrived at Fresnes, Pierre and Cottin
were led in. They 'chatted quite normally for a while' after which
she had a further conversation with Colonel Henri who told her
that she would be able to send food parcels to the men. The Colonel
Henri who was offering some home comforts to his prisoners was
Hugo Bleicher, who had promoted himself several ranks as he was
so peeved at still being only a corporal.

Bleicher had been told on every recent transmission that Pierre
de Vomécourt was still in Britain, yet if he had doubts in the loyalty
of Mathilde Carré, he never gave them voice. Whether to do so
would mark him out as an Abwehr failure and condemn him to
service on the Eastern Front, or whether he was so sure of his hold
over her despite his latest coup, he was broadly in the same position
as his British counterparts – perplexed about what was really going
on. He had the upper hand now that he had de Vomécourt, but
both sides were in the position of having to re-evaluate their next
moves in the Victoire case, while she herself remained in hedonis-
tic ignorance of this catastrophe.

14

London Dance

Just as Pierre de Vomécourt was supposedly on his way back from 'training', word came from Paris that his 'Lido office searched' and, worse, 'Claude arrested'. The transmission advised that Victoire and Lucas delay their return, and was signed 'Kiki'. The sudden arrival of the original Interallié traitor Kieffer's code name was a terrible and baffling omen for what might be unfolding. The only upside for the British was that one known double agent replacing another on the radio indicated Mathilde seemed not to be under suspicion.

That small chink of espionage hope aside, London had no clues about de Vomécourt's situation and no way of working out what the Germans might be up to in announcing the capture of their own agent, Claude Jouffret. Harmer and his colleagues had to keep transmitting as normal and allow Mathilde to go about her rounds for the time being, even though she currently not only tested MI5's patience, but also threatened their relationship with Special Operations Executive and possibly the very future of the Double Cross organisation.

*

Soon after her arrival, Mathilde had asked her police escort Gale to find her a doctor, and he had taken her to consult the French-speaking E. M. Herbert of Devonshire Place, Marylebone. Herbert was a naturalised Russian, born Herzberg, who now had the plum job of resident doctor at Claridge's hotel; he was 'one of those men who deals with the rich and high-class patients with no particular qualification to do so', according to the acerbic Susan Barton. In Captain Gillson's opinion, there was nothing 'against him from the security point of view' although he 'neither like[d] nor trust[ed] the man professionally'. Mathilde's consultation had 'led to a course of treatment which is designed primarily to raise her morale and make her eat and sleep better', presumably a series of uppers and downers.

As one of the issues around her 'morale', Dr Herbert concluded that she was 'in need of company and distraction', and issued a prescription for both. He was engaged to be married to the artist Anna Mayerson, a refugee from Vienna, and suggested that 'an artistic circle where she would feel at her ease' would be the thing. He would also introduce her to a friend who was 'a lawyer, a lord and … one of the big chiefs of British intelligence.' This was Lord 'Top' Selborne, the fifty-five-year-old scion of a distinguished family of public servants, currently minister for economic warfare and thus in charge of SOE.

Mathilde, Herbert, Mayerson and Selborne met at Claridge's on Friday 1st May. The peer, characterised by Mathilde's handlers as 'a small, stooping figure with protruding grey eyes who would smile at any attractive woman who caught his attention', apparently asked 'Do you know someone called Victoire?' She replied that she did, at which point he said that 'he had always wanted to meet the person with such an interesting history'. Never one to resist flattery, Mathilde recounted her adventures, albeit without talking 'about affairs', or current operations; she added 'some ideas on propaganda etc.' which 'impressed Lord S. very much', so much so that he was surprised 'that nobody had ever thought of them before'. She was not backward in complaining about her lot when she told him that 'she had been kept under observation more or less as a prisoner'. He replied that this 'was outrageous for a person in her position' and that he 'would see to it that she should have everything'. More immediately, he would take her out to dinner the following Tuesday 'unless he had urgent business of state'. The flirtatious peer apparently 'told her that a man who wanted to get on always needed the advice of a clever woman', and offered to 'talk to

Churchill about her', as well as to commission Mayerson to paint her portrait.

Mathilde reported this conversation on Sunday to the startled Greene and Harmer, who concluded 'no doubt that ... it is only a matter of time' before she became 'his mistress'. Susan Barton had been woken up as Mathilde came home to hear all about that night, and in her opinion, Mathilde was merely 'giving herself airs' when she announced that Selborne had 'all the attributes that she admires in a man except that he cannot dance but that for the moment has become a minor matter'.

Nothing in the Double Cross team's training or experience had prepared them to deal with this. And at a time when their work-load was increasing by the day: that month, Colonel Johnny Bevan had joined the Twenty Committee to head the London Controlling Section with orders from Churchill to 'prepare deception plans on a worldwide basis' and to put in train 'any matter calculated to mystify or mislead the enemy'. Harmer passed the Selborne matter upwards, making it Keswick's problem: they could 'let the thing merely go on in a natural way', but whether in the end they owed it to the peer 'to prevent him making a fool of himself' was a matter which Harmer felt he 'must leave for someone else to decide'.

Keswick thought 'that it was most undesirable the association should continue' and he 'would take steps to have the minister warned'. These steps meant that on that same busy Sunday, Brigadier Gubbins went to see the married 'ladies' man' Selborne to put Mathilde's 'true position' to him. Selborne had 'assumed that he was perfectly alright', but nevertheless 'knew how a gentleman should behave', and cancelled their dinner date. However, the relief of Harmer and company was to be short-lived as another of Dr Herbert's contacts and a friend of Selborne's was soon to take yet more of their time and attention – at a point when it was dawning on them that their whole operation had been blown.

*

Bleicher had realised that de Vomécourt was back when his superior, Major Schaefer, 'had given him a few sheets of paper' seized from a courier on the demarcation line, and he spotted 'an agent's report containing a message to be sent off in the Zone Libre'. He was wondering why the handwriting looked familiar when a passage caught his eye: 'HB is still living at the same address but he is sleeping out. I will find him one of these days.' As he was indeed spending most of his nights with Suzanne Laurent, this seemed a direct reference and threat to himself. In a brilliant, or lucky, observation, he recognised from the handwriting that the author of the report, which had been signed 'Sylvain', was de Vomécourt. And if de Vomécourt was back, Roger Cottin must know about it. Bleicher was waiting outside the café when Jouffret had his meeting with Cottin on 25th April.

The former soap salesman had been fearful of this moment since his boss had left for England two months earlier and had been struggling to dissemble through his twice-weekly encounters with Jouffret. Bleicher got straight to the point and asked Cottin where he could find de Vomécourt. Cottin 'refused to answer or even to admit that Sylvain was the same person as Lucas', even when Bleicher said that Cottin's life would be spared for information. The offer that worked on Mathilde failed on Cottin, whose nerves were so far gone he must have thought it unlikely he would survive come what may.

Bleicher went to de Vomécourt's offices on the Champs-Elysées and with his usual good fortune found Léon Wolters there in direct defiance of orders. The Belgian, who was hoping to spirit away any incriminating documents to save his own skin, claimed that 'he had broken down under torture' but Bleicher protested that he had not 'needed to manhandle' him, nor would that have been his style, in order for Wolters to 'give away the rendezvous at the Café des Palmiers' and agree 'to act as stool-pigeon'. As de Vomécourt was driven away from the café under arrest with Wolters and Fincken, he was still calmly analytic enough in the face of the inevitable pain and horrors to calculate that his clearly undamaged transport manager was 'the only other person [than Cottin] who had the knowledge necessary' to enable his capture. Mathilde did not cross his mind.

*

The revolver and phial of potassium cyanide were soon found, after which he was 'set upon by eight Gestapo men' in the incongruous setting of a former bedroom at the Hôtel des Terrasses. They shouted questions over one another in their excitement and rage as at first 'he denied everything' and then 'refused to speak' at all. After the Gestapo had had their 'sport', Bleicher entered. He was 'counting on the element of surprise' quickly followed by his prisoner's 'collapse'. But the arrival of 'Jean Castel', rich Belgian businessman, provider of the car to Vaas and his predecessor as lover of Mathilde Carré fell flat. Although de Vomécourt knew that in the end it was useless to deny his identity, he was determined to have his moment. He punctured the triumphant Bleicher by looking blankly at him as he said, 'You must recognise me. I'm Jean ... ' De Vomécourt repeated that he was Monsieur de Mondore, as attested by his identity card.

Bleicher saw that this man was made of different stuff to the untrained part-timers of his experience and left his colleagues to beat up the prisoner. When de Vomécourt was well-bloodied by their blows and kicks, he calmly said that 'they might make him speak, but under such conditions they were unlikely to make him tell them anything that was true'. His 'nonchalance' worked and 'they stopped knocking him about'. Bleicher came back and ordered he be put in solitary confinement for three days, after which 'he would be willing to tell them anything he wanted to know'.

De Vomécourt and Fincken were handcuffed and shackled at the ankles, transported to the morbid gloom of Fresnes and thoroughly searched for the first time. While the German attention was on Fincken, de Vomécourt decided to take the soldier's way out rather than endure torture. He had managed to stash some morphine tablets in his clothing and not been thoroughly searched in

Bleicher's excitement at his prize, and now took these. The Germans had been so pleased to find his cyanide that they never even considered he had a back-up suicide planned. He was dragged to 'a dark cell' on the damp ground floor with a '*Ständig Kontrollieren*'* notice on the door; the guards looked in every half-hour and assumed the prisoner was asleep as the drug took hold. But by eight o'clock that evening de Vomécourt realised that, 'although he felt very ill', his supposedly fatal dose had failed. After the war he learned 'that in cases of extreme nervous tension an overdose of morphine' can have 'practically no effect' as adrenaline dented its efficacy. Yet he did not give up: he noticed through his torpor that he still had his shoelaces with their metal ends, and began to gouge at his left wrist with this blunt instrument, but by midnight he had only succeeded in making 'a large hole' and was still 'nowhere near the artery'. The self-harm had the good effect, however, of making him realise 'that he could probably stand up to anything the Gestapo could do to him'. So he began to ponder 'hoodwinking' them, 'stopped probing and started to think out a good tale'.

*

Bleicher turned up again on Monday 27th, and this time de Vomécourt cordially said that he had recognised him at once, and had just needed some time 'to sort his ideas out'. He confessed that he had returned to France 'with the idea of creating resistance groups', but 'gave absolutely no information on the people involved'. Bleicher used his most persuasive arguments, starting out with the personal 'If you do not talk, I shall hand the dossier to the military police who shall shoot all the members of your Group', and moving on to the patriotic, 'If all the good men in France are killed, who will rebuild France?' But to no avail. De Vomécourt considered Bleicher the only German he came across 'who knew how to interrogate properly' but nevertheless maintained his image of 'an extremely idealistic, but quixotic French patriot, with entirely

---

* Constant checks.

impracticable ideas'. After three days, Bleicher made the mistake of showing him the report captured at the demarcation line as evidence. By repeating names already included there, and taking 'most of the blame on himself', Cottin and Maître Brault, rather than anyone else the Germans 'had already arrested or might be able to arrest', de Vomécourt appeared co-operative whilst not giving anything away.

Pierre de Vomécourt was lucky that he had the decent Bleicher questioning him. When his brother Jean was captured a few months later, he was brutally tortured, but remained silent before his deportation to Germany, where he was 'beaten and kicked and slugged and starved' and 'put to work in the mines' at Sachsenhausen. When the Germans gave the order to evacuate the camp to the sound of the Russian guns in 1945, he volunteered to stay with those too weak to move and was 'pushed, alive, into the ovens' after the camp commanders decided 'to liquidate all witnesses to their bestiality'.

By 1st May Bleicher was irritated; he decided to up the stakes. The Germans were increasingly carrying out reprisals to subdue the growing French resistance, and had shot fifty French civilians in response to the derailing of the Cherbourg–Paris train. Bleicher told de Vomécourt that they would shoot another 500 if he did not disclose the source of the sabotage. Amongst this batch of executions would be the thirty-four people they had arrested in the belief that they were connected to 'the Lucas Group' and, if he did not volunteer 'all the information required', he too would be shot. If he co-operated, he would be tried as a soldier.

De Vomécourt 'refused to give an answer until he had spoken alone with Roger Cottin, his second-in-command'. The two Frenchmen decided on their story and 'prepared a list of the people involved' who were already known to the Abwehr. De Vomécourt 'had learned from Victoire exactly what the Germans knew' and who was already in captivity, including Abbott and Redding. They added a couple of other names for the sake of verisimilitude, two agents who would almost inevitably be caught soon enough anyway. Bleicher had given his word that anyone they offered up would be tried as a prisoner of war rather than executed, and it was later reckoned that de Vomécourt and Cottin saved at least thirty lives by their deal.

He remained loyal to Mathilde throughout his fifteen days of questioning, greatly helped by Bleicher's 'vanity' that would not allow him to doubt the success of his own operation. De Vomécourt 'assured him that Victoire had come under suspicion during her interviews' in London, but that 'they did not get anything precise from her'; it was because of these British doubts about her allegiance that he had decided 'to come back under a fake identity' unknown even to her. The Germans 'so little doubted this' that de Vomécourt hoped that 'the English services could use the Polish radio to trick the Germans' and do 'great and very useful work' for a long time to come. At the end of the war, Kieffer confirmed that 'Bleicher does not believe that Lucas ever suspected a double-cross' as Mathilde had the Frenchman 'completely under her thumb'. Years later, long after public opinion had made up its mind about her loyalties, Ben Cowburn met Bleicher in Paris, and his former adversary asked, 'Tell me, the Cat – was she really double-crossing us or not?' When 'Colonel Henri' came to write his own account of his time as a spy-hunter, he barely mentioned his first great coup, Interallié, and in his shame never referred to Mathilde, the only agent who turned his own tables on him.

*

In London, the continued absence of news was the source of great anxiety and increasing gloom to B1a at a critical moment for their grand schemes. Dusko Popov, Agent Tricycle, had always cost the Abwehr a great deal of money to which the FBI were also contributing to finance his Gatsbyesque life in the United States. He had managed to spend a staggering $86,000 in just nine months and the decision had been taken to get him to England before his extravagance led to his discovery; but just days after Mathilde and de Vomécourt arrived in London, B1a received an intercepted Abwehr telegram from Bletchley Park that indicated Berlin suspected Popov 'to be working for both sides and recommended extreme caution when dealing with him'. Tar Robertson faced a choice between 'bringing him back into the fold' or cutting him loose; if he was let go, Robertson estimated Popov's survival 'chances were nothing like even money', and if he was uncovered, 'it was pretty certain that he would be tortured to squeeze him dry of information about our system'. So he sent Popov back to Lisbon to carry on his work.

De Vomécourt's courage was not in doubt, but the SOE assumption that a prisoner of the Gestapo would not be able to hold out (or should even try to if they were to save their own lives) for more than twenty-four hours under torture, just enough time for papers to be destroyed and colleagues to scatter, meant the odds of his continued silence were slim. Their carefully primed deceptions could be exposed to catastrophe, and they sought Mathilde's counsel.

She was clear that 'they had to keep going as if nothing had happened': it would be 'fatal' to let on that they feared failure. Harmer reckoned that 'although [de Vomécourt's] moustache was not very far advanced' when he had left England and might have flourished since, de Vomécourt could hardly 'have hidden his identity from anyone who had seen him before'. But he agreed that once again they could only keep their side of the pretence going.

Kieffer's next message, sent on the same day that Bleicher was threatening de Vomécourt with reprisals for the train derailment and Mathilde was meeting Lord Selborne, said there was still no news of Cottin or Wolters, but pushed for a decision on her and de Vomécourt's return. It suggested that they might even go straight to the unoccupied zone as they were 'too precious to be exposed to the present graver risks'. If the British were not giving anything away, nor were the Germans, and they both became vague on the airwaves: the British exhibited concern for Jouffret and what he might give away 'in captivity'; the Germans claimed that his arrest made it unsafe 'to approach any agent at present in the Lucas organisation' but nevertheless instructed her to 'send fresh funds urgently'. They did not forget their prisoner Czerniawski either, and made a fresh demand for the 250,000 francs 'demanded by lawyer'.

By the middle of the month, a note of petulance had crept in about the non-arrival of money or her return date. The British were running out of time, and no longer looked to be still in the game. They had no spies in place to give them news and stopped their demands for operational detail. They turned their attention in wards to an urgent reassessment of the traffic now that they had to assume their whole operation had been exposed.

The parameters for the damage review displayed the incalculable logical complexity of the compromised triple-cross: if the Germans understood that the British knew that 'they were controlling the transmitter in Paris', they would work on the basis that 'intent to deceive' had underlain every question since Mathilde's arrival. If, however, de Vomécourt had 'defended Victoire in his interrogations, they may think that the questions asked during April were genuine'. But then again, as the Germans must have known that 'sooner or later' their deception would have been rumbled, questions might have been asked 'not with intent to deceive, but with intent that ultimately they would be known to be false'. After some spins around this circle, Harmer admitted that it was a philosophical topic 'which could be discussed indefinitely, but it would probably be fruitless', before once again trying to imagine himself as a German intelligence officer calculating whether the British 'knew all about' a subject and were just verifying whether the truth was being told, or whether 'we wanted to find out what the Germans wanted us to believe'. In the end he decided that 'it is so difficult to provide any answer that no conclusion at all has been attempted'.

When they turned their attention to the specifics, the spies felt on firmer ground in their mirror-thinking. The Germans would reckon the British had 'no operational intentions against the Seine estuary' because they had repeatedly asked about it; conversely, that they were interested in Normandy, specifically the Cherbourg peninsula, as no questions had been sent about that until late April; and that they must have 'very good agents' in Brittany as they had made so few enquiries there. Although they had asked for 'vulnerable points' on the railway line between Bordeaux and Irun on the Spanish border, the Germans probably worked out 'they were not contemplating any action' against it; likewise the bridges over the River Marne.

Analysis of the traffic coming the other way threw up three main areas where the Germans were planting incomplete or false information: they were 'anxious to have [the British] believe that a new minefield had been laid near the Channel Islands'; they were rearming in Brittany with an armoured formation that had come from the Russian front, which had not been given much credence anyway; and they were 'anxious to hush up the importance of the production' of explosive at Sevran-Livry, which was no surprise. In the end, Mathilde's knowledge and insights about the enemy's 'methods of penetrating espionage organisations and running double agents' represented perhaps the most valuable intelligence gained.

Special Operations Executive (F Section) were deeply disappointed that 'Autogiro as a working circuit was snuffed out before it had got properly alight'. But they recognised that if de Vomécourt had indeed had his career 'cut short before his work could bear fruit', he had 'nevertheless played a very large part in laying the foundations of the future successful development of resistance in France'. But they did not go as far as giving Mathilde any credit for her bravery, acting skills and her eventually loyal single-mindedness that had at least ensured his exfiltration.

The misinformation of the past couple of months was written off for security's sake, and whatever had happened to him in France, de Vomécourt was acknowledged to be out of the war. Amongst the dejection around the loss of such an influential asset, the question of how to handle the expensively high-living Agent Victoire was becoming ever more urgent. But even as these operational discussions were getting under way, the presumed blown asset was tying them up in yet more complications.

*

Lieutenant Richard Dafydd Vivian Llewellyn Lloyd of the Welsh Guards had, like his friend 'Top' Selborne, been introduced to Mathilde Carré by Dr Herbert, who had 'urged him to be friendly to her as she had done great services to the country and had escaped from France'. Herbert 'had no idea how far Ll. Ll. would go' in following up on his suggestion. The handsome, dark officer was taken by her war stories, and by her charm and vulnerability when they met for dinner in the second week of May. He followed up with flowers and an invitation to the cinema. Llewellyn Lloyd was better known as Richard Llewellyn, the author of *How Green Was My Valley*, supposedly rooted in his experiences growing up in South Wales although in fact Lloyd had been born in Hendon, Middlesex, and had spent little time in the principality. The novel, set in a nineteenth-century coal-mining community, had been published in 1939 and had been a worldwide bestseller, while the Hollywood version of 1941 had made its author even richer.

The reliably cynical Susan Barton went to pick up Mathilde from Stratford Court on 17th May, and over lunch got a detailed account of their encounter. Mathilde regarded the evening as 'a great success' (which Mrs Barton was not surprised to hear as she believed her charge to be entirely venal, and that she would have noticed the heft of Llewellyn Lloyd's 'pocketbook') and 'that he was exceedingly charming'. In fact, although she was not 'in love' with him, Llewellyn Lloyd was definitely 'a little in love with her', according to Mathilde. This turned out to be an understatement: it soon transpired that she reckoned it 'was a question of their souls having found each other', she was 'his inspiration, and the 'only other woman in his life', apart from his grandmother. Mrs Barton was relieved that 'indiscreet as Victoire seems to be with regard to her work and adventures, she is exceedingly discreet as regards her love affairs' so that at the least Mrs Barton could be 'convinced from all she has told me' that they were sleeping together without having to hear her 'say so outright'.

Stratford Court was deemed 'not good enough for her' and Llewellyn Lloyd offered her his 'exceedingly nice, very expensively furnished' flat in Upper Brook Street, just off Park Lane, for as long as she wanted while he lived in barracks. Mrs Barton hurried round to vet the resident maid, a suspicious figure because 'she is supposed to be English', yet 'from her very strong accent' was definitely 'foreign'. She later conceded that 'perhaps she is Welsh'. Barton was also alarmed by the 'inspiration' angle, which might mean that Mathilde was giving him 'ideas for books and stories'. She warned her charge that if any of these ideas were based in reality and secrets were spilled, she would not be able to publish her own book after the war.

When the *Mémoires d'une Chatte* were completed in disjointed draft, Part II, about Interallié, carries the dedication 'In memory of Roman C ... who was my "dearest Toto", from "his Spitfire"'. Part III, detailing her time as a collaborator and escape to England, is 'For my chosen brother, Christopher H ... ' Such was her state of infatuation with Llewellyn Lloyd at the time, though, the dedicatee of the whole thing is 'Richard Vivian Lloyd Llewellyn [sic]', under whose name she wrote

> You who took me by the hand without knowing it,
> You who loved me without knowing me,
> I love you too,
> And I offer you all of this long story of your
> CAT FLOWER ... LY* OF FRANCE

At a point when she and her handlers were questioning her usefulness, Mathilde extravagantly attached her faltering esteem to a successful, good-looking lover. She saw herself as his inspirational muse, and in return offered her memoirs to the literary man rather than to the real architects, and saviours, of her war, who got lesser roles. She must have known that her time spent living and working alongside Hugo Bleicher would look inexcusable, and that her account of it glossed over many of her collaborative actions; but maybe her new lover, whose own writings displayed sleight of hand in relocating his life and upbringing, would not judge her as

---

* A contraction of 'Lily'.

harshly as those still engaged with the monochrome struggle that she symbolised.

Llewellyn Lloyd soon began to find her attentions overwhelming. He had left barracks and moved back into his flat with her, but after a few days took himself off to the Savoy hotel for a month, spending only a few days at home to appease her at the instigation of Dr Herbert. She complained to Wotitski on the telephone that Llewellyn Lloyd 'lacked emotion', and was put out when he said that he 'had not had time' to have her manuscript translated, even though he would recommend it to his publisher if her 'Department' allowed. Masterman was worried about the possibilities of loose talk as 'it was only to be expected that a man of this sort would have friends in artistic and film circles', but overcame his suspicions after they met to conclude that the captain could be discreet.

By the time Masterman and Harmer were having these literary discussions, B1a had had some weeks to consider the status of the whole operation and to agonise over the future of their expensive and at times frankly troublesome guest. She had come to London as the person who had 'done great services to the country', but also as a collaborator who had had a hand in committing many of her former agents and colleagues to incarceration and maybe worse. And now that Pierre de Vomécourt was either dead or in German hands and the double-cross useless, some resolution was needed. In common with all tragic protagonists, the direction of her next and final scenes was out of her hands.

15

A Difficult Decision

Mathilde Carré's thirty-fourth birthday fell on the last day of June 1942. She had just delivered the part of her memoirs that recounted her time as a German collaborator to Christopher Harmer. She had a sizeable credit on her moral balance sheet: her nursing career, Interallié, and her connivance to get de Vomécourt to London far outweighed the period with Hugo Bleicher to which she had given a rather self-forgiving account, eventually under the heading of 'A Period of Hate'.

She was 'surprised' that Harmer sent flowers by messenger as she would have expected him to 'come up to see' her in person. The reason for his reticence became apparent all too soon: the failure of her cat-like luck and her own confidence in her survival was about to derail the narrative that was as truthful as she could make it whilst allowing her to sustain her sense of herself. In one of the ironic twists in which war abounds, 1st July was the first day of the battle of El Alamein in the Egyptian desert, the turning point characterised by Churchill as 'the end of the beginning'. For Mathilde, powerless in the complicated web of accommodations between reality and idealism in wartime, it was the other way around.

*

Bleicher ratcheted up the pressure in an attempt to find out what her status was now that he had de Vomécourt in Fresnes. On 13th May the Abwehr signalled their 'impression that you are neglecting us for the profit of Lucas' in answer to the British message that thanks to Jouffret's and Cottin's arrests 'our projects and plans for new organisation have been upset'. Bleicher turned this around to appeal to Mathilde's vanity when he stated that 'the arrest of Claude has demoralised agents greatly who ask every day for news of you', to which the British reply offered personal complicity: it urged the Germans 'to have complete confidence and no impatience', and asserted that she was not 'neglecting you for anybody as you know how much I am altogether for our organisation'. London was giving the impression that she was undetected but treading carefully. Bleicher did not acknowledge this declaration of loyalty, but again insisted she supply a return date and money, as her 'agents are intriguing more and more what to do' and could 'do nothing with promises that are never realised'.

Double-cross upon double-cross had caused stalemate, but Bleicher's bluntness forced London's hand. They could not acknowledge the disappearance of de Vomécourt and needed to begin to wash their hands of the whole deception. Accordingly, they replied to this threat with an uninformative transmission on Mathilde's behalf that 'since situation is so bad and we have no precise news, Lucas and I are going to leave England immediately'. They would come back home 'by a longer and safer route', which implied via Lisbon and Vichy, and would be in Paris at the end of May with the money. A final date that acknowledged the twisted deception had run its course, and brought the spymasters right up against 'a difficult decision'.

Both SOE and MI5 were keen to continue transmitting a bit longer but for different reasons. The former needed 'to try and find something out about the arrest of Lucas' to establish their future in France; the latter 'to close down the case leaving the Germans in as much doubt as possible' about whose side Mathilde was on. F Section, unaware that Bleicher's promise to his prisoner meant de Vomécourt was still in Paris awaiting a military trial, assumed that de Vomécourt had been 'taken to Berlin' as 'a valuable source of information'.

The Double Cross team seeded fresh doubt on 1st June when they claimed they had 'not had any news of Victoire and Lucas for ten days and fear that their voyage has been held up'. The BBC announced '*Victoire visite sa famille*' to signal she was in France amongst their less cryptic evening *messages personnels*. A week later they reported 'no trace of Victoire' and still nothing a week after that. On the tumultuous day after her birthday came the final transmission of the chain that went back to the brilliant intelligence-gathering of 1941, through the dangerous period of Abwehr deception to the B1a's careful use of the 'Polish radio'. The British had the last word when they signalled: 'We have news of Victoire and Lucas. To save those that remain and because of great difficulties, we have decided to close down the organisation. You must hide the set and disappear. In sending this message, the last, we repeat the motto of Walenty in his last message: "Every day and in every way against the Boche. Long live Liberty."'

*

The lack of explanation of what the 'news' might be was meant to tantalise, and masked the intense deliberations between the officers of MI5, MI6 and SOE entangled in Mathilde's case. Dunderdale of MI6 had suggested as soon as de Vomécourt fell silent that they might 'broadcast some of the misdeeds of Bleicher and other members of the German Secret Service over the BBC News Service' as a warning to any resisters unwittingly in contact with Kieffer, Jouffret or Bleicher himself. This could have the disruptive effect of 'stirring up trouble within the Gestapo' as well as 'give the impression that we had been given the information by Victoire under duress', but the idea had been vetoed by the Poles for fear of reprisals against Roman, should he still be alive. Harmer, Mathilde's most compassionate advocate, now raised the possibility of reviving the scheme in order to emphasise her innocence. He restated his opinion that she had 'worked genuinely against the Germans' and only 'co-operated' with them 'to save her own skin'; and that her initial betrayal of de Vomécourt had the unintended good effect of maintaining German 'confidence' in her.

However, Harmer's legal training and complicated induction into agent-running meant that while he could understand Mathilde's

The Villa Baur at Maisons-Laffitte, comfortable home of Abwehr IIIF in 1940.

La Petite Prieuré Villa in Saint-Germain-en-Laye, known as 'The Cattery' after it became the base for the Abwehr's daring double cross.

Pierre de Vomécourt, twice Mathilde's saviour.

The forged *carte d'identité* of Major Ben Cowburn, the adventurous SOE officer who had to put aside his doubts in the heady early months of 1941.

The pride of the German navy escaped the day of the comic failure of Operation Waterworks, in part thanks to the Abwehr's ingenuity in running Agent Victoire.

J. C. Masterman, the Oxford don
and sportsman, who chaired the Twenty
Committee that ran the creatively ingenious
Double Cross team for MI5.

'Tar' Robertson, known as
'Passion Pants' for his tartan trews,
B1a's operational head.

The 'glintingly clever' Christopher Harmer,
Mathilde's handler and confidant.

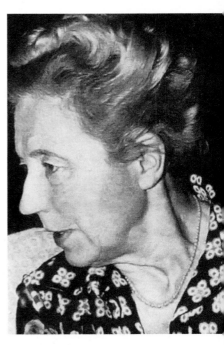

Susan Barton, the only woman on the
team, who kept a close eye on her charge.

The 'macabre' headband, Mathilde gave to her ATS minder, Valerie.

'Klop' von Ustinov, in his First World War German greatcoat, was sent to soothe and charm MI5's 'at times frankly troublesome guest'.

Lord Selborne, Minister
of Economic Warfare, caused
perturbation after spending
the evening with Mathilde.

The author and Welsh
Guardsman Richard Llewellyn
Lloyd, who invited her into
his Mayfair flat.

Mathilde's expression was impassive throughout her trial.

Her counsel, Maître Albert Naud had been a notable *résistant* himself but fought her case with understanding and wisdom.

Renée Borni appeared mortally ill in court.

Hugo Bleicher's post-war life was spent running a tobacconist near Lake Constance.

After her release from prison, Mathilde Carré was rarely seen in public as she retreated from the world and turned to religion.

collaboration, it could never be discounted. Theoretically she still could have 'changed horses in mid-stream' in England to pass intelligence back; after all, the Germans 'did not notice her change of attitude' when she returned to the Allied cause in January.

The fate of the woman whose gift for drama, whose undoubted courage had been tempered by her instinct to survive, and who had tried to keep some control over her destiny before being forced to give way to circumstance, was now completely in the hands of the imaginative, patriotic Englishmen. She had no inkling of the deliberations about her destiny and if she felt any fear about what might happen next, she subsumed it in frenetic social activity and in updating her own account of her life.

*

The first of Harmer's five options was to send her back to France 'en mission'. This would be outside the remit of the Double Cross team, and ultimately a decision for SOE. But he acknowledged that it was patently high-risk to return an agent who had already changed sides twice.

They could return her 'with the object of her contacting the Germans and working again for them'; in other words, to use her as a groundbreaking quadruple agent. Harmer's fertile imagination was fired, and he warmed to this theme. His team would ensure that she appeared convincingly 'anti-British' and would supply her 'with a false questionnaire designed to mislead the enemy' as well as the means of communication with them, 'say ... in secret ink from the unoccupied zone'. They would protect themselves by assuming that 'her messages are dictated by the Germans', all the while giving her cover by 'taking steps to make her disgruntled, such as the failure to supply her with money, instructions and so forth'. The obvious downside was the potential 'present to the Germans of the information she has managed to acquire about the British intelligence services'. F Section were more concerned about their reputation and that she would tell of their 'rivalry' with the spies owing to her 'anti-SOE bias' that stemmed from their separation of her and de Vomécourt. Also, they were still suspicious that 'in his more intimate moments' he might have given her valuable 'knowledge of his organisation'.

Another of Harmer's potential solutions was to 'let her live in this country at our expense for the rest of the war doing nothing'. It is not hard to hear the frustrations of the past couple of months when he rhetorically dismissed his own proposition as 'intolerable and so far from ridding us of the trouble and difficulty it would give rise to a tremendous amount of worry and effort without any result at all'.

They could cut her adrift 'with a present in the shape of a sum of money for what she has done', and then treat her 'as any other alien who enters this country'. The false papers that had been made for her as Madame de Roche would be recalled and she would most likely 'seek employment with the Free French or elsewhere' under her own name without 'any further assistance from the intelligence services'. The danger still remained that 'we cannot be absolutely certain of her from a security point of view', and Harmer's comment that she 'might stir up trouble with the Free French' was something of an understatement. Many patriotic resisters on the ground still felt that the Free French were not contributing enough to the salvation of their country, the realisation that had motivated de Vomécourt's path to SOE two years earlier. Women in the organisation were employed 'as shorthand typists, telephonists, drivers, nurses and social workers', of which only nursing could possibly hold any appeal to Mathilde anyway. Above all, once her backstory emerged, she would be lucky to escape with her life. All of which Harmer summed up as 'it would probably not to be to her liking', with the repercussions 'a constant menace' for him and his colleagues.

Harmer's fifth option was internment, 'undoubtedly the most final method' and the one which would 'rid' them 'of the trouble of looking after her and the danger she may be at large'. But his qualms about this solution encapsulated the issue: she had indeed worked for the Germans 'at one time' but that had been after she was 'just arrested', which counted in mitigation. She had then put things as right as she could by enabling de Vomécourt's exfiltration 'by her efforts' and 'co-operating' fully. Harmer considered that they 'were under some sort of moral obligation not to turn against her'. She had arrived in the country under the auspices of their armed forces, and had been 'encouraged in her belief (or rather not discouraged in her belief) that one day she would be sent out by British intelligence' to work for them in France. On the other hand, she was legally 'an undesirable alien', so internment had to be 'worthy of consideration' alongside cutting her loose to join the Free French or sending her back as a quadruple agent. Harmer's thoughtful memorandum summarised the complexity of dealing with a suspected blown agent in the double-cross world of mirrors, as well as highlighted the dangers for Mathilde.

*

She did at least have freedom in how she passed her days as discussions about her future came to a head: her dalliance with Llewellyn Lloyd continued; she gossiped with Herbert and Wotitski on the telephone in the mornings and went to clubs with them in the evenings. Her minders were 'creating the illusion that she was a free woman'. She regarded her residence in Mayfair as a saving to official funds, and realised that her 'sole chance of returning to France' and to espionage was to 'play [their] game to the full and to create a very good impression as far as the work' with her case officers was concerned, so that she would have 'personal as well as official reasons why she can be trusted'.

On 9th June, a high-level meeting took place in St James's Street with representation from SIS, including Dunderdale and Greene; Keswick and Buckmaster from SOE; and Dick White, Tar Robertson and Harmer from MI5. The first decision was to close down 'the Walenty transmitter' for good later in the month. It had come a long way since Mathilde and Gane had traversed a bog together in search of advice on how to make their radio work in early 1941. The cover of other B1a agents had held, so the next item on the agenda, the chillingly titled 'Disposal of Victoire', was a new procedure. Mathilde had had a change of heart and recently informed Harmer that if she were to be sent home, she 'would certainly be caught and shot' by her countrymen, so that ruled out the quadruple-agent possibility. The North African option she had floated earlier was also was taken off the table at SOE's request as they were still not concerned about information gleaned from de Vomécourt; for the same reason, they could not countenance her remaining 'in this country in complete liberty', which left being paid off to take her chances with the Free French or internment as the only possibilities.

The officers from the different services were divided, and savage in their criticism of Mathilde, particularly when Harmer ventured that 'she was writing a book' which she had told him would include 'an exposure of the malfeasances of SOE'. Dunderdale declared that unless they were 'prepared to liquidate Victoire altogether' it was best not to intern her as 'after the war' she would be able 'to do immense damage'; he would prefer to 'subscribe to giving her a present'. Keswick was too upset about the failure of the de Vomécourt mission and not inclined to celebrate his earlier exfiltration: he snapped that they were 'under no obligation to her' and that 'she was too dangerous to be allowed her liberty'. Dick White worried that if she were interned 'in an ordinary camp on the Isle of Man' there would still be 'much danger of leakage'; he was with SIS in paying her off, accompanied by the threat that if she spoke of her work in France or England she would be immediately interned. SOE retaliated that she knew too much even to take this risk.

Operational needs had to take priority, and it was agreed that if SOE submitted a written case for internment, MI5 would apply to the Home Office for an order. Dunderdale wanted it recorded that 'SIS had no primary reasons for wanting Victoire interned' before the meeting moved on to the last two items of the day, approval of her expenses and a *message personnel* 'to put her parents' mind at rest'. The childish message with its affectionate nickname is the more poignant for the discussion of liquidation, treachery and internment that preceded it: '*La petite Fee-Menouche va bien et embrasse son père et mère.*'

*

The case for Mathilde Carré's detention was a simple enough one when it came to it, and General Lakin, MI5 head of security, made his submission within three days. His first point was conclusive on its own: 'she admits to having collaborated with the Germans and to having been responsible for the arrest in France of various British or Allied agents'. Next came the days before her confession to de Vomécourt: 'while collaborating with the Germans she betrayed to them another British agent whom they did not arrest because they hoped by leaving him at liberty to arrest later the whole of his organisation'; and 'that she did not reveal to this man the fact that she was working for the Germans until taxed by him'. There was no mitigation offered for her work in getting him out of France, instead 'she had shown herself to be disgruntled' with SOE and 'has threatened to write a book exposing' the service. Lakin's final reason for the removal of her liberty was the card that could be played against her whatever the persuasive contrary evidence: 'there is great danger that at any moment, if this has not already happened, she might decide to work against the British' for unstated 'personal reasons'.

The last speculation aside, it was unarguable. Tar Robertson requested an 'amplified statement' before she was 'interviewed'. Its author, Captain A. H. Robertson, pulled no punches in his indictment of her character: she had not been 'entirely discreet' with Lord Selborne, and she could be 'a valuable agent' only if her 'appetite for luxury and lovers' could be satisfied. When he concluded that she was little better than 'an expensive nuisance', it added a dismissive coda to the watertight legal case, but one that could not countenance its object's human contradictions and vulnerabilities, and her strenuous, sometimes heroic, attempts to overcome those.

*

Mathilde's last two weeks were spent enjoying London oblivious to these deliberations. She dictated her memoirs to a French typist found by Wotitski, walked in Kew Gardens, lunched at Chez Victor and gossiped on Llewellyn Lloyd's telephone. When he wanted to go with her to the Ballets Russes, she offered to get the tickets but asked Wotitski to buy them instead as she was needed by her new '*famille*', MI5, in the morning, after which she was going to the cinema to see *Joan of Paris*. She might have hoped that the film, about five RAF pilots shot down over occupied France and their escape to England with the help of a brave barmaid who outwits the Gestapo, would strike noble chords with her story; but the following morning she was vociferous in her complaints to Anna Mayerson 'that the Americans and the British must be decadent to have made such a film'. She was eager to get hold of a copy of Antoine de Saint-Exupéry's memoir *Pilote de Guerre*,* his account of flying reconnaissance flights in May 1940 and nearly all his fellow pilots being killed 'like a few glasses of water' thrown 'into a vast burning forest', but did not report back whether either that or Maurice Baring's knotted Edwardian love story, *Daphne Adeane*, had more resonance for her.

Primarily through the well-connected Dr Herbert, she had a widening social circle, vetting of which still took up Bıa's time. There was a Hungarian painter of miniatures named Lengyel, who had befriended Mayerson in an air-raid shelter during the Blitz and was thought 'to be mixed up in a spy ring' but on closer inspection was deemed 'too timid and too much of a rat to undertake any sinister activities'. His relationship with Mathilde, the spies decided, was a 'normal social outcome'. Gaston Boudou was 'well known in French circles in London' and as he had 'previously been hairdresser to Queen Mary, and having acted in that capacity to many people in society to some of whom he appears to act as confidant',

---

* Later translated into English as *Flight to Arras*, the memoir was a huge bestseller in the United States in 1942, strengthening public opinion behind the war in Europe. It was nevertheless banned by the Free French as the generally apolitical author viewed General de Gaulle as self-seeking rather than interested in national unity.

he was not suspect. It was even feasible, they concluded, that she was introduced to him solely 'on account of his hairdressing activities'. Espionage now seemed far from her mind after the exhausting activity of the previous eighteen months; even her account of Interallié and her collaboration seemed like tales from a long-gone time. But the watch on her had to remain as the formalities to end this socialising were being drawn up.

*

Harmer prepared the paperwork for Colonel Hinchley-Cooke, legal adviser to MI5, in the last week of June. He was keen to stress that although the arrest would have 'collective responsibility' from the combined intelligence services, its impetus had come from SOE, 'while SIS and ourselves rather favour her'. The ambivalence the lawyer felt about the agreed course of action runs through his outline of her case: he did not believe that she had taken any money from Interallié funds for herself, as her detractors, including Włodarczyk, claimed; his tortured syntax gave away his conflicted feelings about his proposal when he wrote that 'one cannot say for certain that any given agent would not have been arrested' in the first days of her collaboration with Bleicher; 'her usefulness was at an end' only when they had told the Germans she was on her way back.

Hinchley-Cooke's final address to Mathilde Carré would state that she had 'come to this country as a person who had collaborated with the Germans', and had 'made mis-statements about the extent of her co-operation with them'. Most damningly, she had 'originally betrayed Lucas voluntarily' to Bleicher until the Frenchman 'taxed' her with her true allegiance. The crux of the case was that 'having once collaborated with the Germans, she can never be allowed again to go anywhere where she could possibly contact them' and thus 'her continued liberty in this country is too dangerous to be allowed'.

Harmer followed his distasteful task by handwriting a letter to her in French. He addressed her as 'My Dear Sister' and thanked

her for delivering the third part of her memoirs, about her time
with Bleicher, the day before. He had not managed to start reading
them, as they had arrived 'at a difficult moment'. He elided the
events of the past week when he said that he had just been to a
meeting at which it had been decided that his part in the business
of sending the messages and so on was nearly over, and he was
handing over that side of things to 'Robson', as A. H. Robertson
was known to her. He was going to be busy for the next few days,
and could not come to her flat for a cup of tea that afternoon. He
would also be unable to join her to celebrate her birthday, which
he 'sincerely regretted'. He would 'telephone her in a few days
when he was back' but would at least 'give her the necessary explanation' when he could. Things had been 'up in the air for him' over
the past few weeks and 'that was why he had to take some holiday'
now. Before offering his regrets about her 'soirée anniversaire' once
more and warmly signing off for the last time before she was
locked up, he left a heartfelt, open sentence hanging that perhaps
expressed his personal sadness at the outcome: 'It's the war, I
suppose.'

*

If Harmer sent his bunch of flowers on her birthday mainly out of
embarrassment, Llewellyn Lloyd and Dr Herbert were both genuinely out of town. Mathilde told Wotitiski when they dined together
that the day had been 'awful'. In the afternoon, Robertson had rung
her to say he would call for her at the Upper Brook Street flat the
following day at 4.45 p.m. without giving any reason. He took her
to the Embankment entrance of Scotland Yard where Hinchley-
Cooke met them, escorted her to an interview room, delivered his
address and informed her that she 'was to be interned for the duration of the war'. She was 'astonished and furious' as the police drove
her the fifty miles to Aylesbury Prison. An inmate there commented that she looked 'like a poor cat' in her bedraggled dejection
on arrival, far from Roman Czerniawski's 'Chatte' stalking about
her espionage business.

At the same moment, John Masterman was putting Llewellyn Lloyd in the picture. He suggested the captain ring his maid to tell her that his house guest had 'gone away' and that someone would be 'coming round to pack her things'. Llewellyn Lloyd himself was 'advised not to return to the flat until about 7 o'clock in the evening', which gave Susan Barton time to take an inventory as her last duty in the Victoire case. Items to be confiscated included 'a copy of the instructions given to Lucas before he left the country', copies of 'the various messages which have passed via the Walenty transmitter', the 'part of her book which relates to her association with Walenty', her diary containing the 'various events of last winter', any 'maps and documents ... which have reference to her collaboration', any letters from Greene or Harmer, and 'all her literary efforts and papers'. Harmer would also like his typewriter back. Everything connected to her life in France and her multiple wartime allegiances was deemed to belong to British intelligence.

Richard Llewellyn Lloyd took up residence in his own home again, and the following morning his batman was on the telephone to Fortnum & Mason to order a case of beer. The novelist enjoyed spinning tales about his conquest: a couple of weeks later a B1a secretary reported that she was regaled in the dentist's chair with tales of how important leaks had been traced to a brilliant spy who had worked for 'the British government for many years, previously in Syria' as well as for the Germans and the Vichy government; but now, thanks to the intrepid Welshman who had lured her into his confidence and his flat, the wicked Madame de Roche was in the Tower of London awaiting execution.

*

'I am neither in tears nor in a rage', Mathilde wrote to Harmer on her first day in prison, just after he had used her name to send the final signal to Paris that ironically ended 'Long live Liberty'. He had her 'story, truthfully told' in his hands, how she had 'risked everything' to 'save as much as she could' and yet she was now a criminal, no better off than Kieffer or Jouffret. She echoed his words of a few days earlier when she wrote, 'I suppose, as you do, that this is simply the war', but was still stunned by the injustice. She wanted only to help the British from 'Richard's flat', but if her services were no longer required, she could perhaps put her prejudices aside and restart her service to her country as a nurse for the Free French. Harmer would understand that if she stayed where she was, she would, 'to put it simply, die one evening'. Mathilde ended her letter 'affectionately' thanking Harmer for her birthday flowers and, 'above all', for their 'beautiful fraternal friendship'. Her life had pivoted again, but this time there seemed to be nowhere else to turn, or be turned.

16

Two Prisoners and a Breakout

Mathilde was 'behaving like a little angel' a week after she was 'safely installed at Aylesbury' and Harmer accepted that her letter to him was 'written more in sorrow than in anger'. Her corrupting influence of boredom was ever-present: she had spent the past two years involved in great causes and the inactivity of prison life was a constant threat to her equilibrium. Her mind retreated to her days of undivided work for France, and to the adventures she had shared with Roman Czerniawski and Pierre de Vomécourt, two undoubted patriots, men judged by other men, whose futures were shortly to change. One of them would re-enter the war, with some alarming missteps along the way; the other would leave it with his honour intact. Both would have another role in the life of their former comrade.

*

The spies remained uncomfortable about Mathilde's treatment. She was interned under a Home Office Detention Order 12(5A), covering 'non-enemy aliens' rather than for any of her collaborative actions. Dunderdale asked for it to be put on the record that SIS had 'no primary reasons' for wanting her locked up at all, and Dick White had approved the request 'not without reluctance'. SOE took responsibility: they were keen to protect anything that remained of de Vomécourt's network, including his brothers, and regarded it as 'most important ... that she should be under maximum control until the end of the war'. Harmer was most of all worried about the repercussions that would visit them when she encountered the company she would be keeping.

Stella Lonsdale, the only other inmate held under 12(5A), was the wife of the 'Mayfair Playboy' John Lonsdale, a member of a gang of thieves led by the Marquess of Bristol. She had been visiting her French mother-in-law at the time of the Armistice, teaching English at the Berlitz school in Nantes while registering daily with the occupiers. Her garbled claim was that a German intelligence officer had suggested she get herself to England from Marseilles to pave the way for him to discuss a peace plan; she had intended to go to MI9, British intelligence's escape and evasion arm, to tell all, but was rumbled and had to flee to Britain. MI5 could establish no evidence of whether she was an Abwehr agent, but her various excuses about why she was carrying plans of fuel depots when she was apprehended were suspicious enough to get her locked up. Mathilde felt Stella Lonsdale was 'rather trying' as 'a third party in one's affairs', and did not mix with the others as she could not bear the 'foolish and malicious gossip'.

The other women were all being held under Defence Regulation 18B, deemed Nazi sympathisers. In this category were the 'moribund' Duchesse de Château-Thierry who had presided over a fashionable Eaton Square salon that fronted for an Abwehr recruitment organisation; her servant My Erikssen, later swapped for an SIS agent held in her native Stockholm; and Mathilde Krafft, the German-born widow of a wealthy English coconut planter in Fiji who had most recently been the housekeeper for a naval officer on the south coast and was suspected of distributing Abwehr funds in England.

Mathilde was well treated by the governor, Miss Mellanby, to begin with but their relationship changed when she wrote a letter to the Home Office requesting French books and an English grammar and Mellanby brought her some titles in Spanish and others suitable only 'for young children or kitchen maids'. She was given extra ration coupons to acquire new underclothes, of which she was 'in bad need'. It was eventually agreed that she could have her 'literary effects which do not relate to confidential work', letters and cards which had nothing to do with the intelligence services, her cigarettes and chewing gum, her medicines (once they had been tested by MI5's scientific section to check they were 'not useful for secret writing'), and her 'photographs of Lucas'. 'In view of the good work Victoire has done for us in the past' and as a salve to official consciences, her salary continued to be paid and she was encouraged to complete her memoirs to amuse herself.

After a week on the Special Wing, Mathilde wrote to General Legentilhomme, commander of the Free French Forces in Africa, that her work for Bleicher had been planned 'to save the maximum' number of lives and 'to do the Germans the maximum of harm'. She claimed she would never 'have betrayed a Frenchman or an Englishman', and professed her 'absolute loyalty and devotion and an honesty which [the British] cannot find very often'. She begged the general to get her released so that she could return to nursing. The letter was not sent on, and Harmer tried to get her to understand that it would 'be hypocrisy to pretend that the high-ups who made the decision' to intern her would change their minds; he implored her to make the best of her situation. On the same day, Buckmaster, noticeably failing to acknowledge that she had managed to bring one of his brightest stars to London, thanked Harmer for 'the wind-up of a troublesome affair which has only had the merit of causing us to exercise our brains in concert'.

On Harmer's next visit, he found 'a very changed woman' from two weeks earlier. She found it 'hard that she was shut up with a collection of Nazi women' who fell with glee on any newspaper item which could be interpreted as 'indicating any weakening of morale in this country'. She wanted a 'proper hearing', was even prepared to serve 'a definite sentence' rather than exist in this limbo, and swore she would be totally discreet if she could 'be granted her liberty and allowed to work'.

He was moved by her misery and floated the idea in Whitehall that now she had 'experienced the unpleasantness of prison life' she might be trusted to work under the threat of reincarceration as 'the dire consequence of possible indiscretions'; she had 'learnt her lesson and will be very careful not to give offence in the future'. It was an appeal that stood no chance of success. Tar Robertson was writing a memorandum to the Twenty Committee that boasted his unit now had 'in MI5 double agents, a powerful means of exercising influence over the OKW*' that same month.

By the early autumn, Mathilde was baffled. She was unable to understand why she had recently been so well treated yet now she was being 'literally buried alive … consigned to this dungeon'. She had no notion why she was considered 'dangerous' or, her worst fear, 'useless'. She begged MI5 'to employ me in whatever manner you please instead of leaving me here', but she was a largely forgotten distraction.

*

Pierre de Vomécourt was informed that his trial would take place in December. Few lawyers wanted to come up against the occupiers in such a high-profile trial: the first turned Madame de Vomécourt down as it was 'a quite hopeless case'; the second passed it to his secretary to handle, who in turn 'did very badly', not even finding out the court date until it was almost too late and then informing her client that it was likely 'the sentence would be the death penalty'. In the end, de Vomécourt took charge of his own defence.

He and Fincken were brought out of their cells on 7th December and the proceedings got under way with the prosecutor's statement that the men had lied to the Gestapo when arrested. De Vomécourt demanded to be seen alone, and 'took this opportunity to protest that they had been promised on the word of honour of a German officer that if they told all they knew, they would be treated as prisoners of war'. To his astonishment, he 'was told that he had kept his side of the bargain' and as the Gestapo appeared to have no evidence against him, that aspect of the case would be dropped. De

---

* Oberkommando der Wehrmacht, the High Command of the German armed forces.

Vomécourt drove home his advantage to say that 'it would make a very bad impression in France when it became known that the word of a German officer had been broken', that his 'wife knew of the bargain' and had informed 'several prominent people' of it. The prosecutor referred the case to the 'general in charge of the Paris region' who said the word of an officer must be kept, ignoring that Bleicher was neither commissioned nor 'was empowered to give them' such a 'guarantee'.

After that, the trial proceeded 'in a very amusing way' to its main defendant. He was 'given a chair at the back' and asked to clarify various points, and 'in this way ... was able to cover up many slips by his friends'. The only tricky moment was when the peasant farmer from Vaas who had agreed to bury the dropped containers 'persisted in denying everything'. De Vomécourt had 'fabricated a story about black-market goods' to explain the farmer's presence at the aborted drop, but the farmer had been briefed by the lawyer to repeat that they must be talking to the wrong man, probably 'another farmer of the same name'. As the whole case revolved around *marchandises*, by which Autogiro meant arms but could equally well denote illicit foodstuffs, this was problematic. Somehow, de Vomécourt got himself 'a private interview' with the peasant and persuaded him that he had seen black-market goods after all. On his return to court, the farmer 'covered up his slip by saying Bleicher had interpreted the word "*marchandises*" in the way he wanted, when it in fact meant just what it said'.

The prosecutor commented in his closing speech that 'it was a very good thing' that de Vomécourt had 'mentioned his wife and the very bad impression that would be made in France' if Bleicher's word had been broken. The accused were sentenced to serve out the war as prisoners and returned to Fresnes. They were fortunate that the occupiers cared enough about their image before the Resistance and SOE were more of a menace that an irritant, and leniency became in short supply. In 1943 Pierre de Vomécourt was moved to Germany, and eventually on to Colditz Castle. Although his war was over, he had one final, and crucial, appearance to make in Mathilde Carré's life.

*

Just as one of Mathilde's wartime lovers was preparing for trial in Paris, another, Roman Czerniawski, appeared in Britain on 2nd October 1942. He had spent nearly a year without visitors in his cell in Fresnes contemplating, as his British colleagues put it, that 'a firing squad did not fit in with his grandiose and dramatic ideas of his own destiny' and that he needed to find a way back into the action. Like his former chief of staff, he would be assumed by the Germans to be their double agent in the heart of the enemy's camp, but with the difference that he had fuller control of whom and how he would serve on his way to becoming one of the Double Cross's most 'outstandingly successful' members. The manner of this achievement was remarkable, if not without its missteps and ambiguities, and the contrast with Mathilde's own attempts to work in London shines a light on the national, sexual and moral inconsistencies of the war.

Renée Borni's visit to Roman in November 1941 had been Bleicher's idea. At that point, Roman was considering suicide as he was 'afraid of interrogation "by force"', but Borni's 'assurance that the Germans were very anxious to win [him] over' and the questionnaire he had half-filled in after she had gone gave him pause for thought. He devoted the next few months in solitary confinement to 'plot-hatching, his favourite activity', and came up with something so bold that it could only have emerged from the imagination that had conceived of Interallié.

On 29th November, Roman asked for a letter to be delivered to General Stulpnägel. If the Germans were 'planning the reconstruction of the rights' of Poland after their victory, then he would consider talking to an officer of suitable rank if 'I was convinced I was working for the good of the Polish nation'. It was nothing less than an offer to collaborate, dressed up as if it was a German idea to recruit him.

The following day, Colonel Oskar Reile, the commandant of Abwehr IIIF whose manicured fingernails made Roman surmise that he was not a soldier who spent much time in the field, appeared in his cell with Major Ische, and delivered a torrent of propaganda designed to appeal both to the prisoner's patriotism and his vanity. Reile claimed that his government wanted to work in 'co-operation' with Poland, and that Roman could 'contribute to our programme to advance Europe by several centuries in one leap'. Better to unshackle from both 'capitalist-Jewish England' and 'Communist-Bolshevik Russia' and 'to come under the cultural protection of Germany, since German culture is preferable to barbarian culture'. He was the man who could 'raise the Polish nation on the side of Germany'.

Roman next suggested that he was 'prepared to discuss placing [himself] at the disposal of Germany while at the same time being of use to my country'. If he was got to Britain, he would start to send back information about armaments and aircraft production, troop movements and all 'preparations for, and the possibilities of, a second front'. He demanded that the captured Interallié agents were spared their lives and would be set free. Moreover, that 'Germany would, after winning the war, assist his country and people in a manner commensurate with the valuable work' he would now be undertaking as he prepared 'a fifth column' to be activated as soon as 'Germany attacks England'. He would mobilise 'the Polish *milieu* in London' to 'rise up against the English'.

Reile was convinced by Roman's sincerity, and the improbable scheme was approved by the head of the Abwehr, Admiral Canaris. A few months later, four weeks after Mathilde had been locked up, Roman (code-named 'Hubert') was taken from Fresnes by Propst and Tritche, driven into central Paris, which was clogged by an SS parade, and let go. If questioned, he was to say that he had taken advantage of the car's frequent stops to knock out the guards, roll out of the door and run.

He went to a flat where Ische gave him 10,000 francs, a false identity card, food ration coupons and a tablet of chocolate. He was allowed to send Renée Borni a letter saying that he had escaped from hospital after 'he had surprised the doctor by making a surprise recovery from illness'. This 'escape' was to become one of Roman's many legends. He made the most of his first afternoon of freedom with a haircut and a shave in the rue Pigalle followed by an early dinner in a Russian restaurant on the rue des Acacias before collapsing, exhausted by liberty and his creativity, in a hotel on the Left Bank.

The following morning, he was only 'able to talk with the greatest difficulty', but his spycraft came back to him as he bought some soap, books and a suitcase to 'to make the hotel people' think he was 'a genuine traveller'. He had a hearty lunch before meeting Reile to be given his final instructions, his codes and wireless crystals so that he could build a transmitter in London. He was told to go to the unoccupied zone and find a Polish underground organisation which could get him smuggled to Britain. Kieffer, Gorriot and Jouffret were all active on the Abwehr's behalf in the south and were instructed to trail their former leader without being seen in the hope that he might lead them to another network they could take down afterwards. Hugo Bleicher would also be close by at all times. The lowly military policeman of two years earlier was now regarded as 'a specialist in running double agents' in Berlin, Paris and London, rightly held in the utmost respect by his counterparts in MI5 as 'a man of great ability and ingenuity' as well as one of 'great personal ambition'.

Bleicher took Suzanne Laurent with him for some August tourism in the Rhone Valley at the end of which he met Roman in the toilets of the Brasserie Georges, Lyons. The Pole, who had already been there for two weeks compensating for the deprivations of Fresnes by eating 'enormous quantities' of Chinese food, told him that he was on his way to Aix-les-Bains in the Alps to await further instructions. Bleicher took the unusual step of forcing Roman to sign a contract that acknowledged that he was 'starting to work for the National Socialist State in a military capacity', with the added threat that 'if he failed in his duty the Germans would be entitled to take reprisals' against his family. He and Suzanne Laurent then whisked off to the Hôtel Terminus in Aix.

On their next encounter, Bleicher was 'much more interested in seeing the scenery and very pleased he was having a holiday at the expense of his organisation'. Roman suggested that he visit

Chamonix as they might be in Aix for a while, but then had to retract this advice as he was ordered to Toulouse. Bleicher and Suzanne hurried after him and put up at the Grand Hôtel d'Orléans. The morning after their arrival, a note arrived saying that Roman was off again, asking Bleicher to 'give his regards to everybody', and signed off 'Long Live Hitler, the Great Builder of a New Europe.' Bleicher, who had at least been promoted to sergeant 'as a result of this affair', stayed on in the hotel long enough for Suzanne to get 'a banal postcard with greetings' from Roman in Madrid and later another from Gibraltar saying that Roman was going to see his 'parents', code for London. He did not tell Bleicher that he had 'met by accident' Monique Deschamps, Fernand Gane and another Interallié agent on Gibraltar, and that they would be following him by sea.

*

Roman's account of his 'amazing' escape reconfirmed his status to his exiled countrymen in London as a 'super-spy', although the more hard-headed British, not told of his offer to collaborate, suspected him of 'romancing' when they heard the detail. Once again, they had to decide how far they could trust an agent who had spent time in German custody when their rule book said not at all. In his debriefing, Roman did down his former partner to say 'her guilt is the greater since, although she must have fully realised the extent of the catastrophe, she helped the Germans in their work'. He did not mention that he too had arrived under the auspices of the Abwehr. He was given a desk job by the Poles and a flat in Redcliffe Square, Chelsea, where he was joined by Monique Deschamps. Fernand Gane seems to have taken his dismissal from her bed well enough and earned the high praise from Harmer that he 'appears to have a very balanced disposition for a Frenchman'.

Roman chose to wait five weeks before he dropped 'the bombshell'. He took a sixty-four-page document called *The Great Game* to Colonel Gano in which he told the truth about his recruitment and faked escape, excusing the fantasy version as 'a carefully worked-out plan to fool the Germans' in case they had spies around any of the London intelligence agencies. He admitted that he had whipped up this narrative as 'too sensational'. He produced Reile's wireless crystals, which had been hidden in the heels of his shoes, as good faith, and made his offer to be a triple agent before his grandiloquent finish: 'If I have acted wrong in organising the Great Game, the news that I have perished in an air accident will save my family and my colleagues' from the knowledge that he had shot himself with a revolver if he was 'found to have failed in his military duty'.

Gano was livid. Roman had lied to his superiors and made Polish intelligence look foolish. His plea that 'the pretence' which he 'had been forced to keep up' over the past few weeks 'was exceptionally difficult and unpleasant' was ludicrous. He had clearly been weighing up which side to support. Gano ordered the man he now regarded as a 'sinister individual' to return to Redcliffe Square and hurried to discuss the case with Tar Robertson. If B1a did not believe or could not use Czerniawski, he too would have to be locked up.

Christopher Harmer spent days interrogating Roman and concluded that 'there are considerable doubts about his integrity'. He found 'the circumstances' of the escape and arrival 'somewhat curious'. He had withheld a great deal, significantly that he had offered himself up to the Abwehr as a spy rather than been actively recruited. He had waited over a month before pledging himself and his crystals to the Allies, which meant he had almost certainly been hedging his bets. What saved Roman was that behind his 'intensely dramatic and egotistical nature' (partly the result of his lack of height, they thought) lay his loyalty, which was 'entirely to his own country'. Harmer was for employing him and cited his 'very great service' with Interallié, but met many of the same objections as had been thrown at Mathilde: mainly, as MI5's John Marriott put it, that they could never 'tolerate any person who has worked for our service agreeing in any circumstances to work for the Germans'.

In the end, Harmer's psychological and strategic assessment of Roman prevailed where he had failed with Mathilde, and he came up with the Pole's most lasting code name: 'Roman Czerniawski had been turned by the Germans, and then re-turned by us, so I thought, "*Et tu, Brute?*"' Harmer ruminated on his 'very brave mission in Paris during the first year of the Occupation when most people thought Germany would win the war, so I thought of Brutus's final speech from *Julius Caesar* which begins "He was the noblest Roman of them all."' The newest recruit to Double Cross was given the elevated identity of 'Brutus' as a literary pun, and was on his way to becoming one of their most influential agents. Roman wrote excitedly to Harmer that 'the NEW GAME is beginning'.

Brutus joined Agents Tricycle and Garbo as double agents run by B1a, although he later regarded Garbo with 'disdain' as he lacked purity of motivation in being paid for his work. Just after Roman's recruitment, Harmer also intervened in the case of Elvira de la Fuente Chaudoir: Masterman 'did not want a woman on the team' and pointed out that 'an indiscreet, cash-strapped "Lesbian" with a gambling habit represented a serious security risk'; but Harmer's observations that she was truthful, and that as 'a typical member of the cosmopolitan smart set' would be ideally placed to report back to Berlin 'all sorts of misleading political and social gossip from the gaming tables and salons of London', won the day. Once again, he was deft in his code-naming when he dubbed her Agent Bronx after a 'rum-based cocktail' served in the Hyde Park Hotel.

These new signings were made as Mathilde Carré had been railing against being 'useless' in her 'dungeon' for five months. She put herself on a brief hunger strike in November and was moved to the hospital wing where she was restored with milk and soda. Had she known of Roman's arrival and status, she would have been justified in becoming even more upset by her own situation. The cardinal rule about not using someone who had been a German prisoner seemed to have been bent in his favour because, whatever his intention on his release and in the weeks before he offered his services, he had not actively betrayed anyone in France; because he was Polish and therefore able to claim patriotism without the complex nuances of living as a French civilian in the occupied zone; because he had not been involved with an operation that failed; because he displayed his characteristic self-confidence; and because he was a man who furthermore had not slept with his German controller. Harmer must have been grateful not to explain any of this to Mathilde.

*

Masterman and his team were faced with a dilemma common to double-cross operations, but especially 'ominous' in this case: even if they were confident of 'Brutus and his motives', could they be equally 'sure that the Germans really trusted him'? They would be naïve if they did not contemplate that he had been turned and that his escape was a ruse, as indeed had been the plan. Masterman could understand that they 'might well feel that his loyalty to German interests might not be proof against British propaganda' and the Twenty Committee decided that he 'should not be used for operational deception' for now, rather a close watch be maintained and his telephone bugged. They were braced for the possibility that he might have to join Mathilde under lock and key if his period as a 'sleeper' did not work out, but meantime they built a transmitter using the crystals excavated from his shoes and set about arranging a closely supervised triple-cross. Harmless information about Polish troops in England were sent to establish Roman's credentials, before he went late in the year to the south coast with Harmer and Hugh Astor to report deployments which the Germans found 'exceedingly good'. He had still never fully grasped the French language and soon established his own voice on the airwaves, 'with very distinctive faults'.

Roman had told Reile that 'several of my old agents' were very 'discontented' thanks to their treatment by the British but were still 'bound' to him 'by intense personal loyalty' and would work for him 'without question'. He even suggested that the Germans might want to offer peace terms to the Polish government through him. His honesty was tested by both his masters: the Abwehr asked questions such as his mother's date and place of birth; Astor tricked him into addressing some envelopes as he was worried that the misspellings in the transmissions were a signal to the Germans that he was not operating freely, but was reassured when the errors were repeated by hand.

Roman read Mathilde's *Mémoires* and damned her for her collaboration, made all the worse in his view by the fact that 'she was completely at one with the Organisation ideologically and [they] had organised it together'. But he admitted that her account was 'on the whole true'. He was disappointed that she did not dwell more on his brilliance in 'essential matters such as the evolution of our methods of work ... the training of agents and our development, the way in which we traced the organisation of the German army and the distribution of its units', to conclude 'her guilt ... consists chiefly in having facilitated to the Germans the quick arrest of other and numerous agents'.

He was at last able to 'solve' Kieffer's arrest, and was surprised, perhaps saddened, that it was 'after all due to an ordinary denunciation lodged against him with the police dictated by personal spite' that his Big Network had suffered 'catastrophe'. The Germans had 'no right to be proud' of their counter-intelligence methods, and had 'lost the game as soon as La Chatte got to England'. He did not offer a word of praise for her escape or mention its more heroic cast than his own, but reckoned that now he too had arrived, the enemy was 'entering the final stage of losing the game'. It was his confident 'ambition to conclude this affair in grand style'.

Both Roman and Bia knew 'it would look rather peculiar' not to mention Mathilde to the Abwehr, but had to work out a form of words that would convince them that even if she had been blown, 'Hubert' was still their loyal agent. Tar Robertson concocted a message for him to send in January 1943 that said nothing the Germans had not already surmised: 'For some time [La Chatte] was seen in London but always accompanied by somebody. She is now held somewhere by the British.' Roman reported that he had 'found a great disinclination to talk about her' but the Germans 'ought to assume she has told everything'. Robertson's most creative flourish was to add that Czerniawski thought 'it is possible that they may contemplate sending her back to France to try to secure the release of Lucas' as 'the British appear to be worried by lack of news of him'. Robertson had no idea that de Vomécourt's honourable court martial had already taken place and hoped that by these additions 'there is just a possibility that the Germans may think it is worthwhile keeping Lucas alive to recapture Victoire with or without a large sum of money in her possession'.

*

Mathilde was a continuing source of aggravation and guilt to the British at the same time as her traces were being eradicated. She petitioned the Home Secretary to be released, but was rebuffed before her letter reached the Home Office. She continued to write to Hinchley-Cooke, contrasting her period in London 'when I was shown so much admiration' and 'wished so much happiness' with this miserable existence as the only one of her fellow detainees 'who has neither family nor friends in England'. She was 'a lemon squeezed to the last drop', pleading that if England was at war 'for justice, truth and liberty', she should be shown some of those virtues.

These outpourings hastened a visit from Harmer, who managed once again to shore her up by praising her outstanding work and importance for the Allies. Miss Mellanby reported her charge 'appreciably more cheerful' afterwards. Harmer tried to contact her brother Pierre, now a lieutenant in the Régiment Tirailleurs Algériens, 'principally to keep her quiet' and hoping for 'credit' even though he could find 'no trace of him'.

Mathilde was allowed luxuries such as soap as well as some new clothing. She had extra food ration coupons, and an allowance of ten shillings per week on top of the £58 she possessed on her arrival in Aylesbury, the remains of the SOE cash given to her by Hugo Bleicher. She even found herself accepting that she had entered the 'settled life of an indeterminate period'. But she craved the contacts of her few friends, including Dr Herbert. Her teeth had always been 'slack', as she put it, and the Double Cross team would only pay for 'vulcanite denture implants' rather than gold. She asked for Herbert to examine her self-diagnosed rheumatism, anaemia, weak heart, and 'violent migraines', and his arrival gave her such a boost that the prison authorities asked him if he could 'visit her again, as a friend', but MI5 blocked that and the pair never met again. She wrote to Inspector Gale, her *'Ange Gardien'*, begging him to visit, but received no answer.

She and her four companions on the special wing were moved to the sprawling, castellated Holloway Prison in north London in July 1943. The former *saloniste* Château-Thierry wrote to a friend 'in a way which indicates that she is almost as pleased as if we had given her a suite in Claridge's', and Stella Lonsdale and My Erikssen 'exhibited nothing but the highest praise for their new quarters', MI5 reported. But Mathilde did not share their enthusiasm and dubbed 'the extension' of Holloway 'the House of the Dead', describing it as 'an old house, partly covered with Virginia creeper, dilapidated, rickety and horribly sad' in the grounds between the mortuary and the graveyard for the executed.

Even though MI5 found 'no evidence' that she had 'made any effort to communicate vital information through the medium of any of her fellow internees' and 'she could not now do serious harm' anyway, she was appalled to be once more placed with Nazi sympathisers. She lived in the married couples' wing recently vacated by the leader of the British Union of Fascists, Sir Oswald Mosley, and his wife Diana Mitford, where her neighbours included Christabel Nicholson, who had been charged under the Official Secrets Act after being found in possession of a document from the US Embassy, and Magdalena Colledge, a skating champion who was reported to be 'violently pro-German'.

A letter from 'a keen fascist' to a friend who regarded 'the war as a fight between the Powers of Light (The Nazis) and the Powers of Darkness (The Jew-Controlled Bolshevik democracies)' was brought to Harmer's attention by the censor. The 'keen fascist', who had just shared a cake she had been given with the duchess and Stella Lonsdale, soon aired her resentments about the 'alien' Mathilde who was 'a protégée of the W[ar] O[ffice]' and who was 'receiving benefits in cash and kind' from the government, if that was not just her 'yarn'. When the writer was interviewed, she confirmed that 'the statement about the money, lingerie and dentist's bills' had been made to her directly by Mathilde. She could not understand why this person who was not an '18B' was in with them, and assumed that she had been infiltrated to 'spy on us'. There was a rumour that she had a ring with 'enough poison to kill six people' supplied by the War Office. If 'the whole business' was 'most distasteful' to the other inmates, it was profoundly uncomfortable for Mathilde neither to be believed nor allowed to stand apart. She requested a transfer to the Isle of Man, but once more heard nothing back.

*

Roman was working to restore his good name, and Robertson sought evidence from 'Most Secret Sources', as the German intercepts deciphered at Bletchley Park were known, for 'evidence that he is fully trusted ... in which case he would be eligible for use in deception'. The answer came that the Abwehr reports on 'Agent Hubert' contained 'no qualification to suggest that the source was not a genuine one' and he was regarded as a 'very valuable wireless agent'. Masterman now agreed he was 'the best placed of all our agents for sending over military information', and 'as confidence grew both in him and the Germans' belief in him', he was to be used 'more and more'.

But Roman nearly sabotaged his new career before he was unleashed. Flush with his own importance, he 'threw his weight around and gave himself airs' with his countrymen until he was 'at loggerheads with all the other officers'. Harmer observed that he was 'a vain and conceited man who spent a considerable period of the war in exciting activities and now found himself doing a largely academic job' without the stimulation of constant jeopardy. Roman even suggested setting up a new intelligence network in Britain with his lover Monique Deschamps as his first recruit, and was 'hurt' when Harmer quashed the idea on the grounds that it would be 'courting disaster' for him to 'recruit subagents to work for the

Germans'. That was their job. The irritable Colonel Gano was keen that this 'infernal nuisance' be sent to the Middle East to stop him being 'inordinately ambitious, prying into everything' and 'making very damaging criticisms of other people's work'.

Roman's 'boundless capacity for intrigue' soon found a target. In April and May of 1940, as many as 14,000 Polish officers and intelligentsia had been taken out of Soviet prisons, massacred and buried in mass graves on NKVD chief Lavrentiy Beria's orders. Three years later, the bodies were discovered and the world heard of the Katyn Massacre; shortly after that, the inspector general of the Polish air force, General Stanislas Ujejski, attended a reception at the Soviet Embassy in London to mark the Red Army's twenty-fifth anniversary. Roman was incensed at this 'cosying up to a murderous regime' and in June 1943 published a blistering attack on the general called *In Defence of Our Colleagues*. He ran off several hundred copies of his pamphlet relating 'the latest crisis in our internal relations as well as in our international politics' and insisted that Ujejski be sacked as it was 'unworthy for the head of the Polish air force to go to a tea party where they danced on the newly made graves of many Polish soldiers'. Scotland Yard immediately arrested Roman on a charge of 'the gravest military indiscipline'.

Harmer rushed to his latest troublesome charge's cell to find him unrepentant, and was faced with the urgent problem of how to pass this off to the Germans to preserve the Brutus operational cover. If MI5 sprung him and the Germans got to hear about the affair, it would trigger a disastrous lack of trust in the other Double Cross agents. Harmer came up with a transmission which he somewhat wearily presented for approval to Masterman and Robertson as 'a bit long-winded, but [Brutus] is in any event long-winded' and yet was close enough to the truth to let them off the hook with the Abwehr:

20th June arrested in the clandestine anti-Russian affair. Detained in Scotland ... Await trial in September. Foresee light punishment and probably after the war. Fear I am being watched at present. Until the end of the trial too dangerous to transmit but could write if you gave me immediately an address in Lisbon and the best method of secret ink … I regret difficulties. Morale good. Am hopeful. Greetings.

Roman apologised 'for the harm he had done the Great Game' when his court martial came around in August. He was found guilty of gross insubordination and sentenced to two months' imprisonment, postponed until after the war. He 'declined' to promise to Harmer that 'he will not interfere in Polish internal affairs', and left his handler wondering 'whether the Germans will ever accept Brutus as one hundred per cent reliable'. But the fiction had to be maintained, and Harmer hoped that the looming invasion of France would 'become sufficiently exciting to occupy his thoughts'.

Roman's first act on his release was to ask Deschamps to marry him. She was surprised by this 'most unorthodox proposal', but told MI5 that 'you must remember he is a super-man, and supermen are always eccentric'. For security reasons, he was not allowed to tell Renée Borni, whom he believed 'was still in love with him', of his marriage. In stark contrast to Roman's romantic liberty, his former colleague Mathilde remained 'alone and defenceless' a few miles away with no freedom in prospect and no allies working to keep her in the war.

17

Fortitude and Frustration

Between Mathilde's incarceration and Czerniawski's court martial in the late summer of 1943, the balance of the war had tipped towards the Allies. Germany had been defeated at Stalingrad in November 1942, the Axis powers had surrendered in North Africa in May 1943, Sicily had been taken in August as the Allies fought in Europe for the first time since 1940, and Italy surrendered in September, although the fighting there continued. Maurice Carré was killed during an enemy counter-attack whilst commanding a company of the 1st/4th Tunisians at the Battle of Monte Cassino in the snowbound January of 1944. He was recommended for the highest rank in the Légion d'Honneur for his courage.

The Tehran Conference between Churchill, Roosevelt and Stalin in November 1943 finalised the second front in Europe to set up a pincer movement on Germany. Secret deception campaigns on a scale unseen in history would be needed to enable this to succeed, and Roman Czerniawski was a key player in the Double Cross team's strategy. He was now married and living freely in Chelsea, his path into espionage legend assured. Apart from the fact that both had been authorised to leave France by the Abwehr, his and Mathilde's situations could not have been more different as Agent Brutus began to perform his greatest work, and Agent Victoire languished in misery. The end of the war was in sight for them both, but for her the prospect of peace held the potential for catastrophe.

*

The final report on Mathilde had been signed off in March 1943. Harmer summarised the 'valuable insight into the methods employed by the Germans' that it offered, as well as noting that the Abwehr allowed their recruits 'a very large amount of liberty', even, as he understatedly put it, 'to the extent of making them personal friends'. Although they had shown 'great imagination' in coming up with the double-cross of both Mathilde and Roman, 'in detail they were very slovenly', most obviously in failing to prepare 'Victoire's cover story in this country with any care'. Harmer highlighted a crucial difference between his own successful outfit and the Abwehr: they were 'playing for results rather than safety' at a time when B1a were achieving both and about to pull off their greatest coup.

Hitler's Führer Directive No. 40 of March 1942 had ordered the construction of an *Atlantikwall* of concrete fortresses, pillboxes, massive artillery batteries and mortars, and tens of thousands of troops around the coast of France, Holland and Scandinavia. It was crucial that the eventual Allied invasion did not smash against the Wall, and to that end enough uncertainty would have to be sown to ensure as many troops as possible were moved away from the Normandy landing sites. Operation Fortitude was conjured up to trap the Wehrmacht into the belief that when the invasion came the landings would be around the Pas de Calais at the shortest crossing point of the English Channel; it was credited by no less an espionage expert than Kim Philby as 'one of the most creative intelligence operations of all time'. The physical deception involved dummy landing craft, rubber and cardboard tanks scattered along the coast of Kent and huge orders for Michelin maps of the Calais region; technical deception took the form of 'great waves of radio traffic, a blizzard of electronic noise mimicking great armies training and assembling' and right at its very centre was Tar Robertson's team of double agents, notably Roman Czerniawski. Only spies trusted to the utmost by both sides could be used for the delicate edifice to succeed, and B1a were relieved that Bletchley intercepts indicated that the Germans still believed in 'Hubert'. Any earlier doubts about his loyalty had been forgotten, just as the existence of Mathilde Carré had left nearly all their minds.

A massive and entirely fictitious fighting body was created: the 1st US Army Group (FUSAG) consisted of the 1st Canadian Army (II Canadian Corps and VIII United States Corps), the United States 3rd Army (XX Corps and XII Corps), with support from the US 9th Air Force. This phantom military behemoth was commanded by the colourful, hard-driving General Patton, and was larger than Montgomery's 21st Army Group in Operation Overlord, the real landings that were planned for Normandy. FUSAG's task was to be a threat to the Calais region, and remain so even after D-Day to keep German reserves pinned down; Roman's role was to tell the Abwehr about this vast secret army.

He reported first from Scotland on FUSAG's order of battle, including made-up naval exercises on Loch Fyne and soldiers in Arctic uniform preparing for landings in Norway. He went to Staines in Middlesex to a new section formed to recruit the numerous Poles working in the coalfields east of Calais who would join the army immediately after the Allies had landed. On 9th May 1944, he reported airborne troops congregating in Lincolnshire, and 4th US Army Division and XX Corps in Bury St Edmunds, Suffolk, drawing attention to East Anglia rather than the vast mobilisation further west. He impressed 'that FUSAG is liable to attack across the Channel at any moment' to ensure that 'any airborne raid undertaken by the Germans is carried out at [British intelligence's] dictation'. Even as the real troops fought their way on to the Normandy beaches on 6th June, he was transmitting that he was 'very surprised that the army groups ... are attacking separately' and that 'a number of American officers have arrived at Wentworth' in Surrey supposedly to start co-ordinating the next stage of the landings in north-east France.

No agent could ever be given the full nuanced plans of an operation on this scale for security reasons, and FUSAG detail was rationed to Roman to prevent him 'learning too much'. Yet he was sufficiently valued even after D-Day that when a V-1 'doodlebug' flying bomb damaged his flat and cut Monique's face in July 1944,

B1a offered to pay the pioneering plastic surgeon Archie McIndoe's fees and upgraded Roman's accommodation to Hill Street, Mayfair, a couple of blocks from Llewellyn Lloyd's flat.

By then, Patton was in France with his own 3rd Army, and the Germans might justifiably have begun to question the existence of FUSAG, so it was dissolved; the non-existent troops in the south of England on which Roman 'spied' became known as 12th American Army Group, under the command of General Omar Bradley, and the Wehrmacht's 15th Army remained poised to defend the Pas de Calais until the early autumn as a result. Throughout his work as Brutus, Roman shored up his cover by demanding money from the Abwehr, even remembering to request a new Leica camera to replace the one they had seized from his office in the rue Villa Léandre. The ingenious minds at B1a came up with a proposal for the resulting fabricated photographs: they would be sent to the Abwehr concealed in the shafts of second-hand golf clubs sent care of a 'French official' planted in the Hôtel Splendide, Lisbon. Golf clubs were ideal as they would only be 'subject to cursory examination by Customs and Excise authorities to see whether they concealed contraband such as whisky' and any more thorough investigation would expose the films.

*

It was Hugh Astor who came up with the golf-club wheeze, as by that time Christopher Harmer had been in Europe for four months as a major in 21st Army Group, remaining there until the German surrender. He brought his 'unusual skill and ... energy' to secret operations and was 'contributing measurably to the success of Allied military undertakings'. But whilst he was engaged in training American intelligence officers and in working towards 'the closest integration between American, British and French services', he was necessarily no longer able to visit or even to write his calming letters to the beleaguered Mathilde.

The stakes for resisters and undercover operatives were raised through brutal retaliation and reprisals as the German hold on

France became more fragile in 1944, and SOE demanded even greater restrictions on her freedom. They were 'continually pressing that [she] be kept incommunicado, due to the knowledge that she has obtained about [German] activities'. They were also anxious that 'from Lucas she has certainly obtained a first-hand knowledge of [SOE] policy in France and he may well have given her information about their headquarters organisation' when they had been together over two years earlier. MI5 understood that 'the longer she is kept in detention and prevented from receiving visitors the worse she will become', but without Harmer, there was nobody to fight her corner.

A couple of weeks after D-Day, Mathilde wrote to the president of the International Red Cross. She cited her courageous work for the organisation in 1941 before giving a picture of herself now, interned 'in a most unexpected and circumstantial manner', in pain from her 'eyes, teeth and general health', short of 'clothes, woollens and shoes' and without any news of her family. She appealed for anything that might be done, 'however little it may be, it will be the only joy I have had for over two years', but if her plea even reached its intended recipient, it went unanswered.

She was unable to get her 'Dearest Doctor' Herbert in as either physician or friend, although she reported to him that despite her eyes being 'really bad', her 'morale and the nerves [are] perfectly OK'. As the V-1 and V-2 rockets rained down on London, she and her fellow inmates hid under a metal table to protect themselves from flying glass. She wrote fruitlessly to an Algerian acquaintance asking for word of her brother, to the Home Secretary again, to Hinchley-Cooke, to 'Uncle Tom' Greene and to the absent Harmer in the desperate hope of contact.

*

When Mathilde made these pleas, her sense of impotence was mingled with fresh fear for her future as the war in Europe entered its last phase. Millions of her countrymen had kept their heads down and not declared their loyalties to save their and their families' liberty as they went to work in factories and on farms that sustained the Wehrmacht, or in the civil service which necessarily had to obey German rules. A few would be acclaimed as heroes; others would be condemned for collaboration or treason as immediate, blinkered hindsight took hold with the liberation of Paris in August 1944 and the new government tried to heal the country's divisions.

However much she resented it, in many ways Mathilde was lucky to be in Holloway. As most of the worst collaborators had fled to Germany, the focus was on those that could be identified, including journalists who had written in defence of the Nazi regime. But before official jurisdiction could begin, between 8,000 and 9,000 French citizens were killed in direct executions by the Resistance, 'mingled with all sorts of obscure settling of scores' in what was known as the *épuration sauvage*, the wild purge. Alleged collaborators were forced to walk across pits filled with broken glass, often stripped naked. Women known to have slept with Germans, or in some cases just consorted with them, would have their heads shaved,* their breasts bared, be tarred and processed through the streets of jeering crowds, many of whom had been involved with the occupiers in various ways themselves. Sexual sadism was rife.

The journalist and MI6 officer Malcolm Muggeridge arrived in Paris at the end of August, and saw mayhem on the streets and 'mounting confusion and shooting' at all hours. In Fresnes, there was 'an extraordinary collection of alleged collaborationists, consisting of former eminent politicians, *préfets* and other senior civil servants, officers from the three services, diplomats, writers and journalists, as well as riff-raff from the street accused of having been informers, agents provocateurs or pimps for the Germans'. The prisoners were packed five or six to a single cell, and 'it was difficult to distinguish between some immensely distinguished admiral or general, dishevelled, but still wearing his uniforms and decorations, and rogues ... between some famous actress from the Comédie Française and prostitutes who had found a lucrative

* Estimates of these *tondeuses* range between 10,000 and 30,000.

clientele among German officers and other ranks'. It was physical and moral chaos.

De Gaulle had formed a new government on 9th September and set up the *épuration légale*, the legal purge, by which he intended to 'wipe the slate clean over so many crimes and abuses' that would otherwise permit 'a monstrous abscess to infect the country forever'. The purge trials, which started with writers who were the most visible supporters of the Occupation, sparked an ethical debate. François Mauriac, who became known as 'St Francis of the Assizes', advocated 'moderation and conciliation' in *Le Figaro*: he was 'increasingly uneasy with the idea of executing writers because of their opinions rather than their actions'. Albert Camus, on the other hand, advanced the claims of 'justice' over 'mercy' in *Combat*: he claimed leniency would mean 'sacrificing the ideals for which resisters had died, as well as betraying the dead by allowing their executioners to go free'.

*

Jean Lucien Kieffer was arrested by the Canadian 7th Armoured Division at Livarot in Normandy on 18th August after crossing the German lines in the hope of returning home unseen. Buckmaster visited him, and a week later, on the same day as the Liberation of Paris, the betrayer of Interallié was in a safe house in Marylebone for interrogation about his career as Bleicher's most prolific traitor. He looked for a way to boost his own stock with his interrogators by telling brutal lies about Mathilde, but said nothing that altered their understanding of her, Interallié, or his own role in its collapse.

There was a risk that Kieffer knew that Roman Czerniawski was supposedly working for the Abwehr and that the Pole's disappearance was not necessarily the great escape of which he boasted. If word got out, there would be little alternative but to arrest Roman in Britain to stop his disinformation becoming invalid while there was still fighting to come. Astor was worried that 'in the event of Brutus becoming blown, the whole of Fortitude would also be compromised and the Germans would become aware of our deception technique'. They even considered closing Agent Brutus down, but Kieffer knew nothing of him. Harmer deployed his skill and influence to ensure that Kieffer would not stand trial until after the war.

At the end of September there was an even greater peril to the Brutus identity. Renée Borni was arrested for collaboration by the Forces Françaises de l'Intérieur, the FFI, uneasily formed the previous February from the Liberation Free Corps, the Francs-Tireurs and the Organisation de Résistance de l'Armée to form 'some kind of unified army of the shadows'. This unwieldy outfit, which had found its numbers swelling since the Liberation and had not always risen above the battlefield justice of shooting suspected collaborators out of hand, was now sharing the Free French's double-barred Cross of Lorraine symbol.

In order to preserve his cover in England, Roman had 'on several occasions asked the Germans to pass on messages of goodwill to Violette [i.e. Borni]', which had enabled her 'to deduce that [he] was communicating with the Germans'. His Abwehr handlers had told him that 'because of our dealings with her she seems to have worked out that you are fighting on our side'. He was told to reply that he was 'very much displeased that Violette should have guessed the real situation because I fear any involuntary indiscretion might destroy all my efforts'. Or rather all Bıa's efforts.

Hugh Astor had an idea to keep the Brutus show on the road. Roman was 'to report in a frenzy of anxiety' that SIS had told him of Borni's capture; they had asked him to 'assist' them in 'that part of the interrogation which concerns the break-up of the Walenty organisation'. He would remind them that Borni knew he was working for them, so would need to be briefed on what they had told her; he suspected that the Abwehr would not reply on this point as it could give away their use of him. As a final safeguard, if all went well he would 'put his cards on the table' and re-recruit Borni as a subagent once she was out of custody. But before this elaborate series of bluffs needed to be perpetrated, Harmer managed to infiltrate himself into the interrogation room in France, and reported back that the 'simple and honest ... Violette' had given nothing away and was loyal to the point that she and her fiancé had been 'instrumental in rescuing nine Allied airmen who had parachuted in the vicinity of Lunéville'. She was released to face her legal retribution later.

*

There was a different atmosphere in Holloway that last Christmas of the war as the Allied advance pushed forward into the Fatherland: there were 'chocolates and clean linen, flowers, Californian honey, scented soap from Virginia, coffee and cigarettes'. Mathilde regarded herself as a 'woman who had been deprived of everything by the will of a few men' being 'spoiled by the kindness of a few women'. She could not understand why she was not allowed to send 'a simple Christmas card' to Mathilde Krafft, with whom she had been locked up for 'nearly two and a half years'. She was still complaining about this to Hinchley-Cooke in April 1945 in a letter which also pointed out that she was not allowed 'to receive news directly' from her family; she had not even been told of Maurice Carré's death. She had not had any visitors for over a year now – the woman who had been so deeply involved and who had consumed such high-level thought and debate in London, was now totally written out of the war and decent human contact.

She was consumed by the injustice of her situation. She wrote to Harmer in desperation to say she could no long live 'cheek by jowl with Mrs Lonsdale' who had been meddling in her 'affairs'. She was furious to be associated with someone who had been collaborating solely because she believed it was the right thing to do rather than, as she had, to save her life, and was clear that 'the analogy between her case and mine is non-existent'. She would be 'anything but flattered to be regarded as her friend'.

By the spring of 1945, the 'Brutus case' rather than B1a's ambivalence about her potential treatment was the only factor preventing her dispatch. The examining magistrate in Paris, Fougères, was already preparing the charges against her and had taken her mother's *déposition* in early April. There had been discussions about her deportation the previous autumn. Ian Wilson of MI5, now her case officer, suggested to Dick White and Hugh Astor in November that if she were to leave they would have 'no control over what the French might do'. If her countrymen made an example of her as part of the painful process of getting their house in order, 'they would certainly interrogate her, and might make her the subject of a trial to which publicity might attach'. Roman was still 'used for operational purposes' so his exposure could not be risked, and MI5 were clear that things would look bad if his pact with the enemy and 'the circumstance of his escape' came out.

De Vomécourt needed protection too: Mathilde could give evidence about how they had got out of France in 1942 which would 'endanger his life' now he 'was believed to be a P/W [prisoner of war] in Germany'. These 'objections' necessitated her remaining in England and that 'MI5 ... be afforded as many facilities for controlling her correspondence and visitors as was possible'. They should not even 'put the details in writing' to the French who, in the person of Captain de Couëdic of the Service de la Sécurité Militaire of the French provisional government in London, were asking for the files on her case to be handed over.

The two men for whom she had worked – one pursuing her own last desired career as a double agent in England after talking his way out of gaol, the other, like her, incarcerated, but with his mission and his place of imprisonment tributes to his loyalty – were helping to keep her from her country's retribution. No wonder the prose in the new MI5 legal advice was contorted when it commented 'whether we like it or not we will be to some degree forced to explain our conduct and I believe that it will be very much easier to do this if we can say we were only holding her in detention pending the time she could be returned to her country and subjected to any treatment which the law of that country provides'.

*

The protection could not last. A message had been sent from the 'Brutus transmitter' that it would be 'discontinued on 17th

December' 1944; for want of anything better, 'the prohibitive price of flats in London' was given as the reason why it would not start up again for some time as Roman would apparently find it hard to find somewhere affordable to rig it up. The Abwehr response asking if he needed more money got no reply and in March 1945 it was closed down for good. After the final transmission, the MI5 telegraphist reported that 'the German operator seemed quite sentimental, thanking him for his excellent work in the past and expressing sorrow that the contact would be temporarily interrupted'. The less emotional Major Billy Luke immediately advocated Mathilde be deported as Roman's immediate cover no longer needed protection and her 'only permanent stable companion', Stella Lonsdale, was shortly to be released, with the ensuing damage of loose talk. If either her defence or the French prosecution attempted to summon Roman as a witness in a trial before the end of the war, MI5 should resist as that would have 'serious reflections on our whole deception plans'. Once again, her fate was decided in relation to others.

*

On 14th April, the German commandant of the high-security POW camp Oflag IVC in Colditz Castle was ordered to evacuate his British prisoners in the face of the American advance. They refused to leave and that afternoon, the Americans began to shell the Saxon town. On the 16th, the camp was liberated and eight days later Masterman reported that Pierre de Vomécourt 'is in the hands of SOE and in this country'. Harmer was asked by his former colleagues if there was anything he wanted to ask in connection with Mathilde, to which he replied that he would just like to clarify whether de Vomécourt believed that Mathilde had sent a coded warning of his return in 1942. The response was, as he expected, negative. Other than that, Harmer was resigned that Mathilde had to return to France soon before she became one of 'these cases' which 'will attract a great deal more public attention' to the detriment of his service's reputation.

Not for the last time, de Vomécourt proved himself Mathilde's defender. He recognised that it had been 'undesirable' for her to remain 'at large' but felt that this 'no longer applied' as 'her services to the British cause outweighed her misdeeds'. Keen to get back into the game himself, he even offered to interview his former lover to establish all she knew about Bleicher, who was regarded 'with respect for his successful activities against the Buckmaster circuits' and was high up the wanted list. His offer was declined.

*

The third great influence on Mathilde Carré's war was himself just about to fall into Allied hands. The under-promoted policeman had had a remarkable career: after Interallié and Autogiro, in March 1943 Hugo Bleicher had taken over the Carte network, led by André Marsac and Roger Bardet, by pretending to be a colonel, naturally, who wanted to defect to the Allies. Operating under the self-aggrandising code name of Großfürst ('Grand Duke'), he visited Marsac each day in his cell at Fresnes until he had 'convinced the tall, thin and gullible [man] that he too hated the Nazis and now wanted to defect'. The following month near Annecy, he pulled off his greatest coup when he captured SOE Captain Peter Churchill, then running the Spindle organisation, and the organisation's courier Odette Sansom. Churchill and Sansom, who later married, only escaped death at the hands of the Gestapo after hideous torture thanks to his pretence that he was related to the prime minister.

Bardet decided to collaborate after one night in prison which he, like Mathilde, knew he could not be able to 'stand', and was sprung from Fresnes in a staged escape similar to Roman's. His work led in the middle of 1944 to the arrest of Henri Frager, who had been commissioned by SOE to head its Donkeyman network, and ultimately to the death sentence. One of the intelligence jewels Frager gave Bardet was the key for decoding the BBC's last-minute instructions to the Resistance before the Normandy invasion, but the Wehrmacht ignored the Abwehr's tip.

At one point the flexible Bleicher even considered coming to England himself 'either to get on favourable terms with the British' or as a 'bold penetration move'. Possibly both. His final job for the collapsing Reich was to go to Utrecht, where he was to 'organise a secret intelligence network among the Dutch population', believed in the final days of self-delusion to be largely pro-German. When Bleicher arrived, he found only 'a nervous captain, a few demoralised foreign agents and one or two of [his] own unit' to work with, but before he could organise this motley crew, the advancing Canadian army swept them on to Amsterdam. There they built a transmitter and receiver that sat idle for three weeks until that city too was liberated – by which time everyone wanted a piece of the 'character of exceptional interest to MI5, SIS and SOE'.

Bleicher was brought to Camp 020, Latchmere House in south-west London, the interrogation centre for captured German agents run by the formidable figure of Colonel Robin 'Tin Eye' Stephens, and questioned for weeks before being handed over to the French in October 1945. He confirmed Mathilde's story of her time with him, whilst inflating his roles as mastermind and a saver of lives. But by then she was already home.

*

St James's Street had once again been the setting for an inter-service discussion about her future on 3rd May 1945. Now there was no reason to 'safeguard the interests' of either Czerniawski or de Vomécourt, Mathilde should go. As she 'could cause considerable mischief if she were at liberty' in either England or France, it was 'assumed' that she would be taken into 'safe custody' on arrival. Indeed, a few days later, word came from Paris that 'the French are very anxious to take action in the Judicial Courts against the principal characters surrounding the Victoire and Brutus cases'. Even those keen to protect their own secrets and avoid any reprisals realised that 'it was virtually impossible at this stage to prevent the French from going forward with the cases'.

On 1st June, three weeks after the Third Reich's unconditional surrender, Mathilde, her few belongings and the fifteen shillings and twopence halfpenny she owned were taken by car from Holloway and driven through the rubble of London to be handed over to Billy Luke at Croydon Airport. They did not exchange a single word on their flight to Paris. She had been told of her departure the day before, and was feeling her familiar numbness at the news: she felt 'neither joy nor sorrow', only her powerlessness. She was resigned to what 'the inexorable machine of destiny' would bring her as her world turned on its axis once again.

England had been Mathilde's home for three years, but she had spent only three months of it in any sort of freedom. She was never to come back, or see any of the Double Cross team, or Roman Czerniawski, or Dr Herbert, or Henri Wotitski again. She was now another of France's myriad problems. It was a very different arrival in Paris to that of November 1940: then she had been crossing the demarcation line on her nurse's identity card, fired up by her Joan of Arc fantasies, sharing Roman's enthusiasm for a new way of setting up a network, impressing her mother. She had been indispensable, organised and, above all, valued. When she had last seen her country in early 1942, she foresaw a continuation of her espionage career from London, double-crossing the Abwehr who had forced humiliation on her. But even after her long and abandoned incarceration, it was only now that she admitted to a sense of 'real isolation' as she realised 'the evil which had piled up' against her in the intervening years of festering collaboration in the country she had tried to serve.

18

Intelligence With the Enemy

Mathilde Carré had to be confronted with many she had not seen since November 1941, and by the ghosts of many others. She had to hear personal abuse about her morals and her loyalties as well as remarkable words of empathy and forgiveness. She had spent her life since the Fall of France in the secret world, her deeds known only to her agents and her fellow spies, but now the needs of the law and her country's desire for reconciliation meant she was about to step on to the public stage. Her case brought to the fore the tangled complexity of the times and delicate questions of where loyalties lie when tested to extremes – as well as her own idiosyncratic strengths and flaws.

She had fought against introspection and boredom, and thrived in danger. She had been valued for her courage and steadfastness, and been a catalyst for the visions of others. But now that she found herself dependent upon the judgement of those over whom she could have no influence and who could not listen to her appeals, she paradoxically came to find herself at some sort of peace with her restless nature.

*

France had to put her alleged traitors on trial to rebuild trust and morale. The provisional government's *cours de justice* were set up to establish a legal footing for hazy war crimes and to halt summary reprisals. But when the French penal code had been drawn up nobody had envisioned 'one version of France putting another version on trial for treason', and a relevant law needed to be brought into play. Article 75, 'intelligence with the enemy', which carried the death penalty, became the catch-all charge. Alongside this, a new, hasty, deliberately baggy ordinance for offenders convicted 'of a clear unpatriotic act' was concocted of *indignité nationale*, national unworthiness. This could encompass those who might have done nothing more than have contact with the Vichy government, whilst, for example, those who had become wealthy through financial collaboration rarely came near the courts. A conviction under the Act brought the punishment of *dégradation nationale*, which included the removal of the right to vote, hold public office, military, legal, teaching, media or trade union employment, or be a director or manager in a private company. On top of this relegation to second-class citizenship, property could be confiscated and gaol sentences imposed, the latter frequently in solitary confinement. Thousands of civil servants were sacked or demoted, often for doing no more than keeping the wheels of government in motion, leaving the country with a vacuum in expertise. The legal system seized up: by December 1945, the Paris court had a backlog of 4,200 cases, while in Lyons only forty-four cases were heard between November 1944 and the start of February 1945. Jury panels represented a further issue: they had 'to be endorsed by Resistance groups', which meant that there was likely to be a revenge element to any verdict. As one leading advocate who underwent physical and mental torture for his part in the Resistance was to say, the jurors who might have 'served with complete self-sacrifice' were 'incapable of being just in that justice is a balance between good and evil'.

Marshal Pétain's trial was underway when Mathilde returned. It ended on 15th August with the death sentence being imposed by a majority of one from the special jury of twelve resisters and twelve members of parliament. De Gaulle immediately commuted the sentence to life imprisonment on the grounds of Pétain's age and his military service; his execution would have exacerbated the country's wounds. Pierre Laval was not shown such clemency for his fanatical pro-Nazism, including his D-Day broadcast to his compatriots that forbade them to help the Allied forces. His lawyers' plea that the proceedings were conducted more in a political than a judicial spirit had some force, but either way the outcome was inevitable. Laval took poison on the morning of his execution in order, as he wrote in his suicide note, to spare the soldiers of the firing squad committing a judicial crime. But his aged phial was ineffective and repeated stomach-pumps ensured he faced his prescribed end.

Other than Laval, only two of Vichy's top officials were executed: Joseph Darnand, who as an SS officer led paramilitary groups who hunted down members of the Resistance; and Fernand de Brinon, who had fled to Germany in September 1944 to become president of Vichy's government-in-exile. General Weygand, army chief of staff in 1940 and later the minister of defence who drove Jewish children out of the schools and colleges, was acquitted as the court ruled that he had never acted against the interests of France; he spent much of the rest of his long life writing books defending his actions but de Gaulle denied him a funeral at Les Invalides, the country's military shrine, as late as 1965.

*

Mathilde arrived back into this febrile moral, political and legal atmosphere. She was taken to the building at 11 rue des Saussaies that had been the Gestapo headquarters and now was once again the home of the Sûreté Nationale. On 22nd June she was transferred to the Napoleonic Charenton Fort in the old walls of Paris which had been used by the Nazis as an ammunition dump and radio transmitting station. From her solitary confinement there, she was driven each day in a Black Maria to Fougères' chambers in the rue Boissy d'Anglas, off the place de la Concorde, for the *interrogatoire* as the prosecution case was prepared. The *juge d'instruction*, or examining magistrate's questions, were to continue intermittently for over three months. It was the first time she faced those she had known in both the glorious and the corrupted days of 1941.

She was composed for her introduction to the proceedings. Fougères asked few questions on the first morning but they clarified the scope of his investigation: what were the different addresses at which Bleicher lived, where were the Interallié radio sets and which of those addresses were already known to the Germans? She was relieved that he was 'calm, poised and unbiased'.

Madame Belard gave evidence for the second time. She spoke of her anxiety when her daughter did not telephone her on the day of her arrest; and the frosty lunch at which Bleicher 'preached collaboration'. Jeanne Belard knew when her daughter reached London she would 'tell all' if only to 'be arrested' and safe, so was relieved when Cottin came to see her with 'the happy outcome of the journey'.

For the next few days, Mathilde was led through her arrest and her alleged betrayal of the Interallié agents. She found an advocate with impeccably patriotic credentials: Maître Albert Naud had been in the Resistance himself and imprisoned in La Santé. He had recently refused to act for Pierre Laval, so his acceptance of her case felt like confidence in her at a time when few loyal lawyers had to look far for work. She appreciated her advocate's 'talent and sensitivity'.

Her testimony about the days of November 1941 followed each street she had walked the morning of the arrest, her imprisonment, and the 'plentiful breakfast' Bleicher had provided for her in the Edouard VII at which he revealed that he 'had all the documents and knew everything'. She told of her call to 'Oncle Marco' to confirm their rendezvous, and his and her old friend Aubertin's subsequent arrest, without showing any regret, self-justification or anger. She was taken through Lipski and his daughter, the frail de Rocquigny, Tabet, Poulain, Legrand, Jeannine, and the others who had been taken away in front of her without offering blame or qualification. She might have thought that she should save any defence for her inevitable trial; she may have come to terms with the passions that had run through her war and concluded that the death sentence would be inevitable after she had used so many lives up in the preceding four years; she may simply have lost interest in her own drama and was once again looking down on herself from a different plane.

Fougères' last question on 24th July was 'When did you become de Vomécourt's mistress?' to which she answered, 'Around 20th January 1942, after I had confessed to him.' The case against her had its dates: it was the period between her arrest and the start of her redemptive alliance with de Vomécourt. The possibility of anything that had been brave, noble or patriotic in her war before or after was irrelevant.

*

The parade of witnesses began with the nightmare of Jean Lucien Kieffer, himself in detention. The first question put to him was the dangerously open-ended, 'What do you think of Micheline?' The use of her familiar nickname within the organisation was deliberate and provocative: on nearly every other occasion she was 'the accused' or 'Madame Carré'. Kieffer answered that it was Bleicher who told him she had been Roman's mistress, and that there was a 'great jealousy' between her and Renée Borni, whom Kieffer was quick to say he had never met. Determined to blacken Mathilde to help his own case, Kieffer went on to claim that she had embezzled network funds and was a 'morphinomane'; furthermore, although she had strychnine on her when she was arrested, she was too cowardly to take the noble way out and had instead suggested to Bleicher that he use the poison to 'experiment on the detainees in Fresnes'. She was 'clear-thinking, chilly', and everything she did was 'completely cynical'; she was also 'very sensual'. The legal proceedings were to gather evidence and did not allow for cross-examination, but Mathilde was certainly clear-headed as she understood that to Kieffer she was simply 'an embarrassing witness' who could wreak terrible damage at his own trial and who needed 'at least to be utterly discredited'.

The next people to appear had nothing to gain and delivered their testimony without such mendacious venom. The bacteriologist Henri Collin was confusingly vague when asked about his advice to play along with Bleicher, and denied that he had told his friend Achard that she was 'an agent of the Gestapo'. Mathilde had admired him before but now considered him 'faint-hearted and terrified' before the magistrate, as he had been when confronted by Bleicher in 1942. The unimpeachable patriot Michel Brault told her that she 'lacked courage' in not confiding in him, but he knew now that she had 'already denounced him to Bleicher' by that time.

Mathilde did not deny René Legrand's story about her visit with her arm in a sling 'to ask information about a ship's progress'. André Achard reported de Vomécourt 'evasive' about her loyalty when he visited Vichy in early 1942 in the attempt to limit the rumours that would damage his chances of exfiltration. Achard added what seemed at the time a gratuitous opinion, but it was a forewarning of how the case that was being assembled against her might play to the male jury she would inevitably face: 'In my opinion, the question of sex had a large role to play in Madame Carré's choices.'

Despite the urgency and deprivations of the times, the French took August off in 1945 and Mathilde had to wait until mid-September before her next session in front of Fougères. The radio engineer Max Desplaces described how he had been identified from his signature on transmissions at Arthault's studio; he spoke of being quizzed about Włodarczyk's capabilities, his assumption that La Chatte was languishing in prison after the collapse of Interallié and his hope that the crystals for the radios had been destroyed. Claude Jouffret, who stated that he had collaborated in order to care for his frail parents, told Fougères that Mathilde could not have been Czerniawski's mistress because she was always telling him off for 'being so dirty', but confirmed that she was jealous of Renée Borni not because she held the insalubrious post of Roman's lover but because of the undefined 'nefarious influence that she exercised over' the chief. He did not deny working with Mathilde after he left Fresnes, or with Kieffer in Normandy and in the south, but apparently had no idea that he was being used as 'bait' in the arrest of Roger Cottin, or 'for several days' that de Vomécourt's right-hand man had been imprisoned after their meeting.

The only testimony which provoked Mathilde to speak out was that of Pierre Belle of La Palette as he described the arrest of Jacques Collardey. She had felt great affection for 'the Paris ragamuffin' who had been the only sector head brave or naïve enough to enter the restaurant that day, and who had not been heard of since. Belle told Fougères that he had had no knowledge of the 'German trap', had been in the flat above the restaurant at the time it was sprung and would never have served 'hot drinks to the Germans in the cloakroom area'. Mathilde retorted that even though she had had a 'bad view', she definitely saw Belle discuss the 'set-up for the trap' and allow soldiers to hide in the cellar. He shrugged that he had 'no idea' they were there, a reflection of the attitude needed for survival during the Occupation as well as to deflect from any imputation of collaboration in this period of reckoning.

The most poignant and painful witnesses were Wladimir Lipski and his daughter Lydia, reunited after their terrible experiences in the camps. All Lipski's teeth had been smashed during his first interrogation, and he appeared a 'sick and broken' figure but displayed no rancour towards Mathilde nor blamed her for his experiences; he was even courteous as he told the vivid story of the day of his arrest. He was instead puzzled by how someone who 'did perfect service for the Allies' could also work so well for the Germans, and concluded that she was 'a very strange woman indeed'.

Lipski narrated how Lucien de Rocquigny, the Polish agent who had loved Mathilde, had become 'the immediate target for the SS bullies' of Mauthausen. He laboured in a quarry, forced to carry huge stones until his delicate hands were cut to ribbons. On 1st April 1943, de Rocquigny was 'knocked senseless in a clearing' by the guards when he was unable to lift a big rock. 'Small and frail' as he was, he died of his wounds a few days later, one of an estimated 320,000 deaths at the camp.

Lipski's daughter, the 'Little Chicken' of Interallié, suffered an appalling war. She arrived at Ravensbrück aged eighteen in 1943 and was singled out to be one of the victims of the medical experiments that caused the camp crematorium chimney permanently to belch smoke. But the murderous Dr Hans Gerhart, who was removing muscle and bone from prisoners in the hope of implanting them into wounded soldiers, was impressed by her pleas that she be shot rather than undergo such operations and instead gave her an injection to which he told her she would react in twenty-five years but which had no ill-effects. Lydia weighed only thirty kilos when the camp was liberated, and in 1960, by which time she was a striptease dancer at the Folies-Bergère under the name Lydia Lova, she was awarded the Croix de Guerre avec Palme and became a Chévalier of the Légion d'Honneur for her wartime courage. She limited her statement in Fougères' chambers to the day of the arrest but was 'very abusive' in her demeanour towards the woman she could not forgive.

The courier Stanislaw Lach was not strong enough to appear. He had been badly beaten as his interrogators tried to get Zarembski's address from him, and passed months in solitary confinement prior to joining thousands of his fellow countrymen in the slave labour camp at Mauthausen. After its liberation, he came back to the apartment from which he had been seized, but was too feeble to be able to find work. Another Polish Interallié agent helped him get back on his feet and he ended his days as the foreman of a lingerie factory.

*

The sightings of Mathilde Carré engaged in 'intelligence with the enemy' mounted up and she took it all in with little change of expression. As her former colleagues told their stories she found she 'no longer knew what to say'. She could change nothing, and could summon 'no regrets' as events took their course. Some of the witnesses understood why she had behaved as she had. Marc Marchal simply said as he left the chambers, 'I bear Madame Carré no ill will.' René Aubertin was too ill to attend, perhaps diplomatically so. Robert Poulain chose to give his testimony by letter as he had had enough and was letting himself 'be carried away by the Parisian stream' rather than join in the retributions. Her 'dear

Mireille' Lejeune, who had tried to warn her on the day of her arrest and who subsequently never saw her police chief husband again, was 'just the same': she shook Mathilde's hand and told her that they were simply 'two unhappy creatures'.

The final encounter was with her rival in Interallié and La Chattière, Renée Borni, now facing prosecution on the same charge. As throughout their relationship in the rue Villa Léandre and La Chattière, they were soon at loggerheads. Borni ran through her testimony first: she claimed not to have given away Mathilde's address, which must have been let slip by the incorruptible Krótki and said she had no 'freedom of action' in the Cattery, unlike Mathilde. 'Dame Carré' retorted that she had been denounced by Madame Borni; 'Dame Borni' made the absurd assertion that she did not even know where Madame Carré lived and that there had been 400,000 francs in the Villa Léandre house which Mathilde must have stolen; Mathilde denied ever hearing about 'such a sum'.

When their confrontation was over, Renée asked for more to be added to the written account: that she had been moved to the Cattery after she had suffered a haemorrhage in La Santé, and that she 'never made an offer to serve the Germans' and, illogically, 'nor was any such offer accepted'. Fougères' response was blunt: it would be 'surprising' if Bleicher were to keep her at liberty 'all day unless she was to give information' about the 'people he intended to arrest'.

*

Fougères' dossier was now complete and he could prepare the case. But despite their haste to get through this stage as quickly as possible and the clear prosecutorial case against Mathilde Carré, her next period of imprisonment without trial was another long three years.

During the periods when she was cut loose from attachment and busyness, including in the days after her miscarriage and in her night in La Santé, she disassociated into a reverie. Sometimes she fantasised about heroism, sometimes about suicide, sometimes she felt nothing at all. She was 'alternately gay and indifferent' as she contemplated 'the duality of life and death'. This moving between extremes might have recalled her two aunts from her childhood, or the change from near-suicide to surging patriotism in Toulouse in September 1940 that had launched her career as a spy. By the summer of 1947, visited in Fresnes only by her mother, father and lawyers, she was keeping herself apart from the reality of her situation. Without anyone or anything on which to pin her character and energy, she could feel 'completely unbalanced' in her inability to regulate between her poles.

She cleaved to memories of better times in an attempt to regain her footing. Dr Herbert had reported that Richard Llewellyn Lloyd had offered to 'help' her if he could and she wrote to him that she wanted for nothing 'materially' as her devoted parents brought her 'big lovely parcels', although 'life in [her] cell' was confined to play-ing occasionally with Whisky, the prison cat. She asked plaintively if 'the people of the I[ntelligence] S[ervice] who employed me', by which she meant Harmer, Astor and Tar Robertson, might find a way of 'freeing' her as a 'reward'. The other way Lloyd could be 'sweet' was to write 'now and then' to bring 'back those happy days when you took me by the hand, showing me the heart of the spring-time in Kew Gardens'. She asked him to keep the copy of her *Mémoires* dedicated to him, musing on how much she could add to it now. As she came to the end of her fifth year behind bars, she listed her yearnings: 'to lay in the grass, to work at all those ideas ... to dance! and drink, and laugh! to voyage, to study, to live!'

As it was, she started to contemplate death, not with the excite-ment and wilful energy to cheat it she had shown in the exhilarat-ing early days of Interallié, but 'cold-bloodedly'. It was no longer just an escape from the discomfort of her situation, rather a point of attraction and fascination, 'rich in indefinable hopes'. But her 'potential for energy' and 'lust for life' would always pull her out of these meditations, and reassert the spirit that could 'win the game with death' as it had before.

*

Mathilde had been desperate for human contact beyond Miss Mellanby and Stella Lonsdale in Aylesbury, and had asked MI5 to allow a priest to visit her. The prison chaplain was 'a very good man' who had brought her 'something to read and even a little chocolate' but did not speak much French, and Mathilde felt the interpreter who accompanied him was only selectively passing on 'what interests her'. In 1942 she had been 'by no means a fanatic for religion' but five years on she was turning to God. She had put her faith in Roman, Bleicher and de Vomécourt, and now there was no human to give her life structure and purpose after each of those had failed her in some way. She spent the night of her thirty-ninth birthday meditating on justice and her fate. She knew that 'logically and reasonably' she 'should be judged' and 'condemned' for her crimes, yet, as she quoted from *Tristan and Iseult*, 'Men see the facts but God sees the hearts, and He alone is the true judge.' She was not denying those facts, or that 'the stupidity of human justice' would run its vengeful force, but choosing to look away from that world to a system of belief that could not let her down.

She was better off than many of her fellows: she had her growing faith, and parents who could bring her proper sheets and food. Her neighbour Paulette, 'a little working-class girl intoxicated by the war', had been arrested in 1945 as well, for rendering 'any service with a smile' to the occupiers. When Paulette had come in she had been plump but the prison fare of 'cabbage and rancid fat soup' had seen to that. Paulette had changed from being 'crazy in the gayest manner' to 'quietly mad'. Another neighbour, sentenced to twenty years' hard labour weeding the Fresnes courtyards, had grown 'enormous and shapeless'. When she was told she was being transferred she began to 'laugh and to mutter to herself', and on arrival at her new prison killed herself by beating her head against the wall. Suzy, who was forty-two but looked like 'a sickly child of twelve', had worked in a brothel; her speciality was to dress up as a girl about to receive her first Communion. Suzy pretended 'to have been a great spy', shared the religious books from the prison library with Mathilde and knitted woollen dogs to pass the time.

Mathilde took refuge from this 'madness, intrigue [and] un-healthy curiosity' in prayer and reading devotional works as well as *The Constant Nymph* and *The Story of San Michele*, playing with Whisky, and spinning herself into her fantasy world. The 'hideous earthenware bowls' used for food and drink made a brief noise as tea was poured into them that reminded her of 'those little bells which you hear in small stations'; from this she was able to imagine herself alighting at Villefranche-sur-Mer and seeing flowers in window-boxes; another day she was at Syam, in the Jura, home of her happiest childhood memories, smelling the pines and cycla-mens at the entrance to a tunnel. The only time she admitted to weeping was when Whisky was taken away from her.

What she could not shut out were the repercussions from the war. Most mornings before dawn, engines idled beneath her win-dow as prisoners were taken away to the firing-squad. She thought of the condemned as 'her enemies' until she came back to reality and the similarity of her situation to theirs, and reckoned that this 'cold, judicial murder' was often worse than the original crimes. In September 1947 she was shackled to 122 others and transferred to a different wing, where the following April she heard the 'noisy, sin-ister procession' as Jean Bassompierre was led to his execution. Although she 'did not know the man' personally, his case may have troubled her: he was charged with 'intelligence with the enemy' for his close military involvement with the Nazis yet had also played a hand in saving many French lives after a mutiny at La Santé prison. A long list of former Resistance fighters published an article in *L'Epoque* in an attempt to have his sentence pardoned or com-muted, but the 'procession' Mathilde heard that morning was taking Bassompierre to face a firing squad degradingly made up of members of his former regiment, the Chasseurs Alpins, with whom he had won the Croix de Guerre in 1940.

*

Maître Naud had been in correspondence with MI5 to ask them to send a witness to Mathilde's trial but got back the 'cold official reply' that 'while Madame Carré had indeed passed on certain information to the British authorities, she had always been considered by them as "eminently suspect"'. She likened this let-down to an unsubstantiated 'bit of washerwoman's gossip' and asked Naud to secure testimony from Buckmaster, Cowburn, Gale and Roman for the court, and that 'a representative', preferably Harmer, attend her trial. No statements or witness were forthcoming and B1a was no more: Tar Robertson was farming sheep in Worcestershire; Masterman had become provost of Worcester College, Oxford, playing cricket and writing detective novels on the side; Astor was Middle Eastern correspondent of *The Times*; Billy Luke had resumed his City career and Christopher Harmer had married a fellow MI5 officer and returned to his life as a solicitor in the Midlands. Czerniawski, who had been awarded 'a secret OBE' yet to his peeved irritation never British citizenship for his service, was struggling to establish himself as a printer in London. SOE had been disbanded in 1946, and SIS and MI5 were by now fighting a Cold War currently characterised by the Soviet blockade of Berlin, far removed from parachute drops over France and the hoodwinking creativity of Double Cross.

Another witness who would not be giving evidence was Hugo Bleicher, who was back in Germany. Naud had requested his presence, but the authorities decided that the witness statements he had already made would be sufficient. The Nuremberg trials were long over, and there was little desire to have an Abwehr operative in a French court – particularly not one who had the potential to stir deep national traumas were he to give evidence about how relatively easy he found it to turn loyal citizens into traitors.

*

Mathilde's fortieth birthday in 1948 began her seventh year of incarceration. Most of her fellow prisoners had been released and she felt her little group 'disintegrating'. For someone who had never been good at getting by on her own resources, she now regarded 'gnawing solitude' as 'the base of [her] balance', and her refuge. She no longer 'cared two pins' for this 'bloody life' by the time her trial date of 3rd January 1949 was set. She was standing outside herself, as she had always in moments of perilous stress, and felt 'more and more balanced' as she finally came to accept she could do nothing to affect the verdict. She had given up trying to influence events, and was now 'indifferent', less judgemental and 'more generous' towards others. Her 'willpower' was still there, 'still superb', and she presented her courageous face to the world but was hollowed out by the expenditure of emotion to the point where she was 'desperately empty inside'.

A few weeks earlier, after she had been to a service in the prison church, Mathilde wrote that she would 'ask God' to allow her to 'slide towards complete detachment', ultimately to

> be detached from everything:
> To feel neither anger nor hatred.
> No more love …
> To forget this prison and TO FORGET YOURSELF.

She had spent years struggling to hold on to her equilibrium and claim her place in society, and had finally achieved serenity just as others were to sit in judgement on her life.

19

Curtain

Moments before her trial began a young lawyer approached Mathilde Carré and said, 'Madame, they tell me that you are very brave ... You will have to be for the Committee of the Resistance has decided that it wants your head.' This unethical remark encapsulates the attitude of her countrymen towards her for the rest of her life, vengeful whilst acknowledging her courage. But even four years on, the war was still throwing up surprising allegiances that would reverberate down the decades to inspire debate about the imperfectability of politics and human nature, as well as pose essential and troubling questions about how ordinary people could behave in demanding and dangerous circumstances.

*

De Gaulle's Courts of Justice, which were to last until 1951, had a busy time in late 1944 and early 1945. They took on a vast number of cases in the attempt to cleanse the nation: by January 1945, a full two months before the Allied forces crossed the Rhine into Germany, over a quarter of the country's judges were involved in the trials and there were 18,700 cases under way out of 50,000 charges brought. Four months later, 1,598 death sentences had been carried out and 17,500 sanctions of *indignité nationale*. By April 1946, over 100,000 cases had been investigated and there had been 3,920 death sentences, 1,508 sentenced to hard labour, and 8,500 imprisoned. Others, including Mathilde Carré, had yet to be heard. Many thousands of offences were relatively minor, such as being forced to join fascist movements purely in order to get employment, and about a third of investigations did not lead to prosecution.

To the numerous voices clamouring that the total was only a fraction of those who had collaborated, and citing more effective precedents, Minister of Justice Teitgen retorted that 'The revolutionary tribunals of 1793 limited themselves to a total of 17,500 convictions. So that if you compare the number of sentences passed by the tribunals of 1793 and those of today's Courts of Justice ... you have to say we did a great deal.' Beside him, 'Robespierre, Danton and the others ... were children.' Despite this bold talk, Teitgen exemplified the delicacy and selective potential for biased hypocrisy when he quoted the Nazi sympathiser, Vichy minister of labour Marcel Déat, who had claimed with exaggerated understatement in March 1943 that there were 'not more than 50,000 collaborators in France'.

The courts eventually heard 124,751 cases, imposed 6,763 death sentences (3,910 in absentia), 13,211 sentences of hard labour, and 26,289 prison sentences, many of them specifying solitary confinement. Some jurisdictions chose not to punish collaborators yet did not achieve reconciliation for generations: the Channel Islands had seen acts of co-operation that included Alderney becoming a deadly slave-labour concentration camp for Russian and Jewish workers, and Jewish inhabitants being handed over to the Gestapo; an estimated 900 children were born to Channel Island mothers by German fathers. Yet not a single 'Jerry Bag', alderman or Islander was tried for collaboration, war crimes or treason. Belgium contained only three per cent of the population of France yet maintained a far higher prosecution rate: it had been overrun by the Wehrmacht while a neutral country, and of the 405,067 alleged collaborators on whom dossiers were opened, 57,254 were prosecuted with 2,940 death sentences and 2,340 life sentences the result. The largest reckoning in Europe was Norway's, where 3.2 per cent of the country's population was investigated for collaboration until as late as 1957, some 90,000 cases in all. Over half of these resulted in sentences, but rather than stabilising the country, the trials had a 'profoundly polarising effect'. Sartre realised that nearly 'every choice' made by the inhabitants of an occupied country, would eventually be 'a bad choice' that threatened either life or conscience. The echoes can still be heard long after the deaths of the protagonists.

*

The charge that would be heard in the first days of 1949 by Judge Drappier, president of the Paris Court of Justice, was that 'in France between the 16th June 1940, and the date of the Liberation, with intent to aid the undertakings of the enemy, being a Frenchwoman, [Mathilde Carré] passed on intelligence to a foreign power or its agents, with a view to assisting the undertakings of this power against France.' She appeared in the courtroom dressed in a black skirt, a black coat with a velvet collar and a silk blouse; her hair was tidy and worn with an unfashionable fringe over her forehead. The dock was made for someone much taller, and she spent most of her trial with her chin resting on her arms in order to get a good view of the proceedings.

Her expression through the four days changed little: her mouth was set in the slight upturn of a 'vague smile' and she had a 'deceptive calm' about her which was belied only by the constant, restless movement of her hands. She often removed her glasses so that she 'could not observe the glances' in the court and could 'retire into a fog', disassociating rather than confronting the possibility of 'meeting hatred with hatred'. There were no favours to be won here, and her myopia contributed to the detachment of her demeanour, although looking to her more hostile critics as insolence. This damaging impression was heightened by the arrival of Renée Borni, already regarded by popular prejudice as more foolish and compliant than treacherous, seriously ill on a stretcher.

The court prosecutor, Maître Becognée, ran through a summary of her case, to which Mathilde listened in silence until he mentioned that Hugo Bleicher maintained he had carried on a 'physical relationship' with her 'only in the line of duty'. She was stung to counter that, 'If Bleicher said that, it was only because I wasn't nice to him.' Later in the week, Becognée came back to the point: 'Did it not shock you, as the widow of a French officer, to become the mistress of a German sergeant?' She said that she had been promised her liberty at the end of that day and had indeed been horrified when he followed her to her room in Maisons-Laffitte. She answered the direct question about why she had slept with him with the retort that might have served as a justification for so many of her compatriots' actions: 'Well, what else could I have done?'

*

Colonel Achard had asked to be called first as he was about to depart on a mission to Indo-China. He spoke decisively of her as 'an admirable woman', and was 'positive that during the time she was working with our services she was not playing a double game. She never betrayed us and yet we would have been a pretty important prize for the Germans.' Simoneau, who as a serving spy was not allowed to appear in open court, gave evidence in camera to pay tribute to her 'immense desire' to help her country.

Madame Belard, dressed in a big hat and a heavy fur stole, was up next. She gave melodramatic testimony, with extravagant hand gestures and sobs, declaring that they were 'an honourable family of France' and asking how anyone could 'imagine' that one of them would betray their country; throughout the war they had had a French flag on their wall next to a photograph of their son 'in the uniform of a Saint-Cyr cadet'. Becognée interrupted her flourishes to point out that this 'did not prevent you, Madame, from entertaining to luncheon, under that flag, Bleicher, the German lover of your daughter'. Her reply was irritating to Mathilde, who muttered to Naud that her mother was 'making herself ridiculous', but it nonetheless showed spirit: 'Yes, but I insulted Bleicher for more than two hours that day.'

*

From then on her accusers processed through the court. René Aubertin was first. Madame Belard had passed him in the corridor and asked him to 'speak up for Micheline', to which he replied, 'I'm afraid, Madame Belard, that I must tell the truth.' He reminded Mathilde of the Hugentoblers, 'among your first victims', and 'little Paul de Rocquigny, who really loved you', and who was 'marked down for massacre' through his association with her. Aubertin had been lucky to survive: after Fresnes, he was kept as a hostage to be shot for reprisal before a transfer in 1943 to Mauthausen where he developed pleurisy, a disease which would lead to his immediate execution on its discovery to prevent contagion. He was saved by a Polish prisoner who stole a syringe and emptied the fluid from his lungs every day until he recovered. After the war, the former tank captain built a prosperous career in business.

Marc Marchal chose not to appear as he could not face the 'atmosphere of prejudice' of the purge trials. For his work for 'the British sabotage operation', the chemist had been sent to Buchenwald and then to Neuengamme where he was ordered to inject prisoners with typhus by SS doctors conducting experiments. He refused and was transported to Mauthausen with a letter ordering his death, but his life was saved by a German NCO who respected his dignity. He was repatriated by the Red Cross at the end of the war and died the year after Mathilde's trial, acclaimed by those who knew him as 'a man who never lost heart and whose spirit could not be broken'. Marchal never blamed Mathilde publicly for his incarceration, and was to write a valuable testimonial on her behalf.

Mireille Lejeune's husband Charles had died of typhus just days after being liberated. She recalled how Mathilde had been with Bleicher as they were taken away. Lipski told his and de Rocquigny's pitiful story; one of the railway spies said it was 'without doubt The Cat who had betrayed him'; Legrand again recounted the broken-arm trick and his entrapment. Michel Brault was articulate and impressive: he described his introduction of de Vomécourt as a mistake, failing to point out that the meeting gave his friend a second chance. The vainglorious lawyer's damning conclusion was 'that woman had dreams of becoming a second Mata Hari – either a French one or a German one, it didn't really matter to her'.

*

The most important witness came last. Pierre de Vomécourt knew her better than anyone who had yet spoken: he had seen through her treachery and then trusted her, had defended her name and character in London, and then again in the face of Bleicher's interrogation. To the French, including the jury, he was a hero. As a British officer, he had been recommended for the Distinguished Service Order in 1945, for 'although his own career was cut short before his work could bear fruit … without his courageous and unselfish work it would have been impossible to have proceeded with the organisation of resistance in the northern half of France'. He probably did not know that it was his involvement with her that led to the DSO being withheld as there was 'sufficient doubt' as to whether, despite his undoubted 'courage and enterprise', he might not have 'given a certain amount of information to the Germans' through his intimate association with Mathilde.

De Vomécourt was his usual 'neat, quiet figure' on the stand. He spoke 'in a precise, factual way' about his experiences of being parachuted back into France in May 1941, the loss of the original Georges, and Brault's Boxing Day introduction. He described his discovery of her double game as a 'confession' on her part, and how he had hit on the idea of turning her back. Naud asked the critical question: whether at that pivotal moment Mathilde 'manifested signs of a sincere desire to make amends'.

There was a pause before de Vomécourt answered. He might have been remembering the doubts that had assailed him about her intentions and the rumours he had to quash in Vichy; he might have thought back to their repeated attempts to leave Brittany and how nearly they came to total failure; he might have been contemplating what he knew about the end days of Interallié. But whatever was running through his mind, he was scrupulous in his reply: 'Yes, on the whole I would.' It was the last time the adventurous couple of the winter of 1941–2 were to see each other, but he had added the counterweight to the scales that had tipped against her.

*

Becognée began the Republic's summing-up by using her own words to damn her. He read the devastating passage from her *Mémoires* in which she had told Borchers, late at night in a restaurant, that were she about to be shot, her last requests would be 'to have a superb dinner, to make love, and to hear the Mozart Requiem'. He construed this as 'perfidy' from a woman 'without any moral feelings ... without any scruples. After all, she was the Chief and she bore heavy responsibilities.' The prosecutor took it upon himself to 'speak in the name of all those who were denounced, in the name of the deported and the dead' to ask the jury 'to punish this woman with the supreme penalty for traitors – with the penalty of death'. Mathilde's expression gave no hint of her emotions.

Maître Naud knew he was up against it as he stood to conclude for the defence. He played up her service for the Resistance and the Deuxième Bureau, and how short her time with Bleicher was: 'If this woman committed treason, it was because she was one of the first to enter the Resistance and was herself denounced. And how long did her period of treason last? Little more than a month and a half – just that brief moment of error – and after that she resumed her work on behalf of the Allies.' He argued that 'many of the best members of the Resistance had at one time or another come to terms with the enemy' and asked a question that resonates through the history of treachery: 'She wanted to live; can she be reproached for that?'

He pointed out that Mathilde was a novice in a deadly game of skill, and it was only human to prefer life to death. He all but admitted that she was guilty as charged, but made a persuasive plea for mercy. Her knew that 'the whole trial hinged' on whether he could persuade the jury that 'the spirit of self-sacrifice and self-denial were easier to apply sitting safely in a court of law than along the path of shame taken by Mathilde with a revolver in her back'. He wanted her to be seen not as the 'diabolical spy with green eyes' of 'fabricated legend' but as 'pathetically human' in her actions. But this was not a jury which could keep an open mind by its very make-up, so he returned to her heroism 'from the beginning of the Resistance', asking if they were really 'going to kill one of those who spread patriotic faith in the early days'. He implored them 'to make a difference between the French agents of the Gestapo who went and offered their services to the enemy and those who were first heroic but who overestimated their own powers'. His final sentence may have been legally flimsy but it encapsulated her predicament and drama: 'I beg you now to spare the life of this woman who during years of heroism experienced only two months of weakness.'

*

Judge Drappier was clinical in his guidance to the jury. There were only two questions to consider: the first was whether the 'widow Carré' was guilty as charged of 'intelligence with a foreign power ... with a view to aiding this foreign power against France'; the second was whether 'the action' in the first question was 'committed with the deliberate intention of favouring the enterprises of Germany'. The same applied to the 'widow Borni'.

The jury did not need to retire for long, but returned with a majority rather than a unanimous verdict of guilty for both women, implying a more nuanced reaction than Drappier's guidance encouraged. Renée Borni was guilty, with the recommendation that she be shown mercy. She was sentenced to two and a half years in prison and a fine equivalent to £50; for now, she could return to the clinic where she was undergoing treatment. She hardly served any of her sentence, and was still alive, married with children, when last on the record in 1961.

Mathilde Carré was guilty without any qualification. Naud was told afterwards that her 'impassivity', most notably during her mother's tearful testimony, had looked to the jurors as if she 'despise[d]' the one person who cared about her, and was a spur to conviction. She maintained that blankness, the 'trace of the smile' that had been near for the last four days still present, as the judge announced her punishment: *indignité nationale*, the confiscation of all her personal belongings, the payment of four-fifths of the cost of her four-day trial, and death. She was taken to the condemned cell at Fresnes. Two weeks later, Naud's appeal for a retrial was rejected.

There is no entry for the day of the verdict in her diary, nor for the next four months. The night before she had written that the combination of the drugs she took in the morning to 'stimulate [her] heart' and the sedative to counteract those at night had made her 'hazy' in court but otherwise offered no reaction to her experiences. She maintained she had 'neither rebelled nor asked for a miracle'. She once again turned to the Bible asking for God's pity on her 'for I have no strength'. The switchback of emotions she had experienced in the previous years had cauterised her feelings.

*

There were other trials in 1949. Suzanne Laurent had been captured by the invading Allies as she awaited her lover in the chaos of Germany. She was hoping to get back to France, see her daughter and recover her belongings from the requisitioned flat near the Etoile. She was caught in Kuhberg, in the Black Forest, carrying false papers that identified her as a French labourer. She managed to get work with the United Nations Relief and Rehabilitation Administration, where she met an American colonel who fell for her charms and offered to marry her 'to make life easier for her and protect her from the French authorities'. She wrote to her sister asking for her birth certificate for the ceremony, at which point it emerged that she was wanted in France 'as an important German spy'.

Suzanne was in the dock alongside Roger Bardet and Jean Lucien Kieffer in November. Not a single witness appeared in her defence and she was sentenced to three years' imprisonment, a fine and confiscation of her possessions. She wrote from prison to Bleicher to tell him how the public prosecutor in the trial 'spoke for a quarter of an hour' in his indictment about him, 'his gifts as a psychologist, his keen intelligence and his decency ... the intrepid Bleicher with his amazing luck'. Bleicher's vanity must have been tickled by such acclaim for a time that was very distant from the small tobacconist's shop he now ran in Tettnang, near Lake Constance. Suzanne later changed her name and became a manageress in 'a provincial hotel'.

Mathilde was called as a witness to Kieffer's trial, but simply answered the 'many questions' she was asked in court, 'I don't know, I've forgotten.' She had 'determined to say nothing which could help this partisan justice'. Despite Kieffer's treachery, and the painful parallels with her own activities on behalf of the Abwehr, she realised that there was no hope of fair treatment by this stage. Months after her death sentence, she felt that some had 'vilified' her because of their own 'guilty consciences' in a war in which few were able to act from entirely unselfish motives; her 'true personality' that yearned to do right had been misunderstood, her 'mistakes' transformed into high treason and her 'shortcomings into vices'. It was not for her to do the same for others. Both Kieffer and Bardet were condemned to death, but Bardet's sentence was commuted to twenty years' imprisonment. Kieffer, the betrayer of Interallié and Donkeyman, who had been fittingly code-named 'Asp' at one point in his career, was eventually granted an amnesty in 1953, after any appetite for judicial killings had passed.

The last of the major Vichy figures to face trial was the elegant René Bousquet, regarded by Himmler as 'a precious collaborator' who had prepared the July 1942 detention of over 13,000 Jews in inhuman conditions that became known as the 'Vel' d'Hiv' round-up'. Bousquet's three-day trial and its outcome were in stark contrast to Mathilde's: his 'contacts with the Resistance', notably the *Vichysto-résistant* François Mitterrand, just starting his rise to becoming the longest-serving president of France, ensured Bousquet's acquittal for 'intelligence with the enemy'. The sentence of five years' *dégradation nationale* was lifted on the same day as the court imposed it, his Légion d'Honneur was restored to him and Bousquet was free to pursue a prosperous business and political career. He was eventually indicted for war crimes in 1991 as the repercussions of French collaboration continued to emerge, but was assassinated in 1993 by 'an unhinged publicity-seeker' before his appearance in the dock with the attendant potential for political disaster.

*

Mathilde wrote a letter in pencil on a tatty piece of paper to Maître Naud. She had 'no reason to keep anything secret', and he should believe her when she said he should not 'give any credence to the evidence given by certain of the witnesses on the subject of my so-called depravity'. She did not want to remain 'in his memory either as a monster or as a woman deprived of all feeling', and had now realised that she had been forced by circumstance to put on a 'mask so as the better to hide my real nature'. It was her 'mastery over myself' that enabled her to wear the fixed smile in court and even now in her shackles in the condemned cell, which was lit day and night and searched daily although she had no possessions and no visitors. She thanked Naud for his 'admirable defence' which had moved her to 'fight back tears'. She who had spurned suicide had 'the right to dispose of' her own life, and would like to achieve more before she died: she begged him 'to do everything you can to try and get me out of this awful cell and this prison'. In place of her signature she drew the seated cat silhouette used to sign off letters to Harmer, Llewellyn Lloyd and others she admired.

Naud addressed a closely reasoned, four-page document to President Auriol. He summarised the valuable work his client had done for the Allies and the Deuxième Bureau, maintaining that she had no choice but to act as she had after her arrest: following the capture of Czerniawski and Borni, 'Bleicher and his agents found at the headquarters of the organisation many documents, including papers with the addresses of all the agents and a complete report on the activity of the network, with the code names of the agents and in some cases their names *en clair* as well.' Sooner or later they all would have been caught without her co-operation. Her role had been a passive one, and 'one which she was unable to avoid under penalty of death'. In legal terms, 'the prosecution appears not to have taken the element of doubt sufficiently into consideration'.

Naud's next argument addressed the tricky subject of her physical capitulation to Bleicher. He believed that 'this unpleasant fact is not in itself incompatible with the intelligence activity of an agent of the importance of this woman who was, in fact, the second-in-command of Armand', and thought that the prosecution had 'exploited' the liaison 'as a heavy presumption of her guilt, so that her trial was carried out largely on psychological grounds'.

His plea for mercy was summarised in four points: she had been 'an authentic, effective member of the Resistance from September 1940 to November 1941'; she had admitted 'her error of two months during the time of her arrest'; she 'revealed herself' to de Vomécourt, an 'Allied agent'; and she 'risked her life by making this confidence' and by 'organising her departure for London'. If Bleicher had known what was going on, she would have been 'pitilessly executed' by him. Legal arguments aside, Naud later ruminated on Mathilde's case as well as the business of running and turning agents in general, to conclude that 'she would have been absolved, if it could have been admitted that at certain times in the life of a spy, a double game is part of "the game"'.

The hundredth day following Mathilde's trial fell on Easter Day, 17th April 1949, and on Easter Monday she wrote to her lawyer again. She confessed that she felt 'calm, strong and in full command of my faculties' and reconciled to her impending death. Her 'stupid pride' was 'hurt' at not being able to go to it 'voluntarily' but she felt death had always been her 'friend', even as she chose not to take her life in 1940 and again a year later.

Mathilde took up her diary once more on 4th May. The preceding entry had been written the day before sentence was passed, and the intervening period had been 'the most disconcerting, painful and spiritually overwhelming days of [her] life' as she struggled to equate her beliefs and motivations with her imminent execution. She had suffered from 'appalling headaches' and 'nightmares which turned to hallucinations' in 'the utter degradation' of prison as she relived the evidence given against her in court. The spur to picking up her pen was the receipt of a reprieve signed by President Auriol and her move out of the condemned cell. She had realised that she was due to face the firing squad the following day when she had asked for, and had been allowed, flowers in her cell, and for her hair to be cut by the prison nurse, whose hand trembled as she did so.

*

Mathilde's sentence was commuted to twenty years' hard labour. In the emotion of the hours after the chains around her feet had been removed, she had wept at the prospect of 'the indeterminate number of years' she now faced behind bars. She was transferred to the solidity of Rennes prison, and once again abandoned her diary, this time for years. She was put to work in the wash house and the misery of the work, particularly in winter, and the 'hubbub and the faces' that were all fascinated by the notoriety of La Chatte, came close to overwhelming her. She tried to keep a hold on her sanity by muttering an incantation: 'If hell exists, it must be something in this nature.' She retreated into herself, preferring isolation to the 'gossip and intrigues' of her fellow inmates; she looked down on 'a body which walks and moves, eats and drinks, evacuates and laughs nervously' but questioned whether the soul existed. Her parents were her only visitors, her mother still raging against the English who had let her daughter down after her 'inestimable service' to them.

By 1953 Mathilde was back in Paris, in La Roquette prison. André Achard had re-entered her life and she now regarded him as her 'best friend'. Achard introduced her to a monk he 'loved and admired' and by whom she agreed to be baptised. The governor gave special dispensation for the ceremony to be held in a small nun's chapel to avoid publicity, and she chose as her godmother and witness 'a kindly street woman' named Marthe. From then on Mathilde was able to commit herself to a cause far removed from her ultimately disappointing earthly ventures. She had at last put aside the 'envy, money, lust and vanity' which 'lead to all the cowardices, all the compromise and all the sin'. In her new-found humility, away from the judgement of mankind, she no longer needed to mention her courage, as she had so often in the past.

*

Mathilde Carré was released in September 1954 after over twelve years in prison, three of them in England, and returned to the avenue des Gobelins flat where her parents still lived. Once word got around that she was free, journalists clamoured to see her, but she gave only two interviews. The journalists found 'a quiet, modestly dressed woman', quite unlike the *espionne fatale* they had hoped for. She did not attempt to justify her actions, nor blame the British for locking her up; she 'did not wish to make any complaints' although they 'did know' that she had been 'of real use' to them. It was disappointing copy and the accompanying photographs did not show her face.

Afterwards, she asked her parents to say that she had left Paris and left the public view. Three years after her release she was reported to be 'half blind and fiercely solitary'. She would now find her own redemption in religion rather than in the society she eschewed. She died in her flat near the Luxembourg Gardens on 30th May 2007, a month short of her ninety-ninth birthday.

*

The day after her trial ended, Mathilde had been visited by the chief commissioner of police from Bordeaux who was following up on Roman Czerniawski's enrolment in the Abwehr in the autumn of 1942. At first she refused to believe such a thing could have happened, but the contract that he had signed in the Brasserie Georges in Lyons was proof. The commissioner even told her that Roman's Abwehr number was 7167. She was outraged: she had always refused Bleicher's invitations to join the service and yet was now living under a death sentence; Roman was at liberty and had not even given evidence on her behalf. Subsequently, her testimony to the policemen was not needed as the case was opened before a tribunal in Bordeaux but 'immediately squashed', no doubt thanks to clandestine British pressure.

Albert Naud must have had Czerniawski in mind when he commented that 'some of those with whom The Cat worked were strong
enough to play a double game with the Germans. That was because
they were professionals at this game. Mathilde Carré was only an
amateur – and she showed the human weakness of an amateur in
the tough game of espionage.' He might have added that post-war
justice was similarly harsh and uneven, despite his best efforts and
clear-sighted advocacy. She became a pawn in that game as well, let
down by her flaws and buffeted by fortune and the confusion of the
times in a country riven with mistrust and betrayal.

Roman, the energetic, visionary and unwaveringly patriotic Pole
who had launched Mathilde on her career as a spy after their chance
meeting in Toulouse, well understood the motivations and subtleties of intelligence-gathering in wartime. He did not see her again
after the night of the Big Network's anniversary party, but was
rightly proud of their joint achievement and its 'people of extreme
courage and hard, self-denying work'. Without naming her, he proposed that of those colleagues who 'broke down and, under
pressure, betrayed others', each had 'to be studied separately to
understand the motives of behaviour, which may have had roots' in
any number of characteristics or experiences; nobody could simply
be written off as a traitor. He grasped an essential truth from his
first-hand experience when he admitted that 'I don't know how I
would have behaved if I had been one of those particular cases.
And you ... ?'

The ambivalence and complications faced by many, particularly
women, during the Occupation contained in that open question
tended to be forgotten as the years passed since that foggy
November day of Mathilde's arrest in Montmartre. Authors and
journalists periodically resurfaced to scratch at France's wartime
history and 'took up their pens against' her as a clear example of a
collaborator. She set aside the 'impulsive or even vicious reaction'
she might have given during the early years of her imprisonment to
emerge without 'inner unrest or anger, no rancour and ... no facile

excuses' about her past. She longed, and did everything she could, 'to be forgotten and left in peace'; but she knew that for her complex actions and reactions at a time when compromise and survival often superseded the purity of patriotism, she was doomed to be 'an unfortunate star'. All she could do at such a point was 'stay absolutely still', an uncharacteristic pose for the restless, passionate spy who had scurried around Paris in her red hat, black fur coat and flat shoes in her country's darkest days.

Acknowledgements

I owe a great debt to Ben Macintyre for our many conversations over the past few years about Mathilde Carré, Interallié, the experience of France in the war, the complexities of espionage and counter-espionage, and for his astute comments on the manuscript in its closing stages.

Over the course of writing this book, I have benefited from many conversations and insights into both the Second World War and the story's characters, motivations and actions with Marie-Elsa Bragg, Carmen Callil, Melissa Cosby, Maurice Gourdault-Montagne, Tam Hoskyns, Robert McCrum, Caroline Moorehead, John Preston, Sonia Purnell, Julia Samuel and Adam Zamoyski.

Gerry Czerniawski, Jeremy Harmer and Sue Harmer were generous with their assistance, particularly with regard to photographs of their fathers; Juliet Brightmore once again proved herself a peerless picture researcher and the staff at the National Archives in Kew were as unfailingly helpful as ever. In France, Sylvie Deroche introduced me to Margaux Dumas, a tireless researcher who produced some unknown treasures from the *Archives Nationales* in Paris and elsewhere; Philippe Sands introduced me to Catalina de la Sota who provided context on the legal system in the 1940s; Kate Philipps and Charlotte Juteau retraced Mathilde's footsteps across the locked-down city. My wife Felicity Rubinstein and Francesca Best both provided important feedback on the text.

My agent Natasha Fairweather has been a committed champion as well as an astute reader from the start, and I am very grateful both to her and to Matthew Marland at Rogers, Coleridge & White. I am extraordinarily fortunate to work with Stuart Williams of The

Bodley Head: his editorial insights and tenacity, allied to his outstanding publishing sense, have made the process of the book a great pleasure as well as greatly improved the finished product. David Milner has proved to be an eagle-eyed, astute and knowledgeable copy-editor, Fiona Brown, a sharp-eyed proof-reader, and Lauren Howard has been invaluable in steering the book to publication. Needless to say its deficiencies are down to me.

My greatest gratitude and love for their constant support and forbearance go to my wife Felicity and my son Nat, to whom this book is dedicated.

Bibliography

Archives

Archives Nationales, Paris
British Library Newspaper Archive, London
Harry Ransom Center, University of Texas
National Archives, Kew

Books

Andrew, Christopher *The Defence of the Realm: The Authorised History of MI5* (London, 2009)

Ashdown, Paddy *Game of Spies* (London, 2016)

Beevor, Antony *The Second World War* (London, 2012)

Beevor, Antony and Cooper, Artemis *Paris: After the Liberation 1944–49* (London, 2017)

Binney, Marcus *The Women Who Lived for Danger: The Women Agents of SOE in the Second World War* (London, 2002)

Bleicher, Hugo *Colonel Henri's Story: The War Memoirs of Hugo Bleicher, Former German Secret Agent* (London, 1954)

Boyd, Douglas *Voices From the Dark Years: The Truth About Occupied France 1940–45* (Stroud, 2007)

Buckmaster, Maurice *They Fought Alone: The True Story of SOE's Agents in Wartime France* (London, 2014)

Callil, Carmen, *Bad Faith* (London, 2006)

Camus, Albert, trans. Robin Buss *The Plague* (London, 2002)

Carré, Mathilde-Lily *I Was the Cat: The Truth About the Most Remarkable Woman Spy Since Mata Hari – By Herself* (London, 1960)

——*Ma Conversion* (Paris, 1970)

Churchill, Winston *The Second World War: Their Finest Hour* (London, 1969)

Costello, John and Tsarev, Oleg *Deadly Illusions* (London, 1993)

Cowburn, Ben *No Cloak, No Dagger: Allied Spycraft In Occupied France* (London, 1969)

Day, Peter *Klop: Britain's Most Ingenious Secret Agent* (London, 2014)

Deák, István *Europe On Trial: The Story of Collaboration, Resistance and Retribution During World War II* (Boulder, 2015)

Deák, István, Gross, Jan T. and Judt, Tony *The Politics of Retribution in Europe* (New Haven, 2000)

d'Harcourt, Pierre *The Real Enemy* (London, 1967)

Foot, M. R. D. *SOE in France: An Account of the Work of British Special Operations Executive in France 1940–44* (London, 1966)

—— *SOE: The Special Operations Executive 1940–46* (London, 1993)

Forbes, Robert *For Europe: The French Volunteers of the Waffen-SS* (Solihull, 2006)

Fourcade, Marie-Madeleine, trans. Kenneth Morgan *Noah's Ark* (London, 1973)

Garby-Czerniawski, Roman *The Big Network* (London, 1961)

Gildea, Robert *Fighters in the Shadows: A New History of the French Resistance* (London, 2015)

—— *Marianne in Chains: Daily Life in the Heart of France During the German Occupation* (New York, 2003)

Guéhenno, Jean, trans. David Ball, *Diary of the Dark Years 1940–44* (Oxford, 2016)

Hastings, Max *The Secret War: Spies, Codes and Guerrillas 1939–1945* (London, 2015)

Helm, Sarah *A Life in Secrets: Vera Atkins and the Missing Agents of World War II* (New York, 2005)

Izbicki, John *The Naked Heroine: From the French Resistance to the Folies-Bergère* (London, 2014)

Jackson, Julian *A Certain Idea of France: The Life of Charles de Gaulle* (London, 2018)

—— *France: The Dark Years 1940–44* (Oxford, 2001)

Kedward, H. R. *Occupied France: Collaboration and Resistance 1940–44* (Oxford, 1985)

Kernan, Thomas *Report on France* (London, 1942)

Kessel, Joseph, trans. Rainer J. Hanshe *Army of Shadows* (New York, 2017)

Levine, Joshua, *Operation Fortitude: The Greatest Hoax of the Second World War* (London, 2012)

Liddell, Guy *The Guy Liddell Diaries, Vol 2*, ed. Nigel West (Abingdon, 2005)

Lloyd, Christopher *Collaboration and Resistance in Occupied France* (Basingstoke, 2003)

Lottman, Herbert R. *The Purge: The Purification of French Collaborators After World War II* (New York, 1986)

Lytton, Neville *Life In Unoccupied France* (London, 1942)

McGilvray, Evan *A Military Government in Exile* (Warwick, 2013)

Macintyre, Ben *Double Cross: The True Story of the D-Day Spies* (London, 2016)

McKinstry, Leo *Operation Sealion* (London, 2015)

Masterman, J. C. *The Double-Cross System* (London, 2013)

Mazower, Mark *Hitler's Empire: Nazi Rule in Occupied Europe* (London, 2008)

Milton, Giles *The Ministry of Ungentlemanly Warfare* (London, 2016)

Moorehead, Caroline *Village of Secrets: Defying the Nazis in Vichy France* (London, 2014)

Muggeridge, Malcolm *Chronicles of Wasted Time*, Vol. II (London, 1973)

Némirovsky, Irène *Suite Française* (London, 2006)

Ousby, Ian *Occupation: The Ordeal of France 1940–44* (London, 2017)

Paxton, Robert *Vichy France: Old Guard and New Order 1940–44* (New York, 2001)

Philby, Kim *My Secret War: The Autobiography of a Spy* (London, 1968)

Pryce-Jones, David *Paris in the Third Reich* (London, 1991)

—— *Signatures: Literary Encounters of a Lifetime* (New York, 2020)

Purnell, Sonia *A Woman of No Importance* (London, 2019)

Renault-Routier, Gilbert *On m'appelait Rémy* (Paris, 1966)

Roberts, Andrew *Churchill: Walking with Destiny* (London, 2018)

Rosbottom, Ronald *When Paris Went Dark: The City of Light Under German Occupation 1940–44* (London, 2015)

Ruby, Marcel *F Section SOE: The Story of the Buckmaster Network* (London, 1990)

Saint-Exupéry, Antoine de, trans. William Rees *Flight to Arras* (London, 1995)

Sartre, Jean-Paul, trans. Lisa Liberman *Paris Under the Occupation* (Los Angeles, 2011)

Sebba, Anne *Les Parisiennes: How the Women of Paris Lived, Loved and Died in the 1940s* (London, 2017)

Shakespeare, Nicholas *Priscilla: The Hidden Life of an Englishwoman in Wartime France* (London, 2014)

Shirer, William L. *The Rise and Fall of the Third Reich* (London, 1991)

Spotts, Frederic *The Shameful Peace: How French Artists and Intellectuals Survived the Nazi Occupation* (New Haven and London, 2008)

Stroud, Rick *Lonely Courage* (London, 2017)

Tremain, David *Double Agent Victoire: Mathilde Carré and the Interallié Network* (Stroud, 2018)

Verity, Hugh *We Landed by Moonlight: The Secret RAF Landings in France 1940–44* (Wilmslow, 1998)

Vomécourt, Philippe de *An Army of Amateurs* (New York, 1961)

Waller, Douglas *Disciples: The World War II Missions of the CIA Directors who Fought for Wild Bill Donovan* (London, 2016)

Young, Gordon *The Cat With Two Faces* (London, 1957)

Notes

TNA – The National Archives, Kew, London. Citations marked FO refer to Foreign Office files, CAB to Cabinet Office files, HS to Special Operations Executive files, KV to Security Service files.

FAN – Archives Nationales, Paris. Translations by the author.

When multiple consecutive quotations are from the same source in the same paragraph, only the last in each sequence has been credited.

Prologue

p. 1   put to sea – Young, *The Cat With Two Faces* p. 108

Chapter 1: A Profound Need

p. 3   black factory town – Carré, *I Was the Cat* p. 15

p. 3   miniature little lady – ibid.

p. 4   martyr for France – ibid. p. 16–17

p. 5   into a passion – ibid. p. 18

p. 5   so in love – ibid. p. 20

p. 5   lack of affection – FAN 72/AJ/39

p. 5   consideration and affection – Carré, op. cit. pp. 20–1

p. 6   love and please – ibid. p. 18

p. 6   modern, active woman – ibid. p. 25

p. 6   never kissed – ibid. pp. 26–7

p. 7   brains and taste – ibid. p. 29

p. 7   carefully phrased, cultured – Garby-Czerniawski, *The Big Network* p. 43

p. 7   drawn towards evil – Carré, op. cit. p. 29

p. 8   a bitterness – ibid. p. 30

p. 8   young as ever – ibid. p. 35

p. 8   sensibility and love – ibid. p. 33

p. 8   of the moment – ibid. p. 31

p. 9   worn out and drifting – ibid. pp. 35–6

p. 9   throbbing with life – ibid. p. 35

p. 9	dominating and vindictive – ibid. p. 38
p. 10	superior class – ibid. pp. 38–9
p. 10	deep-seated loyalty – TNA KV 2/931
p. 10	a complete illusion – Carré, op. cit. p. 41
p. 10	a lamentable man – FAN 72/AJ/39
p. 11	of that woman – Carré, op. cit. p. 41
p. 11	on her part – TNA KV 2/931
p. 11	have no bounds – Carré, op. cit. pp. 42–3
p. 12	nourish its mind – ibid. pp. 46–7
p. 12	restless and unbalanced – ibid. p. 50
p. 13	mad – ibid. p. 52
p. 13	yet magnificent pride – FAN Z/6/696
p. 13	marriage ended – FAN 72/AJ/39
p. 13	dead to her – FAN Z/6/696
p. 14	intended to be – Carré, op. cit. p. 52
p. 14	and beautiful task – FAN Z/6/696
p. 14	at the enemy – TNA KV 2/931
p. 15	lack of morality – ibid.
p. 15	petty [and] gossipy – FAN Z/6/696
p. 15	anyone had foreseen – Churchill, *Their Finest Hour* p. 24
p. 15	bottle of rum – FAN Z/6/696
p. 16	Rabelaisian bonhomie – ibid.
p. 16	morale was high – Carré, op. cit. p. 61
p. 16	is already immaterial – ibid.
p. 16	in real danger – Young, *The Cat With Two Faces* p.20
p. 16	*une volupté extraordinaire* – FAN Z/6/696

Chapter 2: A Useful Suicide

p. 18	hopeless mess – Carré, op. cit. p. 67
p. 18	just as little – ibid. p. 63
p. 19	fifth columnist – ibid. p. 64
p. 19	and in despair – ibid. pp. 64–5
p. 20	goal: the south – quoted Gildea, *Marianne in Chains* p. 22
p. 20	a massive anthill – quoted Jackson, *France: The Dark Years* p. 120
p. 20	but go where? – Spotts, *The Shameful Peace* p. 74
p. 20	by the army – Carré, op. cit. p. 65
p. 20	a Slav accent – ibid.
p. 20	intelligent and charming – FAN Z/6/696
p. 20	along the road – ibid.
p. 21	bending over backwards – ibid.
p. 21	sodden with defeatism – Shirer, *The Rise and Fall of the Third Reich* p. 738

p. 22   airmen and disappeared – Carré, op. cit. p. 66
p. 22   real family – FAN Z/6/696
p. 22   unpleasant in [her] life – Carré, op. cit. p. 66
p. 23   stirring up of insurrection – TNA CAB 301/49
p. 23   two scorpions' tails – Callil, *Bad Faith*, p. 198
p. 23   be your shield – Ousby, *Occupation* p. 340
p. 24   the administrative sphere – quoted in Paxton, *Vichy France* p. xii
p. 24   of the continent – ibid. p. 7
p. 24   what is inevitable – Pryce-Jones, *Signatures* p. 72
p. 24   say 'my love' – Guéhenno, *Diary of the Dark Years* p. 3
p. 25   never go out – ibid. p. 1
p. 26   with a smile – quoted Paxton, op. cit. p. 135
p. 26   the noblest undertakings – Sartre, *Paris Under the Occupation* p. 22
p. 26   traitors at Vichy – Carré, op. cit. p. 88
p. 27   German war economy – quoted McKinstry, *Operation Sealion* pp. 343–5
p. 27   still a country – d'Harcourt, *The Real Enemy* p. 6
p. 27   moral and political asphyxiation – Beevor, *The Second World War* p. 128
p. 27   of France itself – Beevor and Cooper, *Paris After the Liberation* p. 383
p. 28   happy in [her] life – Carré, op. cit. p. 66
p. 28   like any other – ibid. p. 67
p. 28   balance sheet – FAN Z/6/696
p. 28   a useful suicide – Carré, op. cit. p. 67
p. 28   open to patriots – ibid. p. 68
p. 28   invisible weapon, intelligence – Fourcade, *Noah's Ark* p. 51
p. 29   appalling French accent – Carré op. cit. p. 68

Chapter 3: La Chatte

p. 30   like a Spitfire – FAN Z/6/696
p. 30   intelligence and willpower – Carré, op. cit. p. 69
p. 30   the great affection – FAN Z/6/696.
p. 30   friendship became intimate – TNA KV 2/928
p. 31   die for it – Macintyre, *Double Cross* p. 12
p. 31   the Polish people – TNA KV 2/72
p. 31   and egoistical nature – TNA KV 2/4532
p. 31   and thinks spying – ibid.
p. 32   and Lieut. Czyż – Garby-Czerniawski, op. cit p. 16
p. 32   Fourth Force: *Underground . . .* – ibid. pp. 22–3
p. 32   of contemporary warfare – ibid. p. 23
p. 33   their desperate fight – Fourcade, op. cit. p. 51
p. 33   in its cradle – Foot, *SOE In France* p. 148
p. 33   wild mountain passes – Garby-Czerniawski, op. cit. p. 29
p. 33   and experienced general – ibid. p. 30

p. 33   screaming for action – ibid. p. 34

p. 33   against the Boche – ibid. p. 35

p. 34   more unusual woman – ibid. p.36

p. 34   mannered and gentle – FAN Z/6/696

p. 34   and good wine – Garby-Czerniawski, op. cit. p. 37

p. 35   find interesting people – ibid. p. 43

p. 35   his fiancée Eva – FAN Z/6/696

p. 35   amounts to suicide – Carré, op. cit. p. 69

p. 35   and artistic feelings – FAN Z/6/696

p. 35   to be conquered – Carré, op. cit. p. 70

p. 35   war – and defeat – Garby-Czerniawski, op. cit. p. 45

p. 35   render great services – TNA KV 2/72

p. 36   second Jeanne d'Arc – Garby-Czerniawski, op. cit. p. 49

p. 36   d'Arc of Poland – TNA KV 2/72

p. 36   both of us – Carré, op. cit. p. 70

p. 36   if pressed hard – Garby-Czerniawski, op. cit. p. 49

p. 36   scratch as well – ibid.

p. 36   way of life – FAN Z/6/696

p. 37   back on generalities – Kedward, *Occupied France* p. 35

p. 37   profoundly humiliated nation – Deák, *Europe on Trial* p. 55

p. 37   singing the 'Marseillaise' – ibid. p. 200

p. 37   old Jean-Pierre – Garby-Czerniawski, op. cit. p. 53

p. 38   her future lover? – Carré, op. cit. p. 71

p. 38   Deuxième Bureau circles – TNA KV2/931

p. 38   from the Germans – Carré, op. cit. p. 71

p. 38   in occupied France – ibid.

p. 38   and enthusiastic approach – ibid. p. 54

p. 38   felt quite safe – TNA KV 2/72

p. 38   conditions of travel – TNA KV 2/4351

p. 38   very important undertaking – Carré, op. cit. p. 72

p. 39   very serious business – FAN Z/6/696

p. 39   *victoire du monde* – Carré, op. cit. p. 72

p. 39   made a major – ibid. p. 73

p. 39   returned to France – Mount, op. cit.

p. 39   actions – Carré, op. cit. p. 73

p. 40   based on films – TNA KV 2/4351

p. 40   and fine features – Carré, op. cit. p. 73

p. 40   still gingering up – Jackson, *A Certain Idea of France* p. 128

p. 40   was shot down – Roberts, *Churchill* p. 618

p. 40   as a nurse – TNA KV 2/931

p. 40   few days' wages – Garby-Czerniawski, op. cit. p. 60

p. 41   a powder trail – Gildea, *Fighters in the Shadows* p. 58

p. 41   Wehrmacht military signposts – Young, op. cit. p. 29

p. 41   genius with Napoleon – Ousby, op. cit. p. 66
p. 41   more than doubled – ibid. p. 123
p. 41   petrol to coffee – Callil, op. cit. p. 210
p. 42   no soul left – Carré, op. cit. p. 76
p. 42   of such work – FAN Z/6/696
p. 42   *un physique quelconque* – FAN 72/AJ/39
p. 42   information from France – TNA KV 2/72
p. 42   new warships built – Roberts, op. cit. p. 642

Chapter 4: The Big Network

p. 44   night observation – Garby-Czerniawski, op. cit. p. 63
p. 44   in intelligence work – TNA KV 2/72
p. 44   making contacts – Garby-Czerniawski, op. cit. p. 64
p. 44   uneconomical and dangerous – ibid. pp. 64–5
p. 45   have a budget – FAN Z/6/696
p. 45   a naïve goodwill – Sartre, op. cit. p. 8
p. 45   the German army – Rosbottom, *When Paris Went Dark* p. 125
p. 46   all the women – Carré, op. cit. p. 88
p. 47   chief of staff – ibid. p. 77
p. 47   politics and propaganda – FAN Z/6/696
p. 48   conquered – FAN F/7/15157
p. 48   good initiatives – ibid.
p. 49   dawdle or chat – ibid.
p. 49   spoke French inadequately – TNA KV 2/931
p. 49   sure of herself – Young, op. cit. p. 35
p. 50   and conscientious man – TNA KV 2/4351
p. 50   hints and suggestions – Garby-Czerniawski, op. cit. p. 76
p. 50   times a week – TNA KV 2/931
p. 50   charming manners – Garby-Czerniawski, op. cit. p. 75
p. 50   for train allocations – TNA KV 2/931
p. 50   the French Railways – Garby-Czerniawski, op. cit. p. 71
p. 50   and conflicting loyalties – Young, op. cit. p. 31
p. 50   devoted – TNA KV 2/933
p. 51   cheerful, cheeky – FAN Z/6/696
p. 51   broad and solid – TNA KV 2/753
p. 51   efficient and intelligent – TNA KV 2/72
p. 51   able and trustworthy – KV 2/753
p. 51   a Messerschmitt etc. – FAN Z/6/696
p. 51   printed demobilisation forms – Carré, op. cit. p. 81
p. 51   a forwarding address – FAN Z/6/696
p. 52   but always grousing – Carré, op. cit. p. 82
p. 52   ambitious and intriguing – FAN 72/AJ/39

p. 52   great happiness – FAN Z/6/696
p. 52   us as well – d'Harcourt, op. cit. p. 16
p. 52   to obtain results – Carré, ibid. p. 83
p. 52   absolute confidence – FAN Z/6/696
p. 52   thin, sensitive hands – Young, op. cit. p. 36
p. 52   youthful freshness – FAN Z/6/696
p. 53   from huge fire – Garby-Czerniawski, op. cit. p. 73
p. 53   this European prison – Guéhenno, op. cit. p. 42
p. 53   small French industry – TNA KV 2/931
p. 53   would flow in – Izbicki, *The Naked Heroine* p. 53
p. 53   calm and brave – Carré, op. cit. p. 81
p. 54   new possibilities – Garby-Czerniawski, op. cit. p. 79
p. 54   in the town – Carré, op. cit. p. 78
p. 54   leading to B – ibid.
p. 56   flat, red shoes – Garby-Czerniawski, op. cit. p. 79
p. 56   of the dictionary – TNA KV 2/931
p. 57   several weeks later – TNA KV 2/4351
p. 57   value of money – FAN Z/6/696
p. 58   the best people – ibid.
p. 59   despairing letters – ibid.

Chapter 5: In Every Way

p. 60   indispensable – Garby-Czerniawski, op. cit. p. 23
p. 60   at that time – TNA KV 2/931
p. 60   against the Boche – Garby-Czerniawski, op. cit. p. 35
p. 60   a petite blonde – FAN Z/6/696
p. 60   of La Chatte – TNA KV 2/931
p. 61   found celibacy unbearable – Carré, op. cit. p. 86
p. 61   Dostoevsky's 'eternal husband' – ibid. p. 89
p. 61   came often – FAN Z/6/696
p. 61   did not work – TNA KV 2/931
p. 61   felt the same – FAN Z/6/696
p. 61   publicity agent – TNA KV 2/929
p. 61   to harbour regrets – Carré, op. cit. p. 86
p. 62   Monsieur Gestapo – FAN Z/6/696
p. 62   other for courtesies – Carré, op. cit. p. 87
p. 62   music all day – TNA KV 2/931
p. 62   bayoneted in the buttocks – FAN Z/6/696
p. 62   know – these scientists! – Garby-Czerniawski, op. cit. p. 132
p. 62   even a cult – FAN Z/6/696
p. 62   Affectionately. Love – Guéhenno, op. cit. p. 60
p. 63   in every corner – FAN Z/6/696

p. 63   all been marked – Young, op. cit. p. 32

p. 63   being too dirty – FAN 72/AJ/39

p. 64   the salient points – TNA KV 2/4351

p. 64   them for inefficiency – ibid.

p. 64   general situation – Carré, op. cit. p. 87

p. 64   professional customs men – Gildea, *Marianne in Chains* p. 142

p. 65   third-class dominion – Jackson, *France: The Dark Years* p. 178

p. 65   had grown stale – TNA KV 2/933

p. 65   *envichysés* – FAN Z/6/696

p. 65   and his daughter – FAN Z/6/696

p. 65   studies in medicine – Carré, op. cit. p. 91

p. 66   than actually clever – FAN Z/6/696

p. 66   mouth too wide – Carré, op. cit. p. 93

p. 66   black market activities – Garby-Czerniawski, op. cit. p. 131

p. 66   a great deal – TNA KV 2/931

p. 67   high-domed forehead – Young, op. cit. p. 36

p. 67   all the data – FAN Z/6/696

p. 67   and torn clothes – Young, op. cit. p. 43

p. 67   of the world – FAN Z/6/696

p. 67   to British subjects – TNA KV 2/931

p. 67   bit jealous, unnecessarily – FAN Z/6/696

p. 67   anti-aircraft installations – Young, op. cit. p. 42

p. 68   gamblers always do – FAN Z/6/696

p. 68   staunchly pro-British – Young, op. cit. p. 46

p. 68   feigned nasal – FAN Z/6/696

p. 68   with marked interest – Carré, op. cit. p. 95

p. 68   all her charm – TNA KV 2/931

p. 68   of the townspeople – Carré, op. cit. p. 96

p. 68   very amiable meal – FAN Z/6/696

p. 69   and efficient work – Garby-Czerniawski, op. cit. p. 101

p. 69   obvious inner strength – ibid. p. 105

p. 69   and his family – FAN Z/6/696

p. 70   link Stop Valentin – Garby-Czerniawski, op. cit. pp. 105–6

p. 70   the big desk – ibid. p. 107

p. 72   heaven's sake work – Carré, op. cit. p. 92

p. 72   old family servant – Garby-Czerniawski, op. cit. p. 126

p. 72   profits for centuries – ibid. p. 128

p. 72   modern and cute – Carré, op. cit. p. 93

p. 73   Review of the Press – Garby-Czerniawski, op. cit. p. 129

p. 74   new and unusual life – ibid. p. 119

p. 74   swift and successful – Carré, op. cit. p. 98

p. 74   with no education – TNA KV 2/931

p. 74   a true woman – FAN Z/6/696

p. 75   the Maginot Line – Fourcade, op. cit. p. 69
p. 75   occupied Western Europe – Rosbottom, op. cit. p. 161
p. 75   personal reasons – FAN Z/6/696
p. 75   on the black market – TNA KV 2/931
p. 75   conditions of work – TNA KV 2/72
p. 76   disappeared – TNA KV 2/931
p. 76   Franco-Scottish gunnery officer – Tremain, *Double Agent Victoire* p. 59
p. 76   well in – TNA KV 2/933
p. 76   excellent new companion – Garby-Czerniawski, op. cit. p. 151
p. 76   fifth columnist – TNA KV 2/931
p. 76   *La Chatte Communiqué* – Tremain, op. cit. p. 56
p. 77   *Vive la Liberté* – Garby-Czerniawski, op. cit. p. 233
p. 77   and reliable reports – TNA KV 2/933
p. 77   the enemy within – Gildea, *Marianne in Chains* p. 17
p. 77   carried out badly – Ousby, op. cit. p. 215
p. 77   shall be shot – Boyd, *Voices From the Dark Years* p. 125
p. 77   nightmare is beginning – quoted Ousby, op. cit. p. 242
p. 78   green frogs – Garby-Czerniawski, op. cit. p. 121
p. 78   astonished and cross – ibid. p. 124
p. 78   in Africa Stop – ibid. p. 142
p. 79   for RAF Stop – ibid. pp. 143–7
p. 80   complete destruction – ibid. p. 164
p. 80   resistance against Germany – ibid. p. 83
p. 80   inspired total confidence – FAN 72/AJ/39
p. 80   the Colonel – TNA KV 2/72
p. 80   burst of energy – Carré, op. cit. p. 100
p. 81   great international affairs – FAN Z/6/696
p. 81   eating her up – TNA KV 2/72
p. 81   an amazing woman – TNA KV 2/931

Chapter 6: Family Betrayal

p. 82   bestowed on her – TNA KV 2/72
p. 83   will fix date – Garby-Czerniawski, op. cit. p. 171
p. 83   sign radio messages – ibid. pp. 171–2
p. 83   *C'est la guerre* – ibid. p. 180
p. 83   a lovely girl – ibid. p. 182
p. 84   unfavourable reports – TNA KV 2/931
p. 84   a consummate cad – TNA KV 2/4351
p. 84   leave of absence – TNA KV 2/931
p. 84   menace to the organisation – ibid.
p. 84   exceptional bravery – TNA KV 2/72
p. 85   she was working – TNA KV 2/929

p. 85   try and poison – Carré, op. cit. p. 98
p. 85   I had done – ibid.
p. 85   his girlfriends – TNA KV 2/931
p. 86   a little house – Carré, op. cit. pp. 99–100
p. 86   a masterly fashion – TNA KV 2/928
p. 86   some business firm – Garby-Czerniawski, op. cit. p. 187
p. 86   shifted uneasily – ibid. p. 197
p. 86   and make threats – ibid. pp. 197–8
p. 87   Chief's girl – TNA KV 2/933
p. 88   officer in France – TNA KV 2/72
p. 88   to become informers – quoted Guéhenno, op. cit. pp. 121–2
p. 89   most exposed sector – KV 2/72
p. 89   Spanish authorities – TNA KV 2/753
p. 90   not in use – TNA KV 2/72
p. 90   stink of spies – Bleicher, *Colonel Henri's Story* p. 36
p. 91   unobtainable in Germany – TNA KV 2/932
p. 91   as his 'concurrents' – TNA KV 2/2127
p. 91   like an elephant – TNA KV 2/4351
p. 92   countries of Europe – Bleicher, op. cit. p. 24
p. 92   her own country – ibid. p. 30
p. 92   tired of business – FAN Z/6/696
p. 92   flower blooming unseen – Young, op. cit. p. 57
p. 92   muddled espionage case – ibid. pp. 35–6
p. 92   three thousand francs – FAN Z/6/696
p. 92   distrust and repugnance – TNA KV 2/2127
p. 93   running double agents – TNA KV 2/72
p. 93   certain Madame Buffet – FAN Z/6/696
p. 93   out of jealousy – TNA KV 2/753
p. 93   a special courier – Young, op. cit. p. 37
p. 94   force in France – TNA KV 2/72
p. 94   days a month – TNA KV 2/753
p. 94   out the arrest –TNA KV 2/164
p. 94   impatient and inefficient – FAN Z/6/696
p. 94   of the *département* – ibid.
p. 94   trouble in Normandy – TNA KV 2/164
p. 94   address of its chief – FAN Z/6/696
p. 94   short verbal process – FAN Z/6/696
p. 95   and double-crossing – Bleicher, op. cit. p. 39
p. 95   would be shot – ibid.
p. 95   set free – TNA KV 2/753
p. 95   its own needs – TNA KV 2/72
p. 95   Armand's adjutant – FAN Z/6/696
p. 96   full of ideas – Garby-Czerniawski, op. cit. p. 229

p. 96   dear friend – TNA KV 2/933
p. 96   sense any danger – TNA KV 2/931
p. 96   melody if possible – ibid.
p. 97   be present – TNA KV 2/72
p. 97   not noisy atmosphere – ibid.
p. 97   *Vive la Liberté* – TNA KV 2/926
p. 97   take a bath – TNA KV 2/72
p. 97   a little tired – Garby-Czerniawski, op. cit. p. 238
p. 98   all security measures – TNA KV 2/72
p. 98   indescribably bad – Fourcade, op. cit. p. 115
p. 98   refused to reply – FAN Z/6/696
p. 98   Léandre in Montmartre – TNA KV 2/164
p. 99   down the headquarters – FAN Z/6/696
p. 99   of common sense – Carré, op. cit. p. 101
p. 99   sad, fascinating melody – Garby-Czerniawski, op. cit. p. 238
p. 99   move and reorganisation – TNA KV 2/72
p. 99   individual in mufti – TNA KV 2/72
p. 100   an ordinary denunciation – ibid.

Chapter 7: Trapped

p. 101   Continental in Brest – TNA KV 2/72
p. 102   general help – FAN Z/6/696
p. 102   supplementing [their] wardrobe –TNA KV 2/928
p. 102   dropping with exhaustion – ibid.
p. 103   Chatte alias Micheline – FAN Z/6/696
p. 103   was indeed 'Michel' – ibid.
p. 104   on her way – FAN 72/AJ/39
p. 104   Vieux Châlet Café – Carré, op. cit. p. 103
p. 104   and completely Nazified – Tremain, op. cit. p. 111
p. 104   us waiting, Madame – ibid. p. 104
p. 104   shot next day – ibid.
p. 105   like viragos – Carré, op. cit. p. 105
p. 105   a bad night – Friedrich Nietzsche, *Beyond Good and Evil*, Aphorism 157
p. 105   noble – ibid. p. 106
p. 105   two German women – Carré, op. cit. p. 106
p. 106   cold of freedom – ibid.
p. 106   four other people – TNA KV 2/926
p. 106   tall and massive – Carré, op. cit. p. 107
p. 106   comfort or death! – TNA KV 2/4351
p. 106   to facilitate arrests – FAN 72/AJ/39
p. 107   own skin, Madame – ibid.
p. 107   work for them – Young, op. cit. p. 68

p. 107   mainsprings of spying – Ben Macintyre, *USA Today*, 27.9.2018
p. 107   by a sledgehammer – Carré, op. cit. pp. 107–8
p. 107   dirty trick – FAN Z/6/696
p. 107   to the marrow – Carré, op. cit. p. 108
p. 107   in any way – FAN 72/AJ/39
p. 108   of no importance – Carré, op. cit. p. 108
p. 108   looked completely exhausted – TNA KV 2/926
p. 108   like a woman – Carré, op. cit. p. 108
p. 108   great agitation – FAN 72/AJ/39
p. 109   mind at rest – Carré, op. cit. p. 109
p. 109   reproached – FAN 72/AJ/39
p. 109   terrifying activity – ibid.
p. 109   jubilant – Carré, op. cit. p. 109
p. 110   was going on – FAN 72/AJ/39
p. 110   and puzzled eyes – Carré, op. cit. p. 110
p. 110   totally dominated – FAN 72/AJ/39
p. 110   to her toilet – Young, op. cit. pp. 71–2
p. 110   him at once! – ibid. p. 72
p. 111   not extricate himself – Carré, op. cit. p. 111
p. 111   proud and dignified – ibid.
p. 111   was washed out – Young, op. cit. p. 73
p. 111   like a sledgehammer – Carré, op. cit. p. 112
p. 111   safe and sound – Young, op. cit. p. 74
p. 112   shall shoot you – ibid. p. 76
p. 112   deathly weary – Carré, op. cit. p.113
p. 112   after your children – Young, op. cit. p.79
p. 113   for her blood – Carré, op. cit. p. 114
p. 113   obtaining her collaboration – TNA KV 2/931
p. 133   pair of arms – Carré, op. cit. p. 155
p. 133   I have done? – Young, op. cit. pp. 182–3

Chapter 8: Double Agent

p. 114   magnificent black Alsatian – Carré, op. cit. p. 115
p. 114   this German pay – ibid.
p. 114   period of hate – ibid.
p. 115   foolish young idealist – ibid. p. 116
p. 115   four more times – FAN 72/AJ/39
p. 116   well with Armand – Young, op. cit. p. 85
p. 116   greatest distress – Carre, op. cit. p. 117
p. 116   a Levantine trader – ibid. p. 124
p. 117   two German technicians – FAN 72/AJ/39
p. 117   who likes money – TNA KV 2/931

p. 117	accepted with acclamation – ibid.
p. 118	urgently. La Chatte – TNA KV 2/926
p. 118	agents' perennial cry – TNA KV 2/933
p. 118	the free zone – ibid.
p. 118	life's work crumble – Carré, op. cit. p. 120
p. 119	believed [her] perfectly – TNA KV 2/931
p. 119	of the enemy – Carré, op. cit. p. 118
p. 119	deep personal affection – Young, op. cit. p. 87
p. 119	his new address – FAN 72/AJ/39
p. 120	crowded studio apartment – Young, op. cit. p. 88
p. 120	big, strapping – FAN 72/AJ/39
p. 120	stupid, capricious worm – Carré, op. cit. p. 122
p. 120	vitality returning – ibid. p. 121
p. 120	the Mozart Requiem – ibid. pp. 122–3
p. 122	with the hounds – ibid.
p. 123	to their relations – TNA KV 2/931
p. 123	*La Famille Attention* – TNA KV 2/926
p. 123	and his organisation – ibid.
p. 123	hopeful – TNA KV 2/931
p. 124	German trap – FAN 72/AJ/39
p. 124	asked for news – TNA KV 2/931
p. 124	for the Germans – Carré, op. cit. p. 124
p. 124	this spy organisation – ibid.
p. 124	was terribly nervous – ibid.
p. 125	of this war – ibid. p. 127
p. 125	greatest spy network – ibid. p. 124
p. 125	Die Villa Katzensteg – FNA Z/6/696
p. 126	drypoint prints etc. – Tremain, op. cit. p. 134
p. 126	besotted by drink – Carré, op. cit. p. 124
p. 126	could, with Victoire – TNA KV 2/931
p. 127	an abandoned child – FAN Z/6/696
p. 127	to humour her – Carré, op. cit. p. 124
p. 127	dismissive tyrant – FNA Z/6/696
p. 127	a malign fox – ibid.
p. 128	for the Germans – TNA KV 2/931
p. 128	ask any questions – FAN 72/AJ/39
p. 128	frigid atmosphere – TNA KV 2/931
p. 128	unless Armand talked – ibid.
p. 129	vague and anodyne – FAN Z/6/696
p. 129	seemed so normal – FAN 72/AJ/39
p. 130	have been arrested – ibid.
p. 130	and a muffler – TNA KV 2/931
p. 131	money is urgent – ibid.

p. 131   worried about Moustique – ibid.

p. 131   about 1st January – ibid.

Chapter 9: Panther

p. 133   ensuing six months – Mazower, *Hitler's Empire* p. 423

p. 133   our best actions – quoted Shakespeare, *Priscilla* p. 274

p. 134   going east instead – Purnell, op. cit. p. 86

p. 135   heat than light – Gildea, *Fighters in the Shadows* p. 115

p. 135   with the *Tirpitz* – Gilbert Renault-Routier, *On m'appelait Rémy* p. 313

p. 135   now gone ashore – Young, op. cit. pp. 107–8

p. 136   'Colonel Rémy's agent' – TNA KV 2/933

p. 136   Inter-Service Research Bureau – Ruby, *F Section SOE* p. 21

p. 136   support their efforts – ibid. p. 40

p. 136   worth to SOE – Foot, *SOE In France* p. 163

p. 137   other spontaneous organisations – TNA HS 9/1539/6

p. 137   by normal standards – Ruby, op. cit. p.40

p. 137   the conversation himself – TNA KV 2/2127

p. 137   two more agents – TNA KV 2/931

p. 138   initiate mass arrests – FAN Z/6/696

p. 138   trustworthy – ibid.

p. 138   sacred to him – Carré, op. cit. p. 135

p. 139   of their community – FAN Z/6/696

p. 139   took no action – TNA KV 2/753

p. 139   more important episode – Carré, op. cit. p. 130

p. 139   a leisurely pace – TNA KV 2/932

p. 140   this splendid mission – FAN Z/6/696

p. 140   *de cette guerre* – TNA KV 2/931

p. 140   regain her confidence – ibid.

p. 140   chain of events – FAN Z/6/696

p. 140   created confidence – TNA KV 2/926

p. 140   charm and gallantry – TNA KV 2/931

p. 141   abandon our aims – ibid.

p. 141   money to France – ibid.

p. 141   a great power – quoted Tremain, op. cit. p. 156

p. 141   the Russian Front – TNA HS 9/1539/6

p. 142   furious – TNA KV 2/931

p. 142   man in question – FAN Z/6/696

p. 142   certainly be there – ibid.

p. 142   an adjoining table – TNA KV 2/931

p. 142   indescribable joy – FAN Z/6/696

p. 143   energy and enthusiasm – Foot, *SOE In France* p. 163

p. 143   of overkeen men – Carré, op. cit. p. 131

p. 143 German war effort? – Ruby, op. cit. p. 38
p. 144 gallant, friendly – ibid. p. 39
p. 144 salary would be – quoted Gildea, *Fighters in the Shadows* p.106
p. 144 or be killed – Ruby, op. cit. p. 25
p. 144 and lly aerodromes – TNA HS/1539/6
p. 145 with delay fuses – Foot, *SOE In France* p. 164
p. 145 like 10,000 resisters – ibid. p. 175
p. 145 *fn.* 24,000 resisters – TNA HS 9/1539/6
p. 145 death would follow – FAN Z/6/696
p. 146 the necessary drive – Carre, op. cit. p. 131
p. 146 cultivate and perfect – FAN Z/6/696
p. 146 revenge – ibid.
p. 147 decode your message – TNA KV 2/931
p. 147 Secret Agents' Club – Cowburn, *No Cloak, No Dagger* p. 35
p. 147 his left temple – TNA KV 2/927
p. 148 Lucas. Victoire – TNA KV 2/931
p. 148 off their stride – FAN Z/6/696
p. 149 blue funny stories – Cowburn, op. cit. p. 67

Chapter 10: Bait and Switchback

p. 150 being crucified – ibid. pp. 51–3
p. 150 and wireless operator – TNA KV 2/931
p. 151 to become active – Cowburn, op. cit. p. 66
p. 151 assistant – FAN Z/6/696
p. 151 a French chauffeur – TNA KV 2/931
p. 151 anti-German propaganda – ibid.
p. 151 in her power – ibid.
p. 152 Britishers or Jews – ibid.
p. 152 a magnificent one – TNA KV 2/928
p. 152 restrictions of rationing – TNA KV 2/931
p. 153 snow and ice – FAN Z/6/696
p. 153 withstand [his] advances – TNA KV 2/931
p. 153 men is shocking – TNA KV 9/928
p. 153 lack of confidence – TNA KV 2/931
p. 154 at times imprudent – FAN Z/6/696
p. 154 to do that – ibid.
p. 155 do anything silly – ibid.
p. 155 saw there – ibid.
p. 155 via M. Carré – FAN 72/AJ/39
p. 155 German U-boats – Milton, *Ministry of Ungentlemanly Warfare* p. 146
p. 156 or even crippling – quoted ibid.
p. 156 apparently innocent remark – FAN 72/AJ/39

p. 156   could be doing – FAN Z/6/696
p. 157   her shopping bag – Young, op. cit. p. 126
p. 157   in any way – FAN 72/AJ/39
p. 157   his failed arrest – FAN 72/AJ/39
p. 157   had been arrested – TNA KV 2/165
p. 158   sort of work – TNA KV 2/926
p. 158   complicate his escape – Foot, *SOE In France* p. 190
p. 158   chance of escaping – Carré, op. cit. p. 135
p. 158   new rage – FAN Z/6/696
p. 158   for the best – Young, op. cit. p. 128
p. 158   with the affair – TNA KV 2/926
p. 159   knew her well – ibid.
p. 159   perform great deeds – ibid.
p. 159   *toute la Résistance* – ibid.
p. 160   fine work – ibid.
p. 160   warn the British – Carré, op. cit. p. 136
p. 160   the last laugh – ibid. p. 137
p. 161   *pommes de terre à l'huile* – Cowburn, op. cit. p. 70
p. 161   London know quickly – FAN 72/AJ/39
p. 161   cheap spy-thriller – ibid. pp. 72–3
p. 161   turning the tables – de Vomécourt, *An Army of Amateurs* p. 90
p. 162   changed sides again – Ruby, op. cit. p. 51
p. 162   everybody at once – Cowburn, op, cit. p.75
p. 162   would never catch – TNA KV 2/2127
p. 162   their wildest dreams – ibid.
p. 162   the general's trip – ibid. p. 76
p. 162   Radio-Bleicher – ibid.
p. 163   disaster into success – Ruby, op. cit. p. 232
p. 163   Geneva and Washington – ibid. p. 51
p. 163   with the Gestapo – TNA KV 2/165
p. 163   arrested and shot – Young, op. cit. p. 138
p. 164   the glorious catch – Cowburn, op. cit. p. 77
p. 164   out of prison – FAN Z/6/696
p. 165   the parallel network – FAN 72/AJ/35
p. 165   love for him – TNA KV 2/938
p. 165   outside her knowledge – FAN 72/AJ/35
p. 165   in due course – TNA KV 2/165
p. 165   highly evasive – FAN Z/6/696
p. 166   Vomécourt game away – FAN Z/6/696
p. 166   passengers essential condition – TNA HS 9/1539/6
p. 166   to each other – TNA KV 2/165
p. 166   bad climatic conditions – ibid.
p. 167   into occupied France – TNA KV 2/926

p. 167   the intelligence services – TNA KV 2/165
p. 167   another serious organisation – TNA KV 2/931
p. 167   probably military intelligence – KV2/926
p. 167   her so much – TNA HS 9/1539/6

Chapter 11: Operation Waterworks

p. 169   Germans breathing space – Shirer, op. cit. p. 925
p. 169   locomotive at Montauban – Cowburn, op. cit. p. 69
p. 170   discovery and ambush – ibid. p. 77
p. 170   through another channel – TNA KV 2/165
p. 170   truth or fact – Cowburn, op. cit. p. 78
p. 170   danger and discomfort – Young, op. cit. p. 142
p. 170   Gestapo's prisoners there – ibid. p. 143
p. 171   a new organisation – TNA KV 2/931
p. 171   British intelligence officers – Young, op. cit. p. 142
p. 171   and their rivalries – TNA KV 2/926
p. 171   *British Secret Service* – TNA KV 2/933
p. 171   leader in fashion – Carré, op. cit. p. 143
p. 171   up an office – TNA KV 2/926
p. 171   were pressing – Cowburn, op. cit. p, 79
p. 171   act as informer – KV 2/1728
p. 172   kiss her goodbye – FAN Z/6/696
p. 172   for the Germans – TNA KV 2/926
p. 172   dazzlingly red hat – TNA KV 2/165
p. 173   Guirec and Locquirec – Tremain, op. cit. p. 172
p. 173   to the coast – Cowburn, op. cit. p. 81
p. 173   as it came – Camus, *The Plague* p. 142
p. 174   a magnificent sunset – Cowburn, op. cit. p. 83
p. 174   and miserable night – TNA KV 2/931
p. 174   'OK, Edouard' – TNA KV 2/927
p. 175   horrible sensation – Carré, op. cit. p. 145
p. 175   and the boat – TNA KV 2/931
p. 175   roaring and pounding – Cowburn, op. cit. p. 85
p. 175   an upturned umbrella – Foot, *SOE In France* p. 191
p. 175   anything, to scram – TNA KV 2/927
p. 176   furious and dripping – Foot, *SOE In France* p. 191
p. 176   might arrest them – TNA KV 2/165
p. 176   the party complete – TNA HS 9/1539/6
p. 176   on the credulity – Young, op. cit. p. 144
p. 176   of being blown – TNA KV 2/931
p. 177   through the darkness – Foot, *SOE In France* p. 193
p. 177   she had behaved – TNA HS 9/1539/6

p. 177   smiling and saluting – Cowburn, op. cit. p. 87
p. 177   keen – ibid. p. 86
p. 178   absolutely nothing happened – ibid. p. 87
p. 178   pram-dinghies – Cowburn, op. cit. p. 88
p. 178   a wonderful experience – TNA KV 2/927
p. 178   dresses completely destroyed – Carré, op. cit. p. 149
p. 178   painfully slow – Purnell, *A Woman of No Importance* p. 99
p. 178   under a rock – Cowburn, op. cit. p. 90
p. 178   American Embassy – Purnell, op. cit. p. 99
p. 179   with exhaustion – ibid. p. 94
p. 179   other nonsense – Young, op. cit. p. 150
p. 179   many lives saved – TNA KV 2/926
p. 179   at half-speed – Foot, *SOE In France* p. 191
p. 180   very much better – TNA KV 2/931
p. 180   accommodation in future – ibid.
p. 181   the English again – TNA KV 2/165
p. 181   paid that much – TNA KV 2/926
p. 181   impressed – TNA KV 2/165
p. 181   I say so – TNA KV 2/296
p. 181   faithful servant – Foot, *SOE In France* p. 192
p. 182   the early sun – Carré, op. cit. pp. 150–1
p. 182   party at all – TNA KV 2/931

Chapter 12: London Surprise

p. 183   Le Père Blanc – Young, op. cit. p. 156
p. 183   of face powder – ibid. p. 158
p. 183   every possible attention – TNA KV 2/926
p. 183   wardrobe of a man – Carré, op. cit. p. 153
p. 184   and glintingly clever – Macintyre, op. cit. p. 70
p. 184   of general matters – TNA KV 2/926
p. 184   great Resistance leader – TNA KV 2/933
p. 184   legendary fog – Carré, op. cit. p. 153
p. 184   lousy with microphones – Young, op. cit. p. 158
p. 185   an important affair – TNA KV 2/926
p. 185   litre of wine – quoted Andrew, *Defence of the Realm* p. 254
p. 185   to this country – TNA KV 2/931
p. 186   and adventure stories – quoted Macintyre, op. cit. p. 71
p. 186   vigorously anti-Nazi – ibid.
p. 186   telling the truth – TNA KV 2/926
p. 186   and mentally exhausted – Carré, op. cit. p. 154
p. 187   a suitable story – TNA KV 2/926
p. 187   Lucas. Victoire – TNA KV 2/931

p. 187   remarkably good impression – TNA KV 2/933
p. 187   a butler's smile – Ashdown, *Game of Spies* p. 21
p. 188   a marked man – TNA HS 9/1539/6
p. 188   of the old – ibid.
p. 189   sources and agents – ibid.
p. 189   her as genuine – ibid.
p. 189   be absolutely reliable – TNA KV 2/926
p. 189   of the case – ibid.
p. 190   the set-up – ibid.
p. 190   done it themselves – ibid.
p. 191   of the Gestapo – TNA KV 2/927
p. 191   of military information – TNA KV 2/926
p. 191   the Nazi regime – ibid.
p. 191   with her position – ibid.
p. 192   no formal training – ibid.
p. 192   try and save – TNA KV 2/931
p. 192   only real objective – TNA KV 2/926
p. 193   of her experiences – ibid.
p. 193   disappear – ibid.
p. 194   projects in view – ibid.
p. 194   completely reorganised – ibid.
p. 195   last war – ibid.
p. 195   organisation to disappear – TNA KV 2/927
p. 196   pacifist views – TNA KV 2/926
p. 196   *fn.* of vascular origin – quoted Lottman, *The Purge* p. 227
p. 197   recent bomb raids – TNA KV 2/931
p. 197   work can continue – ibid.
p. 198   and their grievances – TNA KV 2/926
p. 198   the bad news – ibid.
p. 198   to work with – quoted Andrew, op. cit. p. 196
p. 198   office for instructions – TNA KV 2/926
p. 199   apartment to herself – ibid.
p. 199   an impossible woman – ibid.
p. 199   the money immediately – ibid.
p. 200   a free woman – TNA KV 2/928
p. 200   French servant girl – TNA KV 2/926
p. 200   Mrs Grist's activities – TNA KV 2/927
p. 201   Victoire and Lucas – ibid.
p. 201   railways being used – TNA KV 2/931
p. 201   real position is – TNA KV 2/927
p. 201   of potassium cyanide – TNA HS 9/1539/6
p. 201   lack of manners – TNA KV 2/927
p. 202   our hospitable shores – TNA KV 2/928

p. 202   open, frank simplicity – Carré, op. cit. p. 155

Chapter 13: Spies' Conundrum

p. 204   in the war – TNA KV 2/165
p. 204   nightmare was behind – Carré, op. cit. p. 154
p. 204   the highest quality – TNA KV 2/165
p. 204   the transport company – TNA HS 9/1539/6
p. 205   formidable intelligence operative – Macintyre, op. cit. p. 71
p. 205   Free French officers – TNA KV 2/927
p. 206   frame of mind – ibid.
p. 206   no anxiety – FAN Z/6/696
p. 206   to dress shops – Young, op. cit. p. 161
p. 207   than an artiste – Carré, op. cit. p. 155
p. 207   too cocksure – ibid. p. 154
p. 207   rather macabre thing – Young, op. cit. p. 162
p. 207   stream of complaints – TNA KV 2/931
p. 207   transferred to SOE – quoted Tremain, op. cit. p. 274
p. 208   'Because I'm stupid' – TNA KV 2/927
p. 208   the end of May – ibid.
p. 208   him in London – ibid.
p. 209   of dreams – imagination – TNA KV 2/928
p. 209   going about with – TNA KV 2/927
p. 209   love to her – TNA KV 2/753
p. 209   a police informer – TNA KV 2/931
p. 209   and make notes – TNA KV 2/927
p. 209   look after security – TNA KV 2/931
p. 210   you many greetings – ibid.
p. 210   largest English organisation – ibid.
p. 210   date of birth – ibid.
p. 211   Tuesday your instructions – TNA KV 2/927
p. 212   own personal safety – ibid.
p. 212   arrange her return – ibid.
p. 212   return this week – TNA KV 2/931
p. 213   gone to ground – Foot, *SOE In France* p. 193
p. 213   thing went wrong – TNA KV 2/165
p. 213   a dropping operation – TNA HS 9/1539/6
p. 213   transport the weapons – TNA KV 2/165
p. 213   amicably – TNA HS 9/1539/6
p. 213   so-called Polish service – ibid.
p. 214   return before interfering – TNA KV 2/165
p. 214   a few maps – ibid.
p. 214   at all costs – TNA HS 9/1539/6

p. 215   a Gestapo centre – ibid.
p. 215   with his business – FAN Z/6/696
p. 215   for a while – TNA HS 9/1539/6

Chapter 14: London Dance

p. 216   Claude arrested – TNA HS 9/1539/6
p. 217   and sleep better – TNA KV 2/927
p. 217   at her ease – TNA KV 2/928
p. 217   of British Intelligence – TNA KV 2/927
p. 217   caught his attention – TNA KV 2/928
p. 218   Churchill about her – ibid.
p. 218   a minor matter – ibid.
p. 218   mislead the enemy – Macintyre, op. cit. p. 123
p. 218   else to decide – TNA KV 2/927
p. 218   was perfectly alright – ibid.
p. 218   gentleman should behave – Chris Gray, *Independent* 28.11.2002
p. 219   one of these days – TNA KV 2/164
p. 219   person as Lucas – TNA KV 2/165
p. 220   the knowledge necessary – TNA HS 9/1539/6
p. 220   eight Gestapo men – TNA KV 2/2127
p. 220   refused to speak – TNA HS 9/1539/6
p. 220   I'm Jean … – TNA KV 2/165
p. 220   knocking him about – TNA KV 2/2127
p. 220   wanted to know – TNA HS 9/1539/6
p. 221   a good tale – ibid.
p. 222   able to arrest – ibid.
p. 222   to their bestiality – de Vomécourt, op. cit. p. 93
p. 222   the information required – TNA HS 9/1539/6
p. 222   what the Germans knew – ibid.
p. 223   very useful work – TNA KV 2/165
p. 223   under her thumb – TNA KV 2/753
p. 223   'double-crossing us or not?' – Young, op. cit. p. 160
p. 224   dealing with him – quoted Macintyre, op. cit. p. 94
p. 224   into the fold – ibid. p. 95
p. 224   about our system – ibid. p. 97
p. 224   present graver risks – TNA KV 2/931
p. 225   demanded by lawyer – ibid.
p. 225   has been attempted – ibid.
p. 226   contemplating any action – ibid.
p. 226   running double agents – ibid.
p. 226   got properly alight – Foot, *SOE In France* p. 193
p. 226   resistance in France – TNA HS 9/1539/6

p. 227   Ll. Ll. would go – TNA KV 2/928
p. 227   say so outright – ibid.
p. 228   she is Welsh – ibid.
p. 228   LY OF FRANCE – TNA KV 2/936
p. 229   and film circles – TNA KV 2/928
p. 229   to the country – ibid.

Chapter 15: A Difficult Decision

p. 230   up to see – Carré, op. cit. p. 157
p. 231   end of the beginning – speech given at Mansion House 10. 11. 42
p. 231   are never realised – TNA KV 2/931
p. 231   a difficult decision – ibid.
p. 231   source of information – ibid.
p. 232   Long live Liberty – ibid.
p. 232   confidence – TNA KV 2/928
p. 233   change of attitude – ibid.
p. 233   en mission – ibid.
p. 234   knowledge of his organisation – ibid.
p. 234   result at all – ibid.
p. 234   trouble with the Free French – ibid.
p. 234   and social workers – Gildea, Fighters in the Shadows p. 132
p. 234   a constant menace – TNA KV 2/928
p. 235   co-operating – ibid.
p. 235   by British Intelligence – TNA KV 2/931
p. 235   an undesirable alien – TNA KV 2/928
p. 235   a free woman – ibid.
p. 235   can be trusted – TNA KV 2/927
p. 235   the Walenty transmitter – TNA KV 2/928
p. 236   in complete liberty – ibid.
p. 236   père et mère – ibid.
p. 237   personal reasons – ibid.
p. 237   an expensive nuisance – ibid.
p. 238   vast burning forest – Saint-Exupéry, Flight to Arras p. 5
p. 239   hairdressing activities – TNA KV 2/929
p. 239   at an end – TNA KV 2/928
p. 239   to be allowed – ibid.
p. 240   war, I suppose – ibid.
p. 240   of the war – ibid.
p. 240   astonished and furious – Young, op. cit. p. 167
p. 240   poor cat – TNA KV 2/928
p. 241   efforts and papers – ibid.
p. 241   previously in Syria – TNA KV 2/929

p. 241   nor in a rage – ibid.
p. 241   Long Live Liberty – TNA KV 2/931
p. 242   beautiful fraternal friendship – TNA KV 2/928

Chapter 16: Two Prisoners and a Breakout

p. 243   than in anger – TNA KV 2/928
p. 244   end of the war – ibid.
p. 244   and malicious gossip – TNA KV 2/928
p. 244   moribund – Liddell, *Diaries Vol.* 2 p. 15
p. 244   or kitchen maids – TNA KV 2/928
p. 244   in bad need – TNA KV 2/930
p. 245   in the past – TNA KV 2/928
p. 245   brains in concert – ibid.
p. 245   allowed to work – TNA KV 2/929
p. 246   over the OKW – TNA KV 2/70
p. 246   leaving me here – TNA KV 2/929
p. 246   the death penalty – TNA HS 9/1539/6
p. 247   of the Paris region – ibid.
p. 247   guarantee – TNA KV 2/931
p. 247   just what it said – TNA HS 9/1539/6
p. 247   made in France – ibid.
p. 248   outstandingly successful – TNA KV 2/72
p. 248   win [him] over – ibid.
p. 248   his favourite activity – Macintyre, op. cit. p. 50
p. 248   the Polish nation – TNA KV 2/72
p. 249   side of Germany – ibid.
p. 249   Germany attacks England – ibid.
p. 249   against the English – FAN Z/6/696
p. 249   recovery from illness – TNA KV 2/72
p. 250   a genuine traveller – ibid.
p. 250   great personal ambition – ibid.
p. 250   to take reprisals –ibid.
p. 251   of this affair – ibid.
p. 251   met by accident – TNA KV 2/4351
p. 251   romancing – TNA KV 2/72
p. 251   in their work – ibid.
p. 251   for a Frenchman – TNA KV 2/929
p. 252   his military duty – TNA KV 2/72
p. 252   difficult and unpleasant – ibid.
p. 252   for the Germans – ibid.
p. 253   of them all – quoted Levine, *Operation Fortitude* p. 175
p. 253   GAME is beginning – TNA KV 2/72

p. 253   disdain – interview Gerry Czerniawski 3.7.2019
p. 253   rum-based cocktail – Macintyre, op. cit. pp. 112–13
p. 254   for operational deception – Masterman, *Double-Cross System* p. 141
p. 254   with very distinctive faults – TNA KV 2/72
p. 254   without question – ibid.
p. 255   of its units – TNA KV 2/4351
p. 255   and numerous agents – ibid.
p. 255   in grand style – ibid.
p. 256   money in her possession – TNA KV 2/4352
p. 256   truth and liberty – TNA KV 2/929
p. 256   trace of him – ibid.
p. 256   an indeterminate period – Carré, op. cit. p. 159
p. 257   *Ange Gardien* – TNA KV 2/930
p. 257   their new quarters – ibid.
p. 257   and horribly sad – Carré, op. cit. p. 161
p. 257   do serious harm – TNA KV 2/930
p. 257   violently pro-German – quoted Tremain, op. cit. p. 308
p. 258   most distasteful – TNA KV 2/930
p. 258   valuable wireless agent – quoted Macintyre, op. cit. p. 135
p. 258   more and more – Masterman, op. cit. pp. 141–2
p. 258   largely academic job – TNA KV 2/72
p. 259   other people's work – ibid.
p. 259   gravest military indiscipline – ibid.
p. 260   Am hopeful. Greetings – ibid.
p. 260   occupy his thoughts – ibid.
p. 260   are always eccentric – ibid.
p. 260   love with him – TNA KV 2/4355
p. 260   alone and defenceless – TNA KV 2/930

Chapter 17: Fortitude and Frustration

p. 262   rather than safety – TNA KV 2/929
p. 262   of all time – Philby, *My Silent War* p. 17
p. 262   training and assembling – Macintyre, op. cit. p. 174
p. 263   at [British intelligence's] dictation – TNA KV 2/72
p. 263   arrived at Wentworth – TNA KV 2/4356
p. 263   learning too much – ibid.
p. 264   such as whisky – TNA KV 2/72
p. 264   and French services – TNA WO 373/147/152
p. 265   she will become – TNA KV 2/931
p. 265   over two years – TNA KV 2/931
p. 265   nerves perfectly OK – TNA KV 2/934
p. 266   settling of scores – Paxton, op. cit. p. 329

p. 267   and other ranks – Muggeridge, *Chronicles of Wasted Time* Vol. II, pp. 223–4
p. 267   the country forever – quoted Jackson, *A Certain Idea of France* p. 340
p. 267   than their actions – ibid. p. 342
p. 267   executioners go free – Déak etc., *The Politics of Retribution in Europe*, p. 195
p. 268   our deception technique – TNA KV 2/72
p. 268   of the shadows – Gildea, *Fighters in the Shadows* p. 338
p. 268   all my efforts – TNA KV 2/72
p. 268   cards on the table – ibid.
p. 269   vicinity of Lunéville – TNA KV 2/932
p. 269   a few women – Carré, op. cit. p. 161
p. 269   receive news directly – TNA KV 2/932
p. 269   as her friend – ibid.
p. 270   publicity might attach – ibid.
p. 270   of his escape – ibid.
p. 270   details in writing – TNA KV 2/932
p. 270   of that country provides – ibid.
p. 271   flats in London – TNA KV 2/4355
p. 271   be temporarily interrupted – ibid.
p. 271   whole deception plans – TNA KV 2/932
p. 271   in this country – TNA KV 2/4356
p. 271   more public attention – TNA KV 2/932
p. 272   the Buckmaster circuits – ibid.
p. 272   wanted to defect – Waller, *Disciples* p. 244
p. 272   stand – TNA KV 2/753
p. 273   bold penetration move – TNA KV 2/164
p. 273   [his] own unit – Bleicher op. cit. p. 165
p. 273   SIS and SOE – TNA KV 2/164
p. 274   machine of destiny – Carré, op. cit. p. 162
p. 274   had piled up – Carré, op. cit. p. 162

Chapter 18: Intelligence With the Enemy

p. 276   trial for treason – Beevor and Cooper, op. cit. p. 157
p. 276   by Resistance groups – Lottman, op. cit. pp. 129–130
p. 276   good and evil – Carré, op. cit.p. 10
p. 278   poised and unbiased – ibid. p. 165
p. 278   of the journey – FAN 72/AJ/39
p. 278   and knew everything – ibid.
p. 279   confessed to him – ibid.
p. 279   very sensual – ibid.
p. 279   be utterly discredited – Carré, op. cit. p. 165
p. 280   of the Gestapo – FAN 72/AJ/39
p. 280   faint-hearted and terrified – Carré, op. cit. p. 165

p. 280   Madame Carré's choices – FAN 72/AJ/39
p. 280   for several days – ibid.
p. 281   the Paris ragamuffin – Carré, op. cit. p. 88
p. 281   no idea – FAN 72/AJ/39
p. 281   strange woman indeed – Young, op. cit. p. 90
p. 281   the SS bullies – Young, op. cit. p. 88
p. 281   small and frail – FAN 72/AJ/39
p. 282   very abusive – Carré, op. cit. p. 166
p. 282   no regrets – ibid. p.167
p. 283   two unhappy creatures – ibid.
p. 283   such a sum – FAN 72/AJ/39
p. 283   such offer accepted – ibid.
p. 283   intended to arrest – ibid.
p. 284   completely unbalanced – Carré, op. cit. p. 168
p. 284   big lovely parcels – letter to Richard Llewellyn, 1.6.47, Harry Ransom Center, Texas
p. 284   in [her] cell – Carré, op. cit. p. 169
p. 284   to study, to live! – letter to Richard Llewellyn op. cit.
p. 284   game with death – Carré, op. cit. p. 168
p. 285   fanatic for religion – TNA KV 2/929
p. 285   of human justice – Carré, op. cit. p. 169
p. 285   a great spy – ibid. pp. 170–71
p. 286   in small stations – ibid. p. 171
p. 286   cold, judicial murder – ibid. p. 172
p. 286   know the man – ibid. p. 188
p. 287   a representative – Young, op. cit. pp. 176–77
p. 287   a secret OBE – interview Gerry Czerniawski 3.7.2019
p. 287   gnawing solitude – Carré, op. cit. p. 189
p. 287   base of [our] balance – ibid. p. 185
p. 288   desperately empty inside – ibid. pp. 194–5
p. 288   TO FORGET YOURSELF – ibid. p. 195

Chapter 19: Curtain

p. 289   wants your head – Carré, op. cit. p. 199
p. 290   collaborators in France – Lottman, op. cit. p. 163
p. 290   profoundly polarising effect – Christopher Clarke, *London Review of Books* 7.11.2019
p. 291   a bad choice – Sartre, op. cit. p. 22
p. 291   power against France – Carré, op. cit. p. 9
p. 291   deceptive calm – Young, op. cit. p. 180
p. 291   hatred with hatred – Tremain, op. cit. p. 369
p. 292   I have done? – Young, op. cit. pp. 182–3

p. 292   immense desire – ibid. pp. 183–4
p. 292   two hours that day – ibid. pp. 184–5
p. 293   marked down for massacre – ibid. p. 186
p. 293   atmosphere of prejudice – Carré, op. cit. p. 201
p. 293   British sabotage operation – ibid. p. 113
p. 293   not be broken – Young, op. cit. p. 77
p. 293   had betrayed him – ibid. p. 187
p. 293   matter to her – ibid.
p. 294   information to the Germans – TNA HS 9/1539/6
p. 294   to make amends – Young, op. cit. p. 189
p. 294   whole I would – ibid.
p. 295   the Mozart Requiem – Carré, op. cit. pp. 122–3
p. 295   penalty of death – Young, op. cit. pp. 191–2
p. 295   reproached for that? – ibid. p. 193
p. 295   pathetically human – Carré, op. cit. p. 11
p. 296   months of weakness – Young, op. cit. p. 194
p. 296   enterprises of Germany – ibid.
p. 296   despise[d] – Carré, op. cit. p. 10
p. 296   trace of the smile – Young, op. cit. p. 195
p. 297   have no strength – Carré, op. cit. pp. 199–200
p. 297   important German spy – Tremain, op. cit. pp. 137–8
p. 298   his amazing luck – ibid.
p. 298   a provincial hotel – Young, op. cit. p.212
p. 298   this partisan justice – Carré, op. cit. pp. 206–7
p. 298   shortcomings into vices – ibid. pp. 200–1
p. 299   unhinged publicity-seeker – Callil, op. cit. pp. 436–77
p. 299   and this prison – Young, op. cit. pp. 196–8
p. 300   sufficiently into consideration – ibid. p. 199
p. 300   pitilessly executed – ibid. p. 200
p. 300   part of the 'game' – Lloyd, *Collaboration and Resistance in Occupied France* p. 133
p. 300   friend – Carré, op. cit. pp. 202–3
p. 300   the utter degradation – ibid. p. 205
p. 301   and laughs nervously – ibid. pp. 207–8
p. 301   inestimable service – Young, op. cit. p. 202
p. 301   kindly street woman – Carré, op. cit. p. 216
p. 302   modestly dressed woman – Young, op. cit. p. 203
p. 302   of real use – ibid. p. 206
p. 302   and fiercely solitary – ibid. p. 220
p. 303   immediately squashed – Carré, op. cit. p. 200
p. 303   game of espionage – Young, op. cit. p. 223
p. 303   And you … ? – Garby-Czerniawski, op. cit. p. 246
p. 304   stay absolutely still – Carré, op. cit. pp. 220–1

List of Illustrations

Section one
The factory town of Le Creusot: Collection Dupondt / akg-images. Mathilde Belard: *I Was 'The Cat'* by Mathilde-Lily Carré, Souvenir Press Ltd, 1960. Mathilde with husband Maurice Carré: Tallandier / Bridgeman. Roman Czerniawski: Archive PL / Alamy Stock Photo. Czerniawski with his regiment: Gerry Czerniawski. Toulouse: Apic / Getty Images. The Champs-Elysées: Sueddeutsche Zeitung Photo / Alamy Stock Photo. Lydia Lipski: John Izbicki, *The Naked Heroine*, Umbria Press London, 2014. Monique Deschamps: Gerry Czerniawski. Rue Villa Léandre: Paul Almasy / akg-images. Renée Borni, Agent Violette: The National Archives: Image Ref: KV 2/929 (1). Roman Czerniawski: Gerry Czerniawski. Hugo Bleicher: The National Archives: Image Ref: KV 2/166. Suzanne Laurent: *Colonel Henri's Story*, Edited by Ian Colvin, William Kimber, London, 1954, (photographer unknown). Rue des Saules: TopFoto / PA Images. La Santé prison: Historic Images / Alamy Stock Photo.

Section two
The Villa Baur: Paul Almasy / akg-images. 'The Cattery': *The Cat With Two Faces*, by Gordon Young, Putnam London, 1957. Pierre de Vomécourt: The National Archives: Image Ref: HS 9/1539/6. Carte d'identité of Major Ben Cowburn: Imperial War Museum / Documents. 12716 Ref/Cowburn_012716_5. *Daily Sketch* clipping: John Frost Newspapers / Alamy Stock Photo. J. C. Masterman: National Portrait Gallery / NPG x90551. 'Tar' Robertson: Private Collection. Christopher Harmer: Private Collection. Susan Barton: Private Collection. Headband: Imperial War Museum / EPH 4086. 'Klop' von Ustinov: Imperial War Museum / HU 57817. Lord Selborne: National Portrait Gallery / NPG x164052. Richard Llewellyn Lloyd: National Portrait Gallery / NPG x23601. Mathilde trial: AGIP / Bridgeman Images. Albert Naud trial: Heckly / AP / Shutterstock. Renée Borni in court: AGIP / Bridgeman Images. Hugo Bleicher: Keystone Press / Alamy Stock Photo. After her release Mathilde Carré: Photo Jean Tesseyre / Paris Match via Getty Images.

Other
The map on page 47: Gerry Czerniawski.

Index